WHY WE FIGHT

Theories of Human Aggression and Conflict

David Churchman

D1313605

University Press of America,® Inc.
Lanham · Boulder · New York · Toronto · Oxford

⊖™ The paper used in this publication meets the minimum
requirements of American National Standard for Information
Sciences—Permanence of Paper for Printed Library Materials,
ANSI Z39.48—1984

For Alita and Mike

Contents

Contents

	Criteria for Good Theory	Conflict Analysis	Human Nature	Aggression & the Mind	Interpersonal Conflict	Gender Conflict	Community Conflict	Dispute Resolution	Business Conflict	Political Conflict	Intellectual Conflict	Causes of War	Interstate War	Asymmetric War	Search for Peace
	1	2	3	4	5	6	7	8	9	10	11	12	13	14	15
Anthropology			■		■							■			
Archaeology			■			■							■		
Biology			■												
Communications					■			■							
Criminology							■								
Economics									■	■	■	■	■	■	■
Ethology			■												
Geography										■		■	■		
History	■					■			■	■	■	■	■	■	■
Labor Studies									■	■					
Law						■		■	■						
Management									■						
Mathematics	■	■						■		■		■	■		
Military Science										■		■	■	■	
Philosophy	■										■				
Political Science								■		■		■			
Psychology			■	■											
Psychiatry				■											
Social Psychology					■			■							
Sociobiology			■			■							■		
Sociology					■	■									
Theology											■				■
Women's Studies						■									

Figure 0.1
Primary Academic Disciplines by Chapter

Preface

The true study of human conflict
is the study of everything else.

—Unknown

This book explores over 100 theoretical explanations of human aggression and conflict and over 75 methods for managing them from over 20 academic disciplines. It proposes six criteria for judging the theories. That is, the book addresses what theorists have said about the nature of conflict, what practioners propose doing about it, and how critics distinguish good ideas from bad. The last may be the most important, as it is applies beyond the realm of conflict management.

Organizing a book around academic disciplines risks becoming pedantic because, like the six blind men describing an elephant based on teaching a different part, each discipline studies only a part of the whole. Arranging a book by type of theory might be useful to a student of ideas but is less so to a practioner. Instead, the book is arranged by seven "levels" of conflict: individual, interpersonal, community, intellectual, organizational, intrastate, and interstate. Examples of conflicts at these levels are a worker "going postal," a divorce, a zoning dispute, global warming, Congressional redistricting, and sanctions against Iraq.

Chapters 1, 2, and 16 are exceptions to the basic arrangement. Chapter 1 deals with the requirements of good theories and with principles for evaluating them. Chapter 2 describes analytical ideas and methods that reappear throughout the book. Chapter 16 synthesizes and assesses conflict theory and suggests directions for future study.

Many will find this book controversial because it questions ideas with which most academics are comfortable. I hope that this generates debate and even more quixotically that the debate will adhere to principles of evidence and logic rather than ideology, wishful thinking, and personal opinion. If everyone's opinion were as good as everyone else's, then Hitler's opinion on race would be just as good as that of Martin Luther King. It was not. One should not confuse the right to an opinion with the rightness of the opinion.

The book draws on a lifetime of reading within and outside the academic literature on conflict and a myriad of other topics. Many points were incorporated from newspapers into lecture notes without any thought of a book ten years later. There is an extensive bibliography of works cited and additional relevant material. Unfortunately, no matter how extensive, bibliographies are necessarily incomplete and immediately obsolete. Some entries lead to earlier sources that often are more insightful and better written than the more recent ones. Some ideas may have their origin in several sources. Some ideas may appear in sources that I do not know, for, as the Preacher said, "there is nothing new under the sun." Sometimes a single phrase provided the inspiration but the original meaning is changed. The title of the book illustrates the point. Taken from the American World War II propaganda films produced by Frank Capra, I use it as a question rather than an explanation.

Acknowledgments

I have had considerable help from many people in writing this book. At the risk of missing someone, I would like to thank a few of them. To the extent that it is cogent, much of the credit belongs to my students, who by their questions and occasional quizzical looks told me when I was unclear, illogical, or just plain wrong. To the extent that it is readable, I am grateful for the suggestions of Les Aucoin, Beth Ahiyjek, Jean Bakewell, Pam Derby, Tia Hatch, Sara Hopkins-Powell, and Sharon Mehdi of the Ashland Writers Group. They along with Robert Hall and Josie Wilson assisted with the tedious task of proof reading. I want to thank George Clark, David Nasatir, Joseph Pendry, Millicent Wood-Harris, and Joseph Wingard for some of the best examples in the text and for their general support and encouragement. Oliver Richmond of St. Andrews University critiqued the entire text and was particularly helpful on the contemporary ethnic conflicts that he knows first-hand from his work in Congo, Cyprus, East Timor, Rwanda, and Sri Lanka. Remaining errors are my responsibility.

Chapter 1
Criteria for Good Theory

It works in practice, yes, but does it work in theory?
—Unknown French diplomat

Theorists from over twenty academic disciplines have tried to explain why we fight. Their disagreements as to causes, consequences and cures raise the question of which theory is best. Six criteria discussed below provide criteria to distinguish good from bad theory.

Usable

How often have you heard someone dismiss an idea as "just a lot of theory," meaning it is useless obfuscation? They are unlikely to be talking about the natural sciences, where theory that does not work is rapidly abandoned and theory that does work leads to practical applications, consequences or inventions. They are more likely to be talking about the social sciences, where failed theories thrive and proliferate.

Theory should explain what happens and how, improve prediction, or lead to better ways to do things. A theory that does not do one or more of these three things fails the usability test. However, theory is not a how-to-do-it manual. For example, a cookbook will tell you the steps you must take to produce a cheese soufflé and anyone who follows the steps will succeed. But, someone had to invent the soufflé based on understanding such matters as the behavior of hot gasses and the nature of emulsions, which is to say, the theory of cooking.

Usability is determined in part by how well a theory explains causes and effects. Western philosophy distinguishes four types of cause. A sufficient cause guarantees the effect regardless of all other causes present. It often is said that, "The president will win re-election if the economy is good." No matter what the challenger says about any other issue, a good economy alone is sufficient to insure re-election. If you know and can create a sufficient condition, you can *insure* a result.

"The president cannot win re-election unless the economy is good," means a good economy is necessary but is not sufficient by itself to guarantee re-election. Other issues such as foreign policy might prove more important. You can *prevent* an effect if you know and can remove a necessary cause.

A cause can be necessary and sufficient. The effect cannot occur without it, and must occur if it is present. Weakest of all, a cause can merely be contributory, meaning that an outcome is more likely to occur when it is present. Smoking is a contributory but not a necessary or sufficient cause for lung cancer.

Some say women are more peaceful than men, so war could be eliminated if women governed. Some say democracies never attack one another, so that war could be eliminated if all governments were democracies. But, are these claims true? Is one, the other, or both a necessary and sufficient, necessary, sufficient, or contributory cause of peace? Readers may wish to test both ideas before reaching the discussion of the first in Chapter 6 and the second in Chapter 12.

Empirical

Theories should be consistent with facts, but the facts must be true.[1] Even the most honest researchers make mistakes. Researchers sometimes define variables poorly or measure them badly, collect data from biased or limited samples, or use inappropriate methods to interpret them. Age, culture, personality, philosophy, politics, rank, religion, and sex of researchers and subjects are among the countless variables that can bias or limit results. An experiment on aggression using undergraduate psychology majors is likely to get very different results than the same research done on marine commandos. Thus, scientists replicate research under different circumstances.

Replication also protects against fraud. The problem is rare but significant, and exists in every field, not just academic research. Jayson Blair of *The New York Times*, Peter Arnett of *CNN*, and Michael Barnacle of the *Boston Globe* are among the high profile cases of fraudulent reporting that led to dismissal. Piltdown Man probably is the most famous but not the only fraud in anthropological history. Manuel Elizalde dressed impoverished Philippine farmers in leaves and passed them off as Tasaday, supposedly a tribe untouched by civilization. Experts estimate that as much as 40% of the work of famous artists that appears on the auction block is forged or so heavily restored as to be worthless.

Four cases of fraud are directly relevant to the study of conflict. The worst case, because it led to the murder of thousands, involves the so-called *Protocols of Zion*, repeatedly proven to be fraudulent, used in Russia to justify pogroms and violence against Jews and still occasionally cited as authentic by hate groups in the United States. Roberta Menchu received the Nobel Prize despite numerous fabrications in her book about the civil war in Guatemala.[2] Michael

---

1. Quantification is but one form of empiricism and some uses of numbers are erroneous, intentionally deceptive, or pseudoscientific. There are many examples in this text of factual but non-quantitative information. The crucial distinction is among facts, conclusions drawn from facts, and opinions.
2. Menchu claimed two brothers were killed by the Guatemalan army but neither ever existed. She claimed that the government took her parents' land, when in fact it was lost to family members in a dispute. If the Guatemalan government was so bad, why could she not have used real instead of fabricated events?

Belleisles was forced to surrender his prestigious 2001 Bancroft Prize for the best book in American history and to resign from Emory University when his study of gun ownership in the American colonies proved to be based on data he had fabricated.[3] Michael Moore received an Oscar for *Bowling for Columbine* and a *Palme d'Or* at the Cannes Film Festival for *Fahrenheit 9/11*. Both are error-laden.[4]

Social scientists, impressed by the success of the physical sciences since Galileo, chose to emulate their methods by emphasizing controlled experiments

---

3. In *Arming America*, Michael Bellesiles clamed that a study of 11,000 probate records proved that very few colonial Americans actually owned functional guns. When scholars asked for his data so it could be reanalyzed, he said he had read them in federal archives in East Point, Georgia. When it became apparent there were no such records, he said he had read them in some 30 different places and that his original data had not survived a flood. When it became clear that much of his data was wrong, he claimed that someone had hacked into his files and changed his data, effectively suggesting that he had put data on his web site that contradicted his own book, but that a hacker had altered it to support his book! Numerous other distortions gradually came to light in follow-up research by Lindren of Northwestern, Roth of Ohio State, Main of Colorado and Gruber of Rice

4. In *Bowling for Columbine*, Michael Moore claims that the NRA callously held a pro-gun rally in Denver immediately after the shooting at nearby Columbine High School. In fact, it was their annual meeting, scheduled years before the shootings. The NRA canceled all events except the annual members' meeting that was required by law. Moore deleted Heston's condolences and joined phrases as much as five paragraphs apart from five different speeches to make Heston seem calloused. Moore tried to make Heston appear racist, ignoring his actual history as the organizer of Hollywood's support for Martin Luther King. Moore linked the NRA with the KKK. In fact, Union officers who opposed the KKK founded the NRA and selected Ulysses S. Grant and Philip Sheridan as NRA presidents in no small part because they worked to crush the KKK.

Over fifty errors—about one every two minutes in a film purporting to be a documentary—have been identified in *Fahrenheit 9-11*. Moore implied that the Florida Secretary of State supervised vote counting: it is done separately in each county. Moore claimed that Bush allowed 142 Saudi citizens to fly home before any other planes were allowed in the air after 9/11: Richard Clarke testified that he not Bush made the decision and the 9/11 Commission confirms that all departures were handled properly. Moore claims Bush extended special favors to Saudis based on his relationship with the Saudi ambassador. In fact the ambassador had been a Washington power broker for decades and was just as close to Bill Clinton. Moore portrays Iraq as a prosperous country with contented citizens. In fact, a sixth of its population had fled, and Saddam's regime tortured dissidents and killed tens of thousands of its citizens. *Fahrenheit 9-11* shows Bush giving a speech on an aircraft carrier saying "Major combat operations in Iraq have ended. In the Battle of Iraq, the United States and our allies have prevailed," but cut out his next words which were, "And now our coalition is engaged in securing and reconstructing that country... We still have difficult work to do in Iraq..." Moore said that. "out of the 535 members of Congress, only one had an *enlisted* son in Iraq," carefully worded to exclude six whose children were serving in Iraq as *officers*. He did not mention that 101 congressman and 36 Senators are themselves veterans.

and mathematical analysis. It now is almost impossible to complete a degree in anthropology, communications, economics, political science, psychology, or sociology without studying statistics and research design; even historians sometimes study "cliometrics." Social scientists have devised ways to measure almost every aspect of human behavior with varying reliability and validity. They have learned ever more refined ways to analyze the resulting data, so that statistical significance often has no practical significance. They have created ever more elaborate but abstract models to guide their research. Whether they have thereby achieved much understanding is an open question.

This may be because the turn to mathematics was only part of the reason that the physical sciences succeeded so phenomenally. The choice of *what* to measure was even more important. Galileo solved this problem also, shifting to questions of how rather than why things happened and focusing his energies on matter in motion. It was not obvious at the time but it insured the rapid progress of astronomy, physics, and technology because his choices proved to explain so many different phenomena. Social scientists have not yet been able to identify and settle on a few key variables with broad explanatory power. Some think human behavior or even any aspect of it such as conflict is too complex ever to identify a sufficiently small number of key variables to make the natural science model work. Some continue the search, but most seem oblivious to the problem and continue to measure everything in sight and subject them to every conceivable statistical test in hope of finding something that at least will get them published and tenured.

Logical

Theories also must be logical. Here we give only one example from each of the eight major categories of logical error (Fisher, 1970).[5] Consider the case of a driver convicted of going through a red light because a witness swore that the light was not green. The jury made two mistakes in logic. First, it accepted a false dichotomy, one of a class of fallacies in question framing, because categorizing the light as only red or green does not exhaust the possibilities. It could have been yellow, or burned out, or even both red and green (some systems use both instead of a yellow light, or there may have been a technical failure). If anyone tries to limit you two choices, *always* ask whether there are other possibilities. Second, the jury accepted a negative proof, one of a class of fallacies of factual verification. Asserting what is *not* does not prove what *is*.

A third category includes fallacies of significance, such as judging friends and foes by different standards. Nazi Admiral Karl Doenitz was spared trial for war crimes on this principle when it was pointed out that the US submarine campaign was little different than that of the Germans except for being so much more successful (US submarines sank 1150 enemy ships totaling 4,859 million

---

5. A more complete list, with very brief definitions, will be found in the Appendix.

tons with much fewer losses than the Germans, while airplanes, mines, and surface craft combined sank 975 enemy ships totaling 2,940 million tons).

You will encounter fallacies of generalization, including special pleading as in the apocryphal case of the boy who killed his parents then asked for mercy because he was an orphan. Fallacies of narration include anachronisms. Among movie anachronisms were the printed leaflets, crossbows, domed buildings and bell towers in *Gladiator*, the Lewis guns in *Lawrence of Arabia*, the boxes labeled "Product of Israel" in *Sound of Music*, and mention of Freud's *Pleasure Principle* (published 1920) in *Titanic* (sunk 1912).

You will encounter fallacies of motivation, such as treating all Jews as avaricious or all Scots as miserly. However, the fallacy should not be confused with useful generalizations. For example, it often is useful to treat American blacks as Democrats although about 10% are Republicans. Analogies can be useful in clarifying complicated ideas, but sometimes are based on mistaken similarities, are taken literally, or confused for complete resemblance. Lewis Carol joked, "Let us speak of many things, of cabbages and kings" because both have heads that can be cut off. You will encounter semantic fallacies, such as writers who use words to mean what they want regardless of the common or legal definition, "terrorism" being a case in point for conflict theorists (Chapter 14), in the manner of Lewis Carol's Humpty Dumpty:

> But, "glory" doesn't mean "a nice knock-down argument," Alice objected.
> "When *I* use a word," Humpty Dumpty said, in rather a scornful tone, "it means just what I choose it to mean—neither more nor less."
> "The question is," said Alice, "whether you *can* make words mean so many different things."
> "The question is," said Humpty Dumpty, "which is to be master—that's all.

Fallacies of substantive distraction shift attention from reasoned argument to the irrelevant and irrational. The most common undoubtedly is the *ad hominem*, but in conflict theory the most dangerous probably is the appeal to authority, including pedantic words, obscure sources, and fallacious mathematics. We can legitimately set "a" equal to "b" then perform a number of perfectly normal algebraic manipulations, always doing the same thing on both sides to keep the equation equal, to prove that every number is twice itself:

Multiply both sides by a:	$a^2 = ab$
Subtract b^2 from both sides:	$a^2 - b^2 = ab - b^2$
Factor:	$(a + b)(a - b) = b(a-b)$
Divide both sides by (a- b)	$a + b = b$
Substitute b for a, as the two are equal	$2b = b$
Thus, any number is half itself	$2 = 1, 4 = 2$[6]

---

6. The error lies in dividing by a-b, which = 0. It is impossible to divide something into 0 parts, so this operation is not allowed.

Finally, you will encounter fallacies of causation, such as mistaking correlation for cause. The supposed correlation between hem height and the Dow-Jones average gives us the advice, "Do not sell until you see the whites of their thighs," which probably is not a reliable guide to managing one's investments. Theories must not only be logical, but must also stand up to factual criticism.

Falsifiable

Theory must be consistent with facts, but facts never can prove a theory. It is logically impossible. The basic reason is that a fact, or any number of facts, may be consistent with more than one theory, some not yet even formulated or imagined. It is for this reason that theories never are considered final, and for this reason that Karl Popper argued that to be considered scientific a claim must be *disprovable* by observation or experiment.

Consider the dispute between Antoine Lavoisier and Joseph Priestly. In the 1770s both conducted the same experiment, heating ore of mercury. Lavoisier interpreted what he saw as an unknown substance being given off by the ore. Priestly, an equally famous and capable scientist, interpreted what he saw as the ore drawing off and absorbing a substance from the air.

Which explanation is true? Or, are both true? Or, for that matter, are both false? If you put yourself in the position of eighteenth century scientists for whom the answer is not yet known, there are four ways to account for the same facts. How do you decide what is right? Karl Popper later argued that no statements can be proved true, but some statements can be proved false. Science, he argued, must not try to prove theories right. Rather, it must try to disprove them. The theory that survives falsification is accepted as a working truth. The effort to falsify characterizes science. The effort to prove characterizes religion. Ideas that are not stated in terms that cannot be tested are not science. Popper, Priestly and his adherents, and Lavoisier and his, acted precisely in this spirit. Experiments were devised to prove the other wrong, leaving Lavosier's oxygen a better explanation than Priestly's phlogiston.

Falsification underlies the logic of statistical research, which is designed to determine whether an independent variable, or cause, affects a dependent variable, or effect. Without getting into the particulars of research design, inferential statistics are used to decide whether to "retain" or "reject" a "null hypothesis" that there is no difference between groups subjected to different causes. Retaining the hypothesis means that the treatment—a weight loss drug or whatever is being tested—probably does not work. Rejecting the null hypothesis means that it probably does work.

Deciding something is false when it is a true is labeled a Type I error (Figure 1.1). A simple example is a union reducing its aspirations on the incorrect assumption that a high wage demand will lead to an unwanted strike. Deciding something is true when it is false is labeled a Type II error. A simple example is making a wage demand lower than management would accept so as to prevent a strike.

	Unknown Reality:	
	Hypothesis is true:	Hypothesis is false:
Reject Hypothesis	Type I error: Hypothesis was correct and should have been retained	Correct decision
Retain Hypothesis	Correct decision	Type II error: Hypothesis was wrong and should have been rejected.

Decision

Figure 1.1
Drawing Conclusions from Research

Other things remaining equal, it turns out that the only way of reducing the chance of making one type of error increases the chance of making the other. Therefore, one has to decide in advance and guard most against the worse error. In the case of labor negotiations, there are so many ways to back off from an excessive demand and so many long-term repercussions for not testing just how far management will go that unions usually want to avoid Type I errors more than they want to avoid Type II errors.

Knowing that science works by trying to prove theories false, careful researchers seek to disprove their own theories before publication. The practice is not limited to the natural sciences but extends, or should extend, to all fields. Donald Foster of Vassar tried to identify the parts Shakespeare took in his own plays by linguistic analysis. He found that words that Shakespeare rarely used first appeared in the words of a single character. He theorized that Shakespeare played these parts himself. These parts often proved to be the first character to come on stage.[7]

Foster then tried to eliminate objections to his theory. He proved that the test never assigned Shakespeare to an improbable role, such as a child. He proved that the unusual words never were scattered in an early play but clustered in a later one. Where the test assigns two roles to Shakespeare in the same play, he made sure they never were on stage at the same time. The theory survived

---

7. John Gower in *Pericles*, Bedford in *Henry VI Part*, Suffolk in *Part II*, and Warwick in *Part III*. The test picks Shakespeare for two roles we know he played, the ghost in *Hamlet* and Adam in *As You Like It*.

these tests, leaving it the best current solution to this small but intriguing problem. Foster used the same techniques to identify Joe Klein as the author of *Primary Colors*, to help police identity the Unabomber (Roberts, April 2002) and to identify Eric Robert Rudolph, who agreed to a guilty plea in April 2005, as the culprit in the 1996 Olympic bombing incident.

Falsification improves theory. Ptolemy proposed a system in which the Sun and planets traveled about the Earth in circular orbits. Copernicus proved it wrong, suggesting a system in which the earth and planets travel about the Sun in circular orbits. Kepler proved Copernicus's circular orbits wrong, replacing them with elliptical ones. Sometimes the theory is correct and the apparent errors lead to new discoveries. Aberrations in the orbits of the outer planets led to the discoveries of Uranus, Neptune and Pluto.

Other examples of falsified and abandoned physical theories are the Aristotelian theory of gravity, the ether, the heliocentric universe, and the plum pudding model of the atom. Examples from biology include Larmarckism, Intelligent Design, the four bodily humors, the miasma theory of disease, and spontaneous generation. More interesting are theories that provide approximate theories that we work with until something better comes along. Although we know the earth is not the center of the universe, the idea remains useful for setting out the coordinate system of celestial mechanics. Newtonian mechanics still works well in most circumstances, although it was made obsolete by the Theory of Relativity and quantum mechanics.

Sometimes falsification is so sweeping that any rational person must abandon the theory in question. Astrology is an obvious case. It is geocentric; the solar system is not. When the most common astrological system (there are many others and they contradict one another) was devised about 100 BC, the sun entered Ares in March. Due to the precession of the equinoxes, it now does so a month later. If the actual situation is important, why has there been no adjustment? If not, what is so important in the ten billion year history of the universe about the heavens of 100 BC? Astrology takes no account of Uranus, Neptune and Pluto. Why do only the visible planets affect us? How can stars influence human lives? Either some astral force must keep billions of us straight, or it must find and fix each individual destiny at the moment of birth. Astrology treats constellations as having an actual existence but constellations actually consist of unrelated stars millions of light years apart, moving at different speeds in different directions. They are given different names and different qualities are inferred for them in different cultures. Believing astrology requires rejecting modern astronomy, biology, and physics.[8]

---

8. To this superstition, we may add the Abominable Snowman, Afrocentrism, alar, Atlantis, the Bermuda Triangle, Bigfoot, Crop Circles, ESP, Kirlian photography, laetrile, levitation, the Loch Ness monster, mediums and fortune tellers, numerology, phrenology, pyramid power, reincarnation, and Tarot cards to mention a tiny fraction of the many frauds and silly ideas that the world has seen.

Theories are developed from facts but tested by falsification. The theory that survives the effort is accepted as a working truth, but the possibility that falsification may occur in the future requires that all theories be treated as tentative. We must remain ready to jettison any theory when it proves untenable.

Parsimony

What if more than one theory that resists falsification? How do we choose the best among them? A fourteenth century Franciscan monk, William of Occam, or *Doctor Invincibilis* as he was nicknamed by those who tried to debate him, provided the answer: "the simplest theory that completely explains the facts is best,"[9] which we now know as "Occam's Razor." This may not seem like much, but without it, Copernicus was no better than Ptolemy. The Ptolemaic System involved an amazing array of epicycles and eccentrics—that is, additional orbits centered on or tangential to the main orbits and to one another. Everything that appeared to move had amazingly complex orbits that needed constant revision as new errors were identified. Indian, Arab, and European astronomers all had different versions of the Ptolemaic system.

Nicholas Copernicus thought the omnipotent and divine Creator would not have created such a mess. He reviewed all the ancient books on astronomy that had been translated from the original Greek through Arabic into Latin during the previous century or so. Inspired by the ancient Pythagoreans' belief in a mathematical universe, by Aristotle's notion of the perfection of circular motion, and the Neoplatonists' exalted idea of the sun, Copernicus suggested that the sun, not the earth, was the center of the universe.

Notice that his inspiration was not more accurate data, or better mathematics, or some brilliant experiment that revealed Truth. Rather, it was a mishmash of mystical ideas and philosophical arguments. Scientific progress often includes an element of inspiration and sudden insight, illustrated by the famous story of Archimedes, whose king challenged him to determine if his crown was made of pure gold or some alloy, without damaging the crown. Archimedes had no idea how to do so till he lowered himself into his bath, watched the water rise, and realized in a flash that the amount of water displaced was a measure of his weight, leading him to run naked through the streets of Syracuse to the palace shouting "Eureka," "I have found it."

When proposed, the Copernican System was no better than the Ptolemaic System at explaining all known astronomical phenomenon, such as the apparent forward and retrograde movements of stars and planets, the annual motion of the sun, the variable brightness of the planets, and the dates of solar and lunar eclipses. It was not much better than the Ptolemaic system because it incorrectly assumed circular orbits for the planets. It replaced the single motion of the sun

---

9 What he actually said is "*entia non sunt multiplicanda prater necessitate*," "assumptions should not be multiplied unnecessarily"

with the dual motion of the earth, rotating on its axis to explain the days and revolving in its orbit to explain everything else. But, it had its own problems. It raised the question of why things did not fly off the moving earth. It implied that stars should be seen at different angles as the earth revolved. But, it eliminated the even more complex Ptolemaic system with its epicycles and other adjustments. Therefore, it was preferable by Occam's Razor. The Catholic Church agreed and based on it adapted the new Gregorian calendar that we still use. It was only a century later as the theological implications began to sink in that the church tried to unseat the Copernican universe.

Parsimony refers to the number of explanatory components and the way they are interrelated. It does not mean that a theory needs to be easy to understand. A theory based on difficult mathematics but on a single formula explaining how to combine operationally defined, accurately measured variables is simple, however difficult the mathematics itself may be. A theory couched in ambiguously worded jargon with elaborate qualifications and limited applicability is not simple.

Generalizable

Generalizability describes the number of different situations that a theory explains. The theory of gravity is generalizable—and consequently powerful—because it explains many apparently unrelated phenomenon, such as the orbit of the moon, the path of a canon ball through the air, and the fall of an apple.

One approach to generalization is taxonomic. Linnaeus developed a hierarchical taxonomy (kingdom, phylum, class, order, family, tribe, genus, species) to show relationships among all life forms. In his system, every living thing animal, plant, fungi, protoctist or prokaryotac fits into one and only one category at each level. There is a perpetual debate as to the proper number of categories in the taxonomy. "Splitters" emphasize differences and devise systems with many categories but few representatives in each. "Joiners" develop taxonomies with fewer categories but more representatives in each.

Conflict theory seeks to explain human aggression and conflict from the intra-personal to the international level. The proper number of categories and subcategories is far from fixed. The arrangement of this book implies a system, but it is neither exhaustive nor exclusive. The first level in the implied taxonomy of aggression and conflict is the individual. It deals with such fundamental questions as whether humans are naturally aggressive or pacific and whether "nature" or "nurture" has the greater impact on personality. Emotions, needs and values are among sources of conflict at this level. Anthropology, biology, ethology, psychology, psychiatry and sociobiology have made the primary contributions to understanding these questions.

The second level involves interpersonal conflict, that between individuals such as siblings, spouses, or teachers and students. It addresses conflicts that stem from personality differences, age differences, communication differences, and gender differences. Communication, gender studies, psychology, social psychology, and sociology have made the greatest contribution to our understanding of these questions.

The third level is small group and community conflict. It includes class and ethnic conflict and the problem of gangs. Arbitration, mediation, negotiation, and torts are considered in this section as major tools for resolving conflicts. Economics, management, political science, and sociology are the major contributors to our understanding at this level.

The fourth level is organizational, primarily business, conflict, including labor-management, competition between corporations, and crisis management. Economics, history, labor studies, management are the major contributors to our understanding at this level.

The fifth level is political conflict, which includes the role of deliberative assemblies and voting systems for resolving conflicts, the problem of gerrymandering for gaining political advantage, and the problem of free riding. Economics, geography, history, law, mathematics, philosophy and political science contribute to our understanding of these conflicts

The sixth level, somewhat arbitrarily placed as it spans many of the other levels, is intellectual conflict, dominated by the five perpetual questions about man, society, history, nature, and God. Philosophy pervades these conflicts, but they also draw on theology and almost all the natural and social sciences as well.

The seventh level is interstate conflict, under which we discuss strategic geography, diplomacy, the causes and methods of war, and the search for peace. Geography, economics, history, and political science are the major contributors to our understanding at this level.

Conclusion

Theories about conflict or anything else should not be judged on whether they fit our beliefs, goals, and hopes, but on whether they increase understanding, help us to make better decisions, and meet the tests of good theory: empiricism, falsifiability, generalizability, logic, parsimony, and usability.

Chapter 2
Conflict Analysis

In as much as mathematical theories relate to reality, they are not sure;
in as much as they are sure, they are not related to reality.
—Albert Einstein

Mathematics has three major roles in the study of conflict. First, descriptive statistics summarize information and make it easier to understand. Examples include batting averages, the Dow Jones average, and median income.[1] Some descriptive statistics more directly associated with conflict include divorce rates, military expenditures, murder rates, voter turnouts, and workdays lost to strikes. Generally, they are well understood although they can be misleading. Standard deviations correct the difficulty by describing how much data spreads out from the mean. For example, the mean temperatures of Madrid and San Francisco are about the same, but the standard deviation is much greater in Madrid, meaning its temperatures are much more variable and extreme.

Second, researchers test theories by the appropriate use of research design and inferential statistics. Reduced to essentials, the process is easy to understand. First, a "null" or "no difference" hypothesis" is stated (*e.g.*, handedness is unrelated to aggressiveness[2]). Then, the researcher devises a strategy to test the hypothesis. Minimally, the strategy specifies a population, a sampling plan, the type of data needed, and how to collect and analyze the data.

The *sample*, those from whom or about whom data actually is collected, should be representative of a *population*, those about whom one desires to draw conclusions. The method might involve laboratory experiment, clinical trial, survey research, content analysis, or something else. Inferential statistics deter-

---

1. Averages take three common forms. Dividing the sum of a set of numbers by the number of numbers in the set gives the mean. Arranging the numbers from smallest to largest and identifying the one in the middle gives the median (think highway divider). Identifying the most common number in a set gives the mode (think fashion). Thus, for the set 1, 2, 3, 3, 3, 4, 5, 6, 7, 8, 8 the mean is 5, the median is 4., and the mode is 3. If all three are identical, the curve is "normal."

2. Charlotte Faurie and Michel Raymond investigated just such a hypothesis. Noting the advantage left-handed boxers have, they wondered if violent societies had more left-handed individuals than peaceful ones. Limiting their study to traditional societies, they reported, for example, that 22.6% of Yanomamo of Brazil (4 murders per 1000 inhabitants) were left-handed, whereas among the Dioula of Burkina Faso (.013 murders per 1000 inhabitants) only 3.4% of the population is left-handed. (*Economist*, 11 December 2004).

mine whether to retain or reject the hypothesis at a specified level of risk. As explained in Chapter 1, errors can be either "Type I" or "Type II". Unfortunately, designing the experiment to decrease the risk of making one error necessarily increases the risk of making the other. For this reason alone, no experiment ever is definitive.

The third role of mathematics, probably the least familiar but the most important for conflict studies, is game theory. The frivolous connotation "game" is unfortunate: it has been applied to deadly serious problems. In World War II it solved the problem of how to set depth charges to maximize the odds of sinking German submarines. Later, it guided US decisions on how many nuclear missiles to build during the Cold War. Mathematics helps conflict managers in assessing risk, making decisions under uncertain conditions, analyzing conflicts, and understanding fairness.

Risk

Starting a war is risky. Running for political office is risky. Hiring a new worker is risky. Getting married is risky. Each decision initiates or risks conflict. The way a person reacts to potential conflict depends in largely on which of four attitudes he has toward the specific risk. A risk-neutral individual is someone indifferent between two choices with an equal payoff. In the same circumstance, the risk-accepting (optimistic, self-confident) person would take the chance, while the risk-averse (pessimistic, insecure) person would not. Finally, the risk seeker seems compelled to take dangerous and unnecessary chances.

More concretely, if the chances were equal that demanding more money during salary negotiation would succeed or result in losing the job, the risk accepting would take the chance. The risk averse individual would not, and the risk neutral one might flip a coin to decide what to do. The risk seeker might start a business rather than do anything so mundane as working for someone else. An individual is likely to be more risk averse after six months unemployment than he would be if he had a perfectly satisfactory job. That is, personality and circumstance interact to determine tolerance for risk at a given moment.

We began to understand risk only after Fibonacci introduced the zero and the Hindu-Arabic numbering system to the west in 1202. Soon after, Cardano calculated the odds for each possible outcome of the roll of two dice, something nobody had been able to do although people had played dice for centuries.[3] John Graunt calculated average life expectancy and Halley (more famous for his less useful discovery of a comet) developed the first mortality tables. This opened the way to offering life insurance

From these beginnings, we have developed methods for dealing with risks of all sorts, whether or not they involve conflict. We have developed many tools to manage financial risk, including portfolio diversification, bond ratings, fu-

---

3. To see why, try dividing CMVI by XVII without converting into Arabic numerals.

tures, hedging, derivatives, puts, calls, and selling short against the box. Federal deposit insurance, unemployment insurance, welfare, social security, pensions, and life insurance reduce financial risks and dampen economic cycles. Health insurance, Medicare, and extended care insurance reduce the risk of financial disaster due to illness. Risk now is more controllable because computers permit calculating the likelihood of almost any imaginable event, and because markets are so good at pricing them.

The conflict in the United States over Social Security reform (in its more rational, less politicized form) is about attitude toward risk. On one side are the risk averse, who believe that the original system is the most certain to continue payments to the retired and who fear the near certainty that retirement for some will coincide with a market downturn, perhaps one even worse than the Great Depression. Of course, in such an unlikely event, the current pay-as-you-go system is likely to become untenable as well. On the other side, the risk-accepting look at the returns obtained through properly managed private investment averaging some ten times that from Social Security. In an attempt to make reform look more attractive, those who advocate change point to four major devices to reduce the risk. First, it should only enroll workers with at least 25 years until retirement. Second, the choice of investments should be restricted to a few simple low-cost funds with varied balances between annuities, bonds, equities, and real estate investment trusts. Third, individuals should rebalance periodically, gradually sacrificing high returns for safety as they age. Fourth, they should practice "dollar averaging," investing a fixed amount each month rather than making occasional large investments.

Despite this, many people spend too much time on small decisions and too little on big ones. Many rely on anecdotes rather than systematic information. Many do not know whether they are dealing with joint probabilities in which one event affects the probability of the next or independent ones in which events have no impact on one another. Many decide based on hope and belief. Many decide before the facts are in and have trouble changing their mind when the facts warrant.

People tend to underestimate big or familiar risks and to overestimate small or unfamiliar dangers. They ignore seat belts or fear miniscule amounts of carcinogens in foods more than driving drunk, medical error, obesity, and smoking. Europeans tend to be more fearful of genetically modified foods than of smoking. Many in Africa fear lightning more than endemic diseases such as AIDS, leprosy, malaria, or tuberculosis. Disputants risk loss in construction, environmental, family and divorce, human resources, insurance, intellectual property, patent, personal injury, zoning and other forms of conflict that pervade our society. Eighty percent of the companies making vaccines in the United States have stopped research and production because of the risk of lawsuits outweighs the profits.

Intelligence agencies fail because attackers practice security and deception to achieve surprise.[4] The best deceptions integrate five basic concepts. First, planners must know exactly what they want enemy to think and do. The objective in 1944 was to keep the Germans from moving reinforcements against Normandy until the beachheads were strong enough to resist counterattack. Second, the deception should exploit the opponent's assumptions. In 1944, the Allies could invade Europe only through Normandy or through the Pas de Calais. They chose the former because the Germans expected the latter, then focused the deception plan on what the Germans expected. Third, the plan should use several different types of information to drop mere hints that add up to the desired conclusion. Fourth, the deception must be carried out at the optimum time, taking account of factors such as how long the opponent needs to discover and analyze information and to draw conclusions. Finally, the deception usually should continue as long as possible. The Allied deception plan continued even after the Normandy invasion. Eisenhower's announcement was worded so as to make the Germans think that Normandy was a feint to draw them from Pas de Calais. Deception involves risk. Seen through, it can lead to disaster, as probably would have been the case had the Germans realized that all the intelligence suggesting the Allies planned to invade Europe in 1944 was an Allied deception, leaving Normandy as the only viable invasion point.

Conflict is inherently risky. Underdogs sometimes win. Successful risk managers (a profession in its own right) must understand both attitudes—the emotional dimension—and payoffs—the rational dimension inherent in any conflict. Theoreticians must give us better ways of integrating the way we think about risk with the causes, processes, and outcomes of conflict.

Decision Making

Prisoners' Dilemma, the earliest significant attempt at mathematical modeling of conflict, extends risk analysis to decision-making. In the basic scenario (Tucker, 1950), the police arrest and separate two suspects. The district attorney is sure they are guilty but lacks evidence so needs a confession to insure conviction. He tells each one, separately, that he can confess or not. If both refuse, the district attorney will book them on petty charges, and they will receive equal minor sentences, B. If both confess, they will receive considerably longer sen-

---

4. Pearl Harbor, the Battle of the Bulge, North Korea's invasion of South Korea, Iraq's invasion of Kuwait, and 9/11 are instances of major US intelligence failures, all of which were "obvious" after the fact. On the other side of the coin, Anthony Cave Brown (1975) tells the story of the brilliantly successful and highly imaginative Allied deceptions during World War II in *Bodyguard of Lies* Brown, 1975, Keegan, 2003). Policy makers, strategists, tacticians and conspiracy theorists all require a deep understanding of its possibilities and limitations.

tences, C. If one confesses and the other does not, then the confessor will receive the most lenient sentence of all, A, while the one who refused will get the toughest sentence of all, D. Figure 2.1 summarizes the situation. Scores within parentheses refer to Prisoner One, those without parentheses to Prisoner Two:

		(Prisoner One)	
		(Not Confess)	(Confess)
Prisoner Two	Not Confess	B (B)	D (A)
	Confess	A (D)	C (C)

Figure 2.1
Prisoners' Dilemma

If the prisoners trust one another completely, both will refuse to confess. If they are unsure of one another, how can each prisoner use the information to make the best decision for himself? The answer is for Prisoner One to add the column payoffs and to select the one with the highest payoff, and for Prisoner Two to add the row payoffs and do the same. That is, Prisoner One will compare (B) + (D) with (A) + (C) and confess or not based on the smaller total (because prisoners prefer short prison sentences to long ones). Prisoner Two will do the same based on B + D and A + C.

Regardless of the actual numbers, a "game" like this with a finite number of players and strategies will produce the same solution no matter how many times it is "played." John Forbes Nash, made famous in the movie *Beautiful Mind*, was awarded the 1994 Nobel Prize in Economics for the discovery many years earlier of the existence of these "stabilities."

Several examples explain why the possibility of identifying stable solutions to conflicts through analysis of payoffs is important. Thomas Schelling (1960) used Prisoners' Dilemma during the Cold War to determine the number of missiles the United States needed to insure that the USSR and the US would continue to choose Cold War over Hot War. A similar analysis suggests that the best strategy against terrorists is to reduce their resources rather than to try to protect potential targets. There simply are too many targets to defend them all.[5] The effective strategy is to go after their training camps and arms caches, choke off their financing, infiltrate their networks, and eliminate their state supporters. Businesses have used Prisoners' Dilemma to analyze price strategies, sociolo-

---

5. To name a few, every plane, every ship at sea, every embassy and consulate, every factory at home and abroad, every reservoir, every bridge, every school, every shopping center, and every sports facility, each (assuming no illnesses or vacations) requiring four shifts of one or more guards working 42 hours a week to maintain a round-the-clock vigil.

gists to explain racial prejudice, and. sociobiologists to explain the evolution of cooperation. The Internal Revenue Service has used it to set penalties for non-payment of taxes high enough to maximize compliance and minimize enforcement costs.[6] Prisoners' Dilemma meets the six tests of good theory reasonably well, one reason it is so prominent in the literature on conflict.

<u>Strategic Choice</u>

Fraser and Hipel (1984) proposed a method for analyzing multi-party, multi-issue disputes involving coalitions, unknown options, and incorrect or misleading information. The details are complex, so it is worth beginning with the essential points, only two in number:

> 1. Each party can rank all possible solutions in preference order.
> 2. Preferences can be analyzed to identify solutions all can accept

Consider the dispute over whether and how to save the California condor. The dispute lasted nearly 40 years. Many groups were involved, but because our purpose is to explain the method we can label as ZOO the groups led by the Los Angeles and San Diego Zoos that advocated intervention to save the condor. We label as FOE the groups led by Friends of the Earth that opposed ZOO.

ZOO believed in making every possible effort to ensure survival of the condor, so advocated captive breeding or double clutching,[7] in preference order. FOE believed in letting nature take its course, so preferred doing nothing, habitat protection, or feeding uncontaminated cattle to condors, in that order. Using binary notation, proposing a strategy is designated "1," while opposing it is designated as "0." Figure 2.2 shows all the possibilities.

Protect habitat	0 1 0 1 0 1 0 1 0 1 0 1 0 1 0 1
Uncontaminated feed	0 0 1 1 0 0 1 1 0 0 1 1 0 0 1 1
Double clutch	0 0 0 0 1 1 1 1 0 0 0 0 1 1 1 1
Captive breed	0 0 0 0 0 0 0 0 1 1 1 1 1 1 1 1

Figure 2.2
All Possible Resolutions of Condor Dispute

An analyst can easily work out every possible outcome no matter how many parties and strategies are involved. Simply alternate 0 and 1 in the first row. Alternate pairs of zeros and ones on the next row. Continue doubling the number

---

6. These examples are explained at the appropriate points in the chapters that follow.
7. Taking a newly laid egg to hatch in captivity knowing that the female would lay a second egg to replace it.

of adjacent zeros in each subsequent row and duplicate them as ones until a row in which all the zeros appear on the left and all the ones on the right is reached. The "do nothing" strategy is shown in column 1 as four "0s." *Every* possible combination is included in such an array.

Next, eliminate absurd combinations. Birds cannot both be entirely in the wild and entirely in captivity, so 0101 is absurd. Similarly, 1001, 1101, 1011, 0111 and 1111 make no sense. Rearrange the strategies in preference order for each disputant. Where two or more disputants have identical preference orders, perhaps because they have formed a coalition, eliminate the duplicate arrays. FOE prefers minimum interference in nature, so from left to right, highest to lowest, its preferences are those of the first four rows of Figure 2.3:

Protect habitat	0	1	0	1	0	1	0	1	0	0
Uncontaminated feed	0	0	1	1	0	0	1	1	0	0
Double clutch	0	0	0	0	1	1	1	1	0	1
Captive breed	0	0	0	0	0	0	0	0	1	1
FOE preference vector	0	1	2	3	4	5	6	7	8	12

Figure 2.3
FOE Preferences

ZOO prefers species preservation by the most cost-effective possible method (explaining why 0001 is preferred to 0011). Its preferences, from left to right, highest to lowest are those of the first four rows of Figure 2.4:

Protect habitat	0	0	1	1	0	0	1	1	0	0
Uncontaminated feed	0	0	1	0	1	0	1	0	1	0
Double clutch	0	1	1	1	1	1	0	0	0	0
Captive breed	1	1	0	0	0	0	0	0	0	0
ZOO preference vector	8	12	7	5	6	4	3	1	2	0

Figure 2.4
ZOO Preferences

Before conducting the analysis, it is useful to convert each binomial column to base ten, resulting in the final row for Figures 2.3 and 2.4 and providing a convenient way to uniquely "name" each possible outcome. The result is designated a "preference vector." To make the conversion, multiply each binomial times the power-of-two value to which the location corresponds, using the top number as the low-order digit. For example, 1110 (the eighth column of numbers in Figure 2.3 and the third one in Figure 2.4) converts as follows:

$$1110 = 1 * 2^0 + 1 * 2^1 + 1 * 2^2 + 0 * 2^3 = 1 + 2 + 4 + 0 = 7$$

These arrays provide a complete description of the conflict between the two parties, with the preferences of each clearly stated. As Einstein noted, all mathematical models clarify at the expense of simplification. In this system, the relative intensity associated with each possibility is lost.

The remaining steps are more tedious than difficult. Begin by identifying "unilateral improvements," designating them with the symbol UI. These improve one party's position without inducing other parties to change their strategy. They occur whenever the *opponent's* preferences do not change from left to right. For example, ZOO can move from its second-choice 0011 solution to 0001, ZOO's first choice solution, because FOE prefers 00 in both instances. While this is the only unilateral improvement for ZOO, FOE has several such improvements, as indicated in Figure 2.5.

Protect habitat	0	1	0	1	0	1	0	1	0	0	
Uncontaminated feed	0	0	1	1	0	0	1	1	0	0	
Double clutch	0	0	0	0	1	1	1	1	0	1	
Captive breed	0	0	0	0	0	0	0	0	1	1	
FOE preference vector	0	1	2	3	4	5	6	7	8	12	
	0	0	0		4	4	4				UI
		1	1			5	5				UI
			2				6				UI
	r	u	u	u	r	u	u	u	r	r	

Protect habitat	0	0	1	1	0	0	1	1	0	0	
Uncontaminated feed	0	0	1	0	1	0	1	0	1	0	
Double clutch	0	1	1	1	1	1	0	0	0	0	
Captive breed	1	1	0	0	0	0	0	0	0	0	
ZOO preference vector	8	12	7	5	6	4	3	1	2	0	
		8									UI
	r	u	r	r	r	r	r	r	r		
	E					E			E		

Figure 2.5
Analysis of Condor Dispute

The next step is to determine stabilities, there being four possible types for each player. The analysis is a matter of inspection and logic rather than calculation. The first type, rational stability, occurs whenever a disputant has no UI to make from an outcome. Figure 2.5 indicates each one by the symbol *r*.

Second, check for sequentially sanctioned stabilities (*s*). These occur when a disputant has a UI that allows the opponent to respond unilaterally and leave the disputant worse off. Identify them by checking each disputant's UIs one by one. There are none in the current situation, but *if* ZOO had a UI from 2 to1, FOE would then have its own UI from 1 to 0, which ZOO regards as a worse outcome to the dispute. Therefore, ZOO would be "sequentially sanctioned" against a unilateral move to strategy 1.

Third, identify instabilities. These occur if a disputant can make a unilateral improvement the opponent cannot respond to with a credible action that results in a less preferred outcome for that disputant. In effect, any strategy not already identified by an *r* or an *s* is unstable and can be marked with a *u*. Figure 2.5 indicates them for both parties.

Fourth, inspect the arrays to identify cases in which a change in strategy would be unstable for all disputants and would leave one or both worse off. Neither disputant would allow such a choice, so these cases are termed "simultaneously sanctioned stabilities." Use the base-ten notation to identify them. Add the base ten values of two unilateral improvements for each player and subtract the strategy being analyzed. Sequential sanctioning exists *only* if the base ten value that results appears on the array to the *left* of the base ten value resulting from the calculation for all disputants. They are exceptionally rare (in this case there are none) but if found are indicated by a slash (/) through the symbol *u*.

An outcome rated *r* or *s* for *all* disputants constitutes a possible resolution to the conflict and is labeled E for equilibrium. In practice, even very complex conflicts have only one to three equilibriums. Each is likely to be meaningful. In this case, they identify the three historical solutions. No action (0000) was taken for 33 years. Double clutching (0010) followed but soon failed. Finally, all surviving condors were captured (0001). By February 1992, captive breeding was working well enough to begin releasing birds into the wild.

The analysis of the condor dispute illustrates how potentially stable solutions to complex conflicts can be identified. How best to use the information rests entirely on the methods (Chapter 8) used to resolve the conflict.

Fair Division

Disputes involving division of property are common. They come up in divorces, settling estates, and dividing the assets of a business that is closing. Allocating resources (*e. g.*, water among farmers, fish, home owners, industry, power, and recreational users) is a related problem. Other cases are dividing the spoils of war, allocating household chores, or developing a wage structure for employees.[8] Differing skills and levels of involvement can complicate the problem of fairly dividing the remaining assets of a small business among its former partners. The division is further complicated when disputants place different values on the items to be divided.

Some animals even seem to have a sense of fairness. Capuchins prefer grapes to cucumbers. In a lab in which capuchins had learned to exchange tokens for food, capuchins who observed one animal receiving a grape for a token refused to give up a token just to get a cucumber, going so far as to throw their

---

8. See Ishmael's negotiation for his share of the profits in Herman Melville's *Moby Dick*.

tokens away or even at the researcher who only offered cucumber slices. It seems righteous indignation is not limited to people.[9]

Many traditional stories raise the complex issue of what we mean by "fair." One is the story of the prodigal son (Luke 15: 11-32). Another is the parable of the man who hired field workers at the first, third, sixth, and eleventh hours of the day but paid them all the same amount at the end of the day. Over the objection of those hired first, the owner insisted that this was fair because he had made a different contract with each and had the right to do with his money as he pleased (Matthew 20: 1-16).

The tenth century Indian *Patiganita*, includes a tale of four dancers who were to perform for four hours for a payment of 48 rupees. However, the best dancer dropped out after one, the second best after two, and the third best after three hours, only the least talented dancer completing her part of the contract. What is fair payment for each?

One possibility is to pay each dancer 12 rupees based on the contract. Another is to divide the 48 rupees based on hours actually danced by each (3, 7, 17 and 25 rupees per dancer). As 48 rupees divided by four dancers for four hours implies an hourly rate of 3 rupees per hour danced, a fourth possibility is to pay the dancers 3, 6, 9 and 12 rupees, the remaining 18 rupees going unpaid as the contract was only partially completed. A fifth possibility is equal division based on ten hours of dancing (4.80, 9.60, 14.40 and 19.20 rupees per dancer). A sixth possibility is to refuse any payment because the dancers did not fulfill the contract for a group performance. Finally, one could pay only the dancer who fulfilled her contract, but should she receive her daily rate of 12 rupees or the entire amount of 48 rupees?

Imagine a failed business in which each partner supplied a third of the capital. One partner provided the management expertise, the second the accounting and legal expertise, and the third provided the marketing expertise. Should the remaining assets be divided equally among the three? Should the partner who took the biggest risk by delaying payment of school loans to start the business get more than the others? Should the one who exaggerated his skills and caused the failure get less? If you chose the first possibility you equate fairness with equality. The second implies that fairness requires consideration of need. If you chose the third, you think fairness requires an element of equity, in this case in the form of accountability.

An American cited for going 17 miles (25 km) per hour over the speed limit might pay a fine of $200. Fairness means treating everyone equally (the justification for a flat tax). In Finland, your fine would increase with your income. This definition of fairness as equity (the justification for progressive taxation) resulted in Anssi Vanjoki paying a $103,600 fine for driving 25 kilometers per hour over the 50 kilometer per hour limit just after cashing in a lot of stock options. Exempting someone from the fine because he was speeding to a hospital

---

9. *Economist* 20 September 2003

with a heart attack victim is an example of fairness as need (the justification for consumption taxes or negative income taxes).[10] Particularly in conflict situations, whenever you hear someone speaking of "fairness," make sure you understand which of the three interpretations is meant and whether or not you agree it is the one that is applicable.

Brams and Taylor (1966) identified four fundamental aspects of fairness in thought experiments involving the division of a piece of cake under various circumstances. Parents know that the best way to divide a cake between two children is to allow the older one to cut it and the other to choose first. This ensures that both children believe they got at least half the cake. A procedure with this characteristic is said to be *proportional*, the first requirement for fair division. In that neither child will feel the other child got a larger piece (although the chooser may sometimes think he got the larger one), the solution also is *envy-free*, the second requirement.

Brams came up with a way to extend the process to three people, but could not solve it for four. He turned to Alan Taylor, who in a Eureka moment saw that dividing a cake among "n" people requires cutting it into $2^{n-2} + 1$ pieces at the start. That comes to five pieces in a four party dispute, reminiscent of the difficulty the four allies had in dividing Germany into occupation zones until they treated Berlin as a fifth "piece." After the first person cuts the cake, the next person has the option of setting one piece aside then trimming any of the remaining pieces so that he perceives all of them to be equal. Each person repeats the process of setting one piece aside and trimming any of the remaining pieces until he feels all are equal. Choosing is done in reverse order, with the condition that anyone who did any trimming must take one of the trimmed pieces if any still are available. The extra piece assures that no player feels he must take second best. The solution was a conceptual but not very practical breakthrough. Other than money there are few things that are as simple to divide as cake—and simple arithmetic suffices for dividing it without such elaborate procedures.

Suppose that half the cake is vanilla and the other half is chocolate. Alita likes only vanilla, but Mike, who likes only chocolate and is the cutter does not know this. The only way Mike is sure to have some of his favorite flavor is to cut the cake so each piece has equal amounts of chocolate and vanilla. In this case, if Mike and Alita announced their preferences, Mike could cut the cake so that he got all the chocolate and Alita got all the vanilla. The solution would remain proportional and envy-free but also would be *efficient*, a third desirable characteristic of fair division. But, if Alita lied about her preference, which really is for chocolate, she will end up with all the chocolate and Mike will end up with the vanilla he despises. Efficiency requires truthfulness, rare among people in conflict.

---

10. Landsburg, S. (n.d.) Highway Robbery. *Wall Street Journal.*

There is a second aspect to efficiency often described as "making the cake larger" so everyone gets more. Take the case of a sister and brother deciding who gets a diamond and who gets a chess set, both appraised at $2000. The sister personally values the chess set at $2500 and the diamond at the $2000 for which she could sell it. The brother values the diamond at $2500 but the chess set at the $2000 for which he could sell it. In this artificially simple situation, giving the diamond to the sister and the chess set to the brother would give $2000 to each for a joint gain of $4000. But, if the diamond went to the brother and the chess set to the sister, each would feel they had received $2500, a joint gain of $5000. The second solution is more efficient. It also is likely to be stable, the characteristic originally identified by Nash

All this speculation helps clarify what we mean by fairness. Sometimes we mean equality, sometimes equity, and sometimes need. Having clarified which we mean, the problem is to find a practical method for achieving it that is efficient, envy-free, proportional, stable, and encourages truthfulness among claimants. Nobody has devised a perfect method to do all this, but four come close and are adaptable to various circumstances

The first technique, Adjusted Winner, begins by having each claimant distribute 100 (or 1000 if a lot of items are involved) points to the items to indicate their relative importance. Let us assume two claimants assign their points among five items to be divided as shown in Figure 2.6:

Items	A	B	C	D	E	Total
Mike	15	25	35	10	15	100
Alita	9	20	30	20	21	100
Total	24	45	65	30	36	200

Figure 2.6
Relative Importance of Items to be Divided

Each item is first assigned to the individual who values it the most, as shown by underlining. The items are re-ordered from left to right based on the *ratios* of the points (always dividing the largest by the smallest number). The underlined points are added to determine the perceived value received by each, as shown in Figure 2.7:

Items	C	B	E	A	D	Total
Mike	_35_	_25_	15	_15_	10	75
Alita	30	20	_21_	9	_20_	41
Ratios	1.16	1.25	1.33	1.50	2.00	1.83

Figure 2.7
Initial Assignments Under Adjusted Winner

We now must determine what and how much Mike must transfer to Alita to equalize the result. Work from smallest to largest ratio, which is to say left to right, through as many items as necessary to achieve the goal. In this case, transferring all of C to Alita would give her 71 points but reduce Mike to 40 points, so it is clear that Mike must only surrender a part of C. We can designate the proportion Mike will retain as C_1, and the proportion that Alita will receive as 1 - C_1. We then write and solve the formula (using the values assigned to item C by each and the total points already received by Mike and Alita):

$$35C_1 + 25 + 15 = 30(1 - C_1) + 21 + 20$$
$$35C_1 + 25 + 15 = 30 - 30C_1 + 21 + 20$$
$$35C_1 + 40 = 30C_1 + 71$$
$$35C_1 - 30C_1 = 71 - 40$$
$$65C_1 = 31$$

C_1 = .477, the proportion of Item C that Mike retains
1 - C_1 = .523, the proportion of Item C that Alita receives

$$.477 * (35 + 25 + 15) + 40 = 16.69 + 40 = 56.69 \text{ points to Mike}$$
$$.523 * (30 + 21 + 20) + 41 = 15.69 + 41 = 56.69 \text{ points to Alita}$$

This system and this order of doing things insure efficiency, envy-freeness and proportionality, and is likely to result in a stable solution. The system also makes it possible to divide goods in any proportion desired. For example, if Alita is entitled to two-thirds, and Mike to one-third of the property, a ratio of 2 to 1, rewrite the equation so tht 2 of Mike's shares equal Alita's share:

$$2[35C_1 + 25 + 15] = 30(1 - C_1) + 21 + 20$$

so that two of Mike's shares will equal Alita's share. The method works only with items that can be subdivided into very small units, only with two claimants, and only if both honestly represent their interests.

When a reasonable degree of truthfulness cannot be assumed, a technique called Proportional Allocation gives up efficiency to insure equality, proportionality and envy-freeness. It also is much simpler to carry out. Start with the same situation as before (Figure 2.6). Assign Mike 15/24 and Alita 9/24 of item A; Mike 25/45 of item B, and so on (that is, square the points assigned to the item by the individual and divide by the column total). Mike would receive 9.37 + 13.89 + 18.85 + 3.33 + 6.25 = 51.69 points. Alita would receive 3.37 + 8.89 + 13.85 + 13.33 + 12.25 = 51.69 points. Alita and Mike each receive equal shares but 8.88% less value than the 56.69 points they would receive using Adjusted Winner. The method remains envy free and proportional but surrenders efficiency to ensure truthfulness. As in the case of Adjusted Winner, the process is limited to two claimants and to items that are easily subdivided.

What if there are many items and claimants? Brams and Taylor did develop a technique (described above) based on cake cutting, but it quickly becomes unmanageable. Imagine three siblings trying to divide an inheritance consisting of $20,000 and fifty items that include such typical family possessions as a piano and a car, items that are hard to "trim." Of course, the siblings could simply agree to sell everything and divide the resulting cash equally. The siblings could even buy the items themselves, knowing they would get back one third of the price paid for anything as part of their equal share of the proceeds from the sale when the cash was divided. However, two siblings might bid against one another for the same item, reducing efficiency

There are two alternatives to selling. The first is the Steinhaus fair-division procedure (Raiffa, 1982). It assumes that each claimant has cash to give to other claimants *if necessary* to equalize the distribution. Each claimant submits a valuation for each item to a mediator. The mediator divides each claimant's total valuation by the number of claimants, designating this amount as the "initial fair share." Each item is assigned to the claimant who values it most highly. The initial fair share is subtracted from the total value each claimant perceives himself to be receiving. The total excess (it will be positive so long as the initial valuations differ) is divided equally among all claimants. Figure 2.12 provides a specific example. The result is efficient, envy-free and proportional. The method is complex, so disputants may not trust it.

Items	Claimants			Total
	X	Y	Z	
A. Chess set	800	850	885	
B. Printer	150	200	175	
C. Rifle	800	500	750	
D. Rug	320	400	290	
E. Television set	465	525	600	
Total value assigned by each claimant	2535	2475	2700	
Initial fair share (total value/number of items)	845	825	900	
Assign each item efficiently	Claimant	B, D	A, E	
Perceived value of items received	800	600	1485	
Excess value (fair share - value received)	-45	-225	585	315
Fair share of excess (total excess/claimants)	105	105	105	315
Target value (initial fair share + share of excess)	950	930	1005	
Cash adjustment (target value - perceived value)	150	330	-480	

Figure 2.8
Steinhaus Fair Division Procedure

The final possibility is an "imaginary auction." If this method is adopted, the negotiation will not be over who gets what, but over the rules for conducting the auction. The most important of these rules are the minimum raise, whether to use the last bid or the appraised value in balancing the books, and exempting any cash from the bidding. Balancing on the basis of the last bid usually is best, if for no other reason than it often is not worth the price to obtain a neutral appraisal. With the rules set, bids are made and can be raised until someone wins the item. Instead of actually paying for items, the winning bid is credited to the winner of the item as value received. After all items have been auctioned off, the total received by each person is determined and cash is used to balance the books. The cash might be part of the property to be divided (the reason for exempting it from the bidding in the first place). Might come from the individual who received the greatest value, or a combination of both. Any remaining cash is then divided among the claimants based on their entitlements. Figure 2.13 shows what might have happened in such an auction.

Sibling	A	B	C	D
Items received	15	19	6	10
Bid totals	23456	25854	32798	27409
Estate cash	9342	6944	0	714
Sibling C cash	0	0	0	1675
Total received	32798	32798	32798	32798

Figure 2.9
Results of Imaginary Auction

A clever claimant could try to gain an advantage if he knows how much more someone else values an item than he does. By overbidding, he can force the other person to pay too much, which will increase the cash he receives in the end. However, it is risky. The person seeking the advantage may over-estimate the amount the other will bid, and end up winning the item for more than he values it, reducing rather than increasing the cash and total value he receives. The danger can be reduced but not eliminated and truthfulness increased, by making sure everyone understands the trick and its implications before the bidding starts.

The imaginary auction insures that each item goes to the person who wants it most, so the result is envy-free and efficient. What we do not know is how much more each person would have bid for the items received. Proportionality is impossible to calculate because we do not know how much more each winning bidder would have paid even assuming they knew themselves.

The method has much to commend it despite its imperfections. In addition to being envy-free and efficient, it can handle almost any number of claimants and almost any number of items. Nobody has to decide in advance how much to bid on an item. Disproportionate entitlements remain possible through cash adjustments. It usually eliminates a lot of bickering and bitterness, and it often vastly reduces the time wasted in trying to reach a solution. It is easy to understand.

Conclusion

Mathematicians have provided vital understanding and tools for conflict theorists. Descriptive statistics provide an efficient way to summarize large amounts of information. Inferential statistics help in testing hypotheses that follow logically from conflict theories. Mathematical games and models help us to think clearly about fairness and risk, although as Einstein reminds us above, we should not expect this clarity to eliminate the passions. Risk analysis and game theory provide theoreticians and practitioners with an important tool for factoring uncertainty into making decisions. Applications are not limited to those involving money, as we will see throughout this book.

A fair resolution to any conflict has four desirable characteristics. First, it should encourage truthfulness and discourage deception. Second, it should be efficient, in that no better solution is possible for one person without hurting someone else. Third, it should be proportional in that claimants feel that the share received equals their entitlement. Fourth, it should be envy-free, in that no disputant wants the share another with the same entitlement received. We also know that envy-freeness can be achieved only if we understand which of three possible concepts of fairness, equity, equality or need is being used by each claimant.

Mathematicians have given us several specific tools for understanding or managing conflict. Of these, Prisoners Dilemma has had the widest impact. The method based on analysis of preferences reduced to an array of numbers can help conflict managers identify proposals that all sides to a dispute are likely to accept and that are likely to prove stable. The imaginary auction provides a simple, practical method for dividing property that meets, or nearly meets, all the requirements for fair division. These ideas are useful across all levels of the conflict spectrum, often influencing other theorists or providing useful tools for practioners.

Chapter 3
The Nature of Man

We were born of risen apes, not fallen angels...
The miracle of man is not how far he has sunk,
but how magnificently he has risen.

—Robert Ardrey, *African Genesis*

The next two chapters deal with the traditional question of whether nature, nurture or a combination of the two best explains human aggression. The first chapter focuses on physical and the second on mental aspects of the question.

<u>Early Man</u>

Anthropologists have long debated whether the first humans were peaceful vegetarians, aggressive carnivores, or opportunistic scavengers: in other words, the familiar debate as to whether we are aggressive by nature, nurture, or some combination of the two.

One reason anthropologists study isolated primitive tribes is the assumption that man's original nature can be learned from people who are least influenced by civilization. The majority of anthropologists conclude from these studies that man is by nature gentle, shy, timid, and non-aggressive. This fits their model of a peaceful vegetarian ancestry for mankind, and the radical image of the noble savage of which many anthropologists and sophisticates have been enamored at least since Tacitus compared fellow Roman citizens unfavorably with German barbarians. Franz Boaz founded Cultural Anthropology on similar assumptions. His students included Margaret Meade and Ashley Montagu, according to whom "...the power of instinctual drives [in humans] has gradually withered away, until man has virtually lost all his instincts (Montagu, 1962a). In the same year, he wrote that "Evil is not inherent in human nature, it is learned... Aggressiveness is taught, as are all forms of violence which human beings exhibit (Montagu, 1962b)."

But, as Robert Ardrey (1965) points out, "Who is going to suffer the deprivations necessary to take from the Eskimo his dinner of whale blubber and his home of ice cubes?" The underlying assumption of most anthropologists may be wrong: isolated tribes may be those that were unable to defend desirable territories so have found a way to survive in areas unattractive to more warlike tribes. After all, some primitive tribes are incredibly warlike.

Raymond Dart's 1924 discovery of a two million year old hominid fossil skull and his follow-up announcement in 1949 that the species hunted baboons gave the debate an interesting turn. He estimated that the adult would have been four feet tall, bipedal, and with a brain intermediate between that of a gorilla and modern man. This was the discovery that pointed to man's emergence in Africa rather than Asia as hitherto believed. Dart later reported finding some fifty baboon fossils that had been killed by a blow to the skull using the humerus bone of an antelope as a club. That is, not only was early man a carnivore but he had used weapons as well. The majority of anthropologists responded that hyenas must have killed the baboons and that the skulls had been found in their dens. Dart (1959) falsified this argument with 24 reasons why the "hyena alibi" as he called it made no sense.

The advocates of a peaceful vegetarian ancestry did not give up. If hyenas did not kill the baboons, it must have been leopards. This is known to be the case (and sometimes baboons manage to kill leopards) but the negative proof does not prove that early man did not *also* kill baboons any more than the fact that cougars kill deer proves that human hunters do not kill them also. The argument continues in the best scientific tradition to this day, with both sides trying to refute the other. Against the considerable evidence that early hominids ate meat, many argued that early man was incapable of hunting so that any meat eaten must have been scavenged. The opponents responded that *Australopithecus africanus* possessed axes, saws, scrapers, poniards, digging tools and clubs, suggesting despite their general inefficiency for hunting that they may have been capable of more than scavenging. In 1959, Dart found an *Australopithecus* skull with a jaw broken by a blow that left the same double depression found on the baboon skulls. As the individual had died of the blow (or at least before it healed), this was evidence of fighting among the *Australopithecines* and perhaps of murder. Another half-dozen skulls with similar injuries have been found since.

Louis Leakey (1965) notes that the vast majority of fossils found associated with the living floors or camp sites of prehistoric man represent the remains of his meals, and these are primarily of bovines ten or twenty times the size of those eating them. If man were only a scavenger, one would expect a more random and less tasty diet. The most parsimonious explanation of the facts is that man has been hunting for a very long time.

In 2001, Ahounta Djimdoumalbaye discovered a skull, two fragments of lower jaw and three teeth from five individuals of a previously unknown human ancestor in what now is Chad. *Sahelanthropus tchadensis* predates Dart's *Australopithecus* by two million years, making it the oldest hominid known. More important, both the location of the find and the mix of primitive and evolved traits "plays havoc with the tidy model of human origins" (Wood, 2002). The braincase and most of the teeth resemble chimpanzees. The nose, brow ridges, facial profile, and base of the skull match those of proto-humans who lived four million years later.

The discovery suggests that hominids were spread through Africa two million years before *Australopithecus*, providing the conditions for the branching off of many species (Brunet, 2002; Wood, 2002), and may spell the end to the long-running search for a single human ancestor and the theory that human evolution is a single file march from ape to man (Pilbeam, 2003). It may be that some were vegetarians, some were hunters, and some were scavengers.

Biology of Aggression

Biology can help us to distinguish the role of nature, nurture, and their interaction in understanding human aggression (Nelson, 2000). Aggression has a biological component that begins with the structure of the brain and the workings of the endocrine system. Emotion, information processing, and decision-making are involved in most instances of aggression and conflict. The limbic system, which developed early in evolutionary history, is the seat of emotions. Information processing is associated with the neocortex. To the extent that the limbic system dominates emotions, people may not be totally aware and in control of their behavior in times of stress.

The hypothalamus is part of the "limbic system," probably the place where the sensation of anger originates in humans. It is a primitive part of the brain that has changed little, suggesting that fundamental emotional responses evolved early. It also suggests that many animals experience emotions and have feelings, which many pet owners understand. Hormones and chemicals may affect brain functioning and neurotransmitters in ways that increase aggressiveness.

Adrenaline, also known as epinephrine, prepares the body for fight or flight. When it is released, heart rate and systolic blood pressure go up, blood flow can double, and blood sugar rises while metabolism is inhibited. In man there also is a feeling of anxiety. Intriguingly, those who argue that fighting is instinctive tend not to attend much to the related, often preferred, instinct for flight, nor do any of these hormones explain which choice is made and why.

Estrogens seem to reduce aggressiveness unless the female is defending its young, but the effects vary among species. Of much greater interest, estrogen has proven effective in reducing hostility and aggression in male sex offenders and in demented patients (Kyomen, 2002).

Testosterone is a logical hormone to suspect of links to aggression because men generally are more aggressive than women. Men have 8 to 10 times more than women. The amount varies from person to person. Levels are higher in the morning than at night. Extreme surpluses or deficiencies are rare. In humans, violence occurs largely in males from adolescence into their forties. By that age, testosterone concentrations decrease, while serotonin, which inhibits aggression, increases, a combination that tends to reduce violent behavior.

Considerable research has linked high testosterone levels with anti-social behavior, poor work history, spousal abuse, extra-marital affairs and divorce. High testosterone levels have been suggested to explain risk seeking (such as playing "chicken" or exceptionally reckless driving) although sociobiology (below) undermines this interpretation. One study of 4462 men found that the high-testosterone men were linked to high levels of delinquency, substance abuse and a tendency toward excess. They had more trouble with authority figures such as teachers, were more likely to have gone AWOL if in service, or to have used hard drugs. A separate study of 692 men in prison found those with high testosterone levels to have been more likely to have committed more crimes of violence, have more convictions and denials of parole, and more prison rule violations, especially rules involving confrontation. Even in women, high testosterone levels were related to crimes of unprovoked violence.

But, this picture is incomplete and oversimplified. First, social rank (hierarchy in higher primates, socio-economic status and education in man) mitigates its effects. Second, it is associated with many positive qualities, such as self-confidence and a sense of well-being. James Dabbs (2000) has conducted dozens of varied and well-designed research studies (including the two cited in the previous paragraph) and published hundreds of books and papers over three decades that have led him to conclude that testosterone affects behavior but that there is no proof that it causes aggression. For example, he found that testosterone levels shot up in the victors and plunged in losers in chess matches. The same phenomenon was found in fans tested immediately before and after the 1994 World Cup soccer final. This suggests that testosterone levels may be a result rather than a cause of aggression. In what anyone who has watched research on human behavior for a couple of decades will recognize as a fairly common phenomenon, researchers now suggest that testosterone deficiency may cause anxiety, depression, diminished libido, insomnia, irritability, physical weakness and poor memory and weakness.

If hormones are linked to aggression, then one might expect that diseases of the endocrine system might be linked as well. For example, hyperthyroidism has been linked to unusual levels of violence. Premenstrual Syndrome (PMS) has sometimes been associated with aggression, and has been used in court defenses of women accused of violent crimes, although there is little support for it as a direct factor in criminal activity. It has four forms and three effects. The first form is associated with fluid retention (PMS-H hyperhydration) and results in bloated stomachs and swollen ankles, knees, hands, and face. The second form (PMS-C) is associated with physical symptoms such as headaches, pains in the legs, arms and back, nausea, and food cravings. The third form, (PMS-A anxiety) and fourth form (PMS-D depression) are associated with mood swings, irritability, tension, depression, anxiety, and disturbed sleep (Reid and Yen, 1981).

Some may think the infamous "Twinkie Defense" to be relevant to this discussion—but it never happened. Dan White murdered San Francisco Mayor George Moscone and City Councilman Harvey Milk. The defense team argued that White had been suffering from long-term untreated depression that diminished his capacity to distinguish right from wrong, and called Dr. Martin Blinder as a witness to testify that the conversion of the previously health-conscious White to a junk-food junkie was evidence of, *not* the cause of, his depression.

Drug abuse also has a strong association with violence, though perhaps less with actual use than with crimes committed to get the cash to buy them, or with wars among sellers. The actual situation is more complex. Marijuana appears to reduce aggression. Hallucinogens except PCP are associated with aggression only when they lead to disorganized behavior or panic. Opiates produce euphoria and lethargy although controlled laboratory experiments have found them to increase the likelihood of unprovoked aggression. The connection between aggression and amphetamines is contradictory. Some researchers report that they stimulate delusions, emotional volatility, hyperactivity, impulsivity, paranoid psychosis, and rage, but their studies are retrospective, involve small samples, and often involve users of multiple drugs, so causation is unclear. Other studies find that amphetamines increase blood pressure but do not lead to aggression. A double-blind experiment that included a placebo suggests that cocaine use increases aggression (Miller, 1996).

Alcohol use has long been associated with violence and aggression. The upper limits in studies of the association between the two report as many as 86% of murderers, 57% of men and 27% of women involved in marital violence, 60% of sexual offenders, and 42% of people who committed other violent crimes had been drinking. A person may become aggressive because he drinks, but a person who intends to commit crime, violent or not, may drink to bolster his courage. Alcohol may increase the risk of violent behavior only for certain individuals or subpopulations and only under some situations and social or cultural influences (Alcohol Alert October 1997, 2000, Potter-Effron, 1997).

One explanation of these data suggests that alcohol weakens brain mechanisms that restrain impulsive behavior. The drinker is less able than the nondrinker (even if the same person) to judge risks, more likely to misjudge social cues as aggressive and more likely to overreact. Another focuses on individual differences in brain chemistry to explain why alcohol results in aggression in some persons but not in others. Research to refine and correct models such as these should gradually improve our understanding of the environmental and biological aspects of violence, and their interaction.

Such models are essential to developing effective strategies not just for alcohol-related violence, but also other problems such as domestic violence, sexual assault, and childhood abuse and neglect. The research suggests that some violent behavior is preventable and some is treatable. One study found decreased levels of marital violence in couples that completed behavioral therapy for alcoholism and remained sober. Another suggests that a 10-percent increase in the beer tax could reduce murder, rape and robbery. Although the reductions were miniscule, the findings do suggest directions for future research. Some anticonvulsants (*e.g.*, carbamazepine), mood stabilizers (*e.g.*, lithium), and antidepressants, (*e.g.*, fluoxetine) have similar potential.

Sex chromosome abnormalities are blamed for some aggression. There are two sex chromosomes, labeled X (female) and (Y) male. An individual inherits one chromosome from each parent. If both are X, the child will be a normal female; if one is X and one is Y the child will be a normal male. In about one case in two thousand, a male child inherits an extra Y chromosome, resulting in Jacobs Syndrome (alternatively, the XYY syndrome). Such individuals are usually very tall and thin; many experience severe acne during adolescence, and their IQ usually is normal but significantly below that of siblings. For a while there was a lot of interest in sex chromosome abnormalities as a cause of aggression. But, a thorough review of the literature combined with a double blind study of 4591 men found no association between either XYY or XXY abnormalities and violence (Schiavi, et al. 1984).

Sociobiology[1]

Sociobiology's most important precursors are Charles Darwin, Herbert Spencer, Konrad Lorenz, and William Hamilton. Darwin suggested partial inheritance of behavior in *The Descent of Man*, although before the discovery of genes he did not suggest how it was possible. Spencer applied evolutionary theory to society, the doctrine known as "Social Darwinism." He, not Darwin, coined the phrase "survival of the fittest." Lorenz discovered imprinting, showing that some behaviors are wired into the brain in some species.

William Hamilton (1964a, 1964b) launched the modern genetic theory of altruism when he realized that genes, not individuals, were the basic unit of evolution. Haldane (1955) anticipated the concept when he remarked that he would lay down his life for two brothers *or* eight cousins, each of which would pass on the same number of his own genes. Genes are selfish: from their perspective, individuals are nothing more than the way genes survive across generations (Dawkins, 1989). If the contest is between individuals, then altruism is detrimental to success. If the contest is between societies, then members sometimes must cooperate (Ardrey, 1969).

All this set the stage for Edward Wilson, an entomologist by training but a renaissance man by inclination. Sociobiology rests on the assumption that animals evolve behaviorally as well as physically for the purpose of maximizing transmission of their own genes, the measure of evolutionary success. Sociobiologists distinguish many types of genetically rooted aggression but emphasize its variability by species and social organization (*e.g.*, the raids of the nomad vs. the conquests of the farmers). Edward Wilson (1975) proposed eight types that he felt have evolutionary roles.

Anti-predatory behavior is primarily defensive but is defined as a form of aggression by Wilson. While most animals prefer fleeing to fighting, most have some form of defense. Prey need not be able to outfight predators, only to injure them enough that the predator no longer will be able to hunt. A zebra's kicks can break a pursuing lion's jaw. A lion so injured will starve, so it attacks carefully,

---

. 1. Recently transformed into "Evolutionary Psychology," this is the more colorful original name.

providing that slight margin that allows zebras to escape most but not every time.

Dominance behaviors exist only in species that live in hierarchical societies and determine each individual's place in it. Subordinates—or those who lose the contests—have species-specific signals announcing their surrender. With rare exceptions confined largely to hunter-gatherer societies, humans live in a hierarchical society. However, the basis for dominance varies widely both within and between cultures. In humans it takes the form of social status, but this has taken many forms across time and place.

Moralistic aggression consists of punishment to enforce behavioral norms and group standards. It seems little different than parental discipline, except it may take the form of punishment by non-relatives including, in human society, formal punishments by authorities such as judges, priests, and teachers.

Parental discipline in many species takes the form of mild aggression to keep offspring close at hand, urge them into motion, break up fighting, and enforce limits. Spanking is an example.

Predatory behavior is seen as aggression by sociobiologists such as Wilson, who sees it as indistinguishable from murder and cannibalism but not as aggression by ethologists such as Lorenz or psychiatrists such as Fromm.

Sexual aggression and rape occurs when males threaten or actually attack females for the sole purpose of mating or sex. In some species, especially among spiders, the female is the aggressor, often eating males immediately after mating in many species. Hamadryas baboons build and maintain their harems by force. Gelada baboons do not. In one experiment, Gelada females placed with Hamadryas males escaped at the first opportunity, but Hamadryas females placed with Geladas had the good sense to avoid returning to the Hamadryas troops!

Territorial aggression involves staking out and defending a territory. It usually begins with vocal or visual signals or by scent marking to define the claim. An incredible variety of patterns exist. Signals warn off intruders, and actual fighting usually is a last resort. Females respond so that males know to change from displays of aggression to displays of conciliation and courtship. In non-monogamous animals, male territories often are larger than and overlap numerous female territories.

Regional conflicts around the globe constantly demonstrate the drive to claim and hold a specific territory. Those who dislike Robert Ardrey's (1966) conclusions dismiss him as a screenwriter,[2] but the *ad hominem* ignores his education as an anthropologist. He based his books on wide reading, conversations with scholars, and his own observation of animals in nature, mostly in Africa. He provides numerous examples from the animal world, extends them to hu-

---

2. *Khartoum, The Four Horsemen of Apocalypse, The Wonderful Country, Quentin Durward, The Green Years, A Lady Takes a Chance, Madame Bovary, The Secret Garden, Song of Love, They Knew What They Wanted,* and *The Three Musketeers.*

mans, and argues that human characteristics such as altruism and love of family are rooted in instinct.

A territory is an area that an animal defends as its exclusive preserve. A territorial species is one in which males, and occasionally females, have an inherent drive to stake out and defend an exclusive property. Defense is directed primarily against members of its own species. Intruders other than predators are largely ignored. There are three main patterns. One is the mating station, a territory that each male stakes out to attract females. Once a claim is established, the owner almost always bests any challenger, often by symbolic combat that minimizes injury and enhances survival. Outside the territory, in the foraging area, males do not fight one another. The pattern is possible only in species in which females rear the young without assistance from the male, one reason that it is found only in about 100 of the world's million or so animals, including at least one insect, the cicada killer, a species of wasp.

The second pattern is the pair territory. Although often first staked out by the male, it becomes the territory of a breeding pair and insures proper care of the offspring. It is found in humans but is most common in birds, exemplars being penguins and gulls. Pairs occupy relatively small nesting territories, which they most often defend by displays at the borders of their territories. Humans may be said to follow this pattern within their communities in dealing with their neighbors. As Robert Frost said, "fences make good neighbors."

The third pattern is the "nation," a territory held by a group as an exclusive possession through joint defense (Carpenter, May 1934). The aphorism "amity toward group members and enmity toward non-members" defines it neatly. Carpenter and others demonstrated that baboon, chimpanzee, gorilla, lemur, and rhesus family groups remain intact even when females are not in season. These findings suggest that joint defense of territory rather than food supplies or sex holds the family group together. Humans also exhibit this pattern.

If biological success is measured only by the extent an individual passes on its own genes, then taking risks to help unrelated individuals makes no sense. Yet altruistic and cooperative behavior undeniably does exist! Most social insects—bees, ants and the like--are hymenoptera. In hymenoptera, siblings are related by 3/4 instead of 1/2, so can pass on more of their own genes by caring for siblings rather than raising their own offspring! This leads to the hypothesis that haplodiploid insects became social due to genetics!

Genetic explanations of cooperative behavior are gradually being identified in other species. Horses generally live in harems of several females and a high-ranking male who fights off all challengers as long as he can. Claudia Feh (March 1999) has added horses to the list of animals that improve the odds of passing on their genes by cooperation. She found instances in France's Camargue of low-ranking males pairing up to maintain their own harem. Both males end up with more offspring than either could achieve on its own, and even more interesting, a higher proportion of their offspring survive than in the harems headed by a single male. Craig Packer and Robert Heinsohn (1995) discovered that lionesses tolerate laggards in defense because they make other contributions to pride survival through better skills at hunting or babysitting. Dugatkin (2003) reports that every school of guppies has one or two risk-accepting individuals that check interlopers, darting back to initiate the escape of all if they are predators.

Weaning in some animals takes the form of gentle attacks to prevent the young nursing and force them to turn to species-normal food. The longer a young animal can nurse, the better off it will be, but the longer the mother must nurse the more her fitness is lowered. Erikson (Chapter 4) specifies weaning as one of eight life crises that can lead to personality disorders.

Aggression exists in species-specific combinations of these eight types. Jane Goodall (May 1979 also personal conversation) reported four different communities of chimps co-existing in Gombe, maintaining separate territories and harmonious relations. But, chimps from Kasakela Valley suddenly began male only "patrols" into Kahama Valley. They moved silently, unusual for chimps. Over several months they singled out lone males and killed them.[3] When all the males of Kahama Valley had been killed, the breeding females were taken over and the territory appropriated. This may combine territorial and sexual aggression.

This sounds very much like conclusions reached by Joseph Manson of Michigan and Richard Wrangham of Harvard (1991), who found that acquiring women was the direct cause of 45% of wars in a study of 87 hunter-gatherer societies, while acquiring resources to pay bride prices caused another 40%. Napoleon Chagnon notes that Yanomamo men who have killed at least one other person have more than twice as many wives and children as those who have not killed. Thus, killing leads to passing on more of one's genes and thus to "reproductive success" as a cause of war (Chapter 12).

By contrast, females are more likely to fight to protect existing young rather than to gain mates. Given the biological cost of bearing and raising a child, female reproductive success depends more on seeing a small number of offspring survive rather than producing large numbers of them. Thus, males and females have different reproductive strategies, one labeled the r-strategy based on producing lots of offspring in the hope that a few survive, found in human males, insects, and other lowly creatures. The alternative, labeled K-strategy is found in species that invest heavily in the care of their offspring, including human females. As a species, humans follow the K-strategy.

Warfare puts a premium on raising males, who do the fighting. An average ratio of 150 boys to 100 girls was found in 600 primitive cultures. Adults are closer to 1:1. Combat evens things up. But, successful warriors have several

---

3. Similar behavior has been documented many times since, and chimpanzees now are known to actively hunt monkeys for food. There now are sixteen documented attacks in Uganda by chimps on humans, primarily infants, resulting in seven deaths (National Geographic Television)

wives. Thus, some adult males remain bachelors, which only increases their aggressiveness. The modern variant is found in China, where girl babies often are aborted, resulting in 50 million Chinese men who cannot find wives.

Those who doubted that genes determine behavior responded with a very logical—and sarcastic—challenge: Which gene determines aggression (or any other specific behavior)? The human genome project, now complete, has found no such gene. However, psychologists, psychiatrists, and geneticists led by researchers such as Caspi (2003), Hamer (1998), Moffit (1993) and Zuckerman (2000, 2002, 2003) began to unlock the mechanisms. True, there are no genes for specific behaviors, but the brain is an electrical chemical organ whose behavior is strongly influenced by genes that affect the way the brain functions. For example, a gene that lies on the X chromosome and makes the monoamine oxidase (MAOA) that breaks down dopamine and serotonin comes in two lengths. One length produces low and the other produces high MAOA. Low MAOA has been linked to aggression in both mice and humans. Men with low MAOA who had been neglected were twice as likely to have engaged in bullying, fighting, theft, cruelty or vandalism or to be convicted of a crime than men with high MAOA who also had been maltreated. Absent such abuse, low MAOA boys were no likelier to be antisocial than others.

Thus, in this case, genes can either exaggerate or moderate a child's behavior. Genes are not switches that make a person aggressive, anxious, or shy. Rather, they determine brain chemistry and that does affect personality. There is nothing simple about it (nor given the variety of human personality would we expect simplicity). For example, geneticists at this point suspect that perhaps a dozen genes together influence the tendency to take risks and court danger.

A logician would say the question of whether nature or nurture explains human aggressiveness is a false dichotomy. A statistician would say that the two variables interact. Biologists have recognized this since at least the 1960s, and are beginning to find mechanisms by which genes may actually be modified by the experience of the animal carrying them—that is, the mechanism behind the interaction between nature and nurture! Such research is beginning to explain the well-known fact that most abused children become well-adjusted, law-abiding, and productive adults, but that a minority become abusive, violent, and criminal adults. If researchers such as Hamer are right, then it should be possible to identify families whose members take more chances than others. When the point is made, many think instantly of the Kennedy family: Joe Jr. was killed in WW2, John was a WW2 hero who was assassinated as was his brother Robert, and his son John died piloting a plane under conditions beyond his skill as a pilot.

In people addicted to danger, the dopamine rush from a particular thrill wears off, and a greater one is needed. Children who graduate from thrill rides in amusement parks to risky driving to bungee jumping or volunteering for the most dangerous jobs in the military may be cases in point. Deborah Capaldi of the Oregon Social Learning Center argues that most problem children are thrill-seekers rather than aggressors. This might seem to make the problem more intractable, but also suggests the cure in that it may be possible to divert thrill-seeking from anti-social to socially useful behaviors such as smoke jumping or venture capitalism.

Conclusion

The question of whether man is aggressive or peaceful by nature or by nurture has long been disputed, is not yet resolved, and may never be. The best evidence suggests that neither position is correct—that the question is a false dichotomy and that the two interact to produce the incredible individual and cultural variety seen across human history. Our ancestors provide controversial evidence as to our evolution from aggressive hunters, peaceful vegetarians, or opportunistic scavengers. Our biology, particularly our hormones and differences between the sexes, provide insights. Fundamental drives, to pass on our genes, to defend territory, to achieve status, and to establish an individual identity, have explanatory power. Furthermore, like other species, we resolve or manage many of our disputes by methods other than fighting, most often verbally. Conflict is common but it is worth remembering that people are more often altruistic and cooperative than warlike and murderous in their relations with one another.

Chapter 4
Aggression and the Mind

The distinction between aggression and assertion is intention.
—Georgia Lanoil

We turn now from scientists who concentrate on the physical origins of aggression and conflict to those who concentrate on its origins in our minds. The psychologists have developed three main theories to explain human aggression, which we take up in turn before considering the contributions of the psychiatrists.

<u>Aggression as Instinct</u>

Our ability to breed animals purposively, such as bulls, roosters, and pit bulls for aggressiveness, and the study of bird songs (inherited in most but not all species) suggest genetic transmission of some behaviors in some species. Konrad Lorenz, who shared the Nobel Prize in 1973 for his work establishing the science of ethology, is an exemplar of this perspective, which assumes that aggression is more instinctive than learned, even in humans. However, he thought humans could learn to control it.

Lorenz (1963) defines aggression as a fighting instinct directed against members of the *same* species: predation is distinct from and not the same as aggression. Lorenz and many others who emphasize instinct often see aggression as serving positive functions. They often emphasize ritualized forms such the tests of strength and dominance common to the males of many species such as monkeys, sheep, and wolves that contribute to species survival usually without physical injury to the losers.

Instinct theorists tend to see anger exploding unexpectedly in the same way a balloon will expand until it reaches its unpredictable limit and bursts. This is the so-called "hydraulic" characteristic of aggression and anger. Unfortunately, it is argument by analogy for which direct evidence is weak.

Related to this hydraulic model is the idea that aggression not diverted or released in controlled fashion—a process known as catharsis—becomes pathological. Lorenz argued that competitive games, mastering skills, cultural activities, and films with aggressive content are cathartic. Lorenz echoed the Olympic slogan when he wrote, "sports promote personal acquaintance between people of different nations or parties, and they unite, in enthusiasm for a common cause, people who otherwise would have little in common." However, they sometimes result in post-game riots. As all humans share the same genetic makeup, but sports riots are largely limited to certain classes and cultures, instinct is not a good explanation for this form of aggression. Furthermore, there is little support in the experimental literature for the efficacy of catharsis (Berkowitz 1993, Bandura 1973).

Most researchers now assert that experiencing aggression strengthens subsequent aggression. Laboratory experiments and studies of the impact of television and movies tend to this conclusion. Earlier researchers came to the opposite conclusion. The change in interpretation may reflect more sophisticated research methods, a change in the type and amount of violence, or a change in the expectations of the researchers—the so-called Pygmalion effect that leads people to interpret data on the basis of their preconceptions (Chapter 1).

Lorenz did include a non-genetic component to his theory of aggression. Rats crowded together eventually begin killing one another. Lorenz felt that crowded inner cities, particularly on hot days, were similarly prone to violence. These triggering mechanisms are at least conceptually reducible through air conditioning and urban planning. However, the causal connection is less compelling when one recalls the hot, crowded but pacific cities of Southeast and East Asia.

Lorenz argues that since we are descended from apes, our ancestors must have acted like apes. Chimpanzees and baboons are aggressive, so our ancestors also must have been aggressive. Put this baldly, most people quickly realize the logical flaws. First, not all apes are aggressive: orangutans and gorillas in particular are very peaceful. Second, physical descent does not insure behavioral descent.

Much of the remaining criticisms of Lorenz's work is from people who do not like the implication of aggression being instinctive, so feel it must be wrong, but have no real evidence to that effect. Criticism of this nature of this or any other theory—and there is a lot of it—is irrational and should be dismissed out-of-hand.

Aggression as Learned Behavior

Another group of theorists think aggression is learned behavior. From this perspective, aggression can be and often is purposeful. Therefore, aggression is best understood from the situation, taking account of the capabilities and mental state of the individual. It follows that aggression can be modified by conditioning and education. Of course, the conditioning can go both ways. Psychologists tend to condition people to be less aggressive, but gang members tend to condition members to be more aggressive.

Albert Bandura is an exemplar of this perspective. Bandura posits that, ". . . the specific forms that aggressive behavior takes, the frequency with which it is displayed, and the specific targets selected for attack are largely determined by social learning factors." In Bandura's most famous experiments, children are observed to determine if they imitate the way adults interacted with a life-size

"Bobo Doll" designed to bounce upright after being knocked down. In one such experiment, children saw the adult who behaved aggressively toward the doll being either punished or rewarded. Children who saw the adults punished proved less likely to imitate the aggression toward the doll (Bandura and Walters 1963, Bandura 1973, 1986), reinforcing the theory that aggression is learned and that people can learn to control it.

Bandura focused much of his energy on whether violence seen on television causes violence in the real world. He postulates three stages leading from the former to the latter. The first is exposure, violence attracting interest because it is frequent, easy to understand, and positively depicted. The second stage is learning how to fight or to use weapons. The third stage is to actually try the violent act oneself. However, few people take the violence they see to this third stage because, as the Bobo Doll experiments demonstrate, they also understand the punishments as well as the rewards. The likelihood of violence is greatly diminished if parents, friends, and teachers punish or even merely disapprove of misplaced aggression.

A woman told American talk-show host Dennis Praeger of a five year old who for no apparent reason walked over and threw her two year old onto the concrete. The boy's mother rushed over and, without even looking at the howling infant on the ground, asked the five year old what was troubling him. Two psychologists, Brad Bushman (2001) and Roy Baumeister (1994) blame such aggression on the constant emphasis psychologists and psychiatrists give to self-esteem, expressing feelings, and "rights" instead of responsibilities. They ask, "Is it not possible that children so raised turned into the adults who shoot up post-offices and schools? Forget about self-esteem and concentrate on self-control." They conclude that we should teach responsibility not rights. If we did so, might we have fewer people who resort to violence, and a society more likely to be protected from those who do (Begley, 13 July 1998; Goode, 9 March 1999)?

Harry Harlow (1974) studied affection, depression, and aggression based on substitution of cloth-covered or wire "mothers" for infant rhesus, pigtail, and bonnet monkeys, with real mothers as controls. One of the more bizarre metal "mothers" also shook violently whenever an infant tried to cling to it. These infants often developed peculiar behaviors who, like some abused children, grew into abusive parents. Harlow concluded that maternal deprivation was one if not necessarily the only cause.

Criticism points to three difficulties in generalizing from such research to humans. First, researchers often select species for experimental studies based on availability, ease of care, and personal preference rather than similarity to human behavior. Second, there is considerable variety among species. Baboons are aggressive and chimpanzees are hyperactive and aggressive, but gorillas and orangutans are calm and gentle. Behavior does not generalize from one species of monkey or ape to another, let alone to humans. Third, the clinical definition of depression includes feelings of worthlessness, excessive guilt, indecisiveness and thoughts of death difficult to infer from animal behavior. Even in humans, psychiatrists recognize that mood and behavior are neither identical nor inferable from one another.

These powerful criticisms suggest that there are no valid animal models for human behaviors such as depression or aggression due to crowding. This has led ethicists to suggest an important "Catch 22."[1] If the monkeys experience feelings such as despair, can the experiments be justified? If they do not experience such feelings, what is the point of the experiments (Gruen and Singer 1987)? Studies of animals to understand their own behavior (such as those of Jane Goodall) remain valid. The use of animal or human subjects in experiments approved by institutional review boards that assess the design of the research, its purpose, and its ethics following accepted guidelines remain valid. However, studies of animals to understand human behavior no longer seem very useful.

Aggression as the Consequence of Frustration

John Dollard and his colleagues Leonard Doob, Neal Miller, and Robert Sears usually are credited with the idea that aggression results from and presupposes frustration. The simplest and clearest formulation of the theory is that, "the occurrence of aggression always presupposes the existence of frustration and, contrariwise, that the existence of frustration always leads to some form of aggression (Dollard, et al. 1939)." That is, frustration is both a necessary and a sufficient cause of aggression. Humans are goal-oriented, and they become hostile when blocked from reaching their goals.

Logically enough, this theory implies controlling aggression by reducing goals and desires. People learn to accept different levels of frustration in different situations. One is more likely to get in a fight on the playground than in the classroom, and more likely to get into one in the classroom than in church. One is more likely to lose one's temper with a subordinate than with a superior. People may not even direct their aggression at the source of their frustration, especially when the source is a powerful authority figure such as a parent or boss who can retaliate severely. This suggests that learning (see above) can overcome frustration.

Within two years of the original publication of the theory, John Whiting (1941) had reported that aggression was only one response among the Kwoma

---

1. From Joseph Heller's book of the same name: "There was only one catch and that was Catch-22, which specified that a concern for one's safety in the face of dangers that were real and immediate was the process of a rational mind. Orr was crazy and could be grounded. All he had to do was ask; and as soon as he did, he would no longer be crazy and would have to fly more missions. Orr would be crazy to fly more missions and sane if he did not, but if he was sane he had to fly them. If he flew them he was crazy and didn't have to; but if he didn't want to he was sane and had to."

of New Guinea to frustration, the other three being avoidance, submission, or dependence. This led the original authors to revise their phrasing to make frustration :

> *likely* to turn to aggression. . . The frustration-aggression hypothesis is . . . intended to suggest to the student of human nature that when he sees aggression he should turn a suspicious eye on *possibilities* that the organism or group is confronted with frustration; and that when he views interference with individual or group habits, he should be on the look-out for, among other things, aggression. This hypothesis is induced from commonsense observation, from clinical case histories, from a few experimental investigations, from sociological studies and from the results of anthropological field work."[emphasis added] (Miller, 1941).

Other researchers picked up the idea and began classifying types of frustration and incorporating additional factors such as fear, learning, and self-esteem to explain whether aggression would result. Berkowitz (1978) provided the best-known reformulation of the theory, arguing that aggression is a more general example of the relationship between unpleasant stimuli and unpleasant emotions and feelings, such as anxiety, anger, annoyance, or pain. These trigger the choice between "fight or flight based on how the individual assesses and controls his feelings. Frustration-aggression theory soon became positively Ptolemaic in its complexity, incorporating every conceivable human response to any situation, and in the end saying little more than "frustration may or may not cause a reaction of some sort." This is not very useful.

Critics argued that war, which clearly is aggression, has other causes than frustration including greed and excitement. Frustration does not motivate the aggression of mercenary or professional soldiers such as those of imperial Rome, 19th century Britain, or 21st century America. In cases where aggression is instrumental, or purposive, the role of frustration is less clear. A simple case is the child teasing the cat or throwing food on the floor to gain the attention of a parent. Other examples of displaced aggression include kicking the dog when mad at the boss, or screaming at the clerk who refuses a refund rather than the inaccessible store manager who set the policy. Some believe, without much evidence, that President Bush invaded Iraq out of frustration with the failure to capture Usama bin Ladin.

Frustration-aggression theory never insisted on aggression directed at the cause of the frustration. However, that makes it difficult to link a particular act of aggression to a particular frustration, and points to a significant problem. Frustration is inferred from aggression, which then is used to explain the aggression. That is, the reasoning is circular, the theory a tautology!

Human Needs Theory

Abraham Maslow (1987) originally published the results of five year's research on the "hierarchy of human needs (Figure 4.1)" in 1943. He postulated a hierarchy of five individual needs each with a minimum level of satisfaction (the grey area in Figure 4.1). The most basic needs, those required for survival such as oxygen, water, food, and shelter, are physiological [P]. Those needs reasonably satisfied, individuals become concerned with physical, psychological and financial safety [S], while still trying to improve the quality of food and housing. When the individual feels safe, the need to belong [B] and to have friends comes to the fore while the individual seeks improvement for the lesser needs through still better housing and even more financial security. A person with friends desires their esteem [E], which requires both personal achievement and recognition. With these needs satisfied, we may expect that self-actualization [SA] will come to the fore as people strive to achieve their full potential.

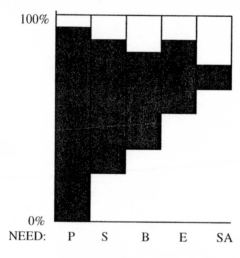

Figure 4.1
Hierarchy of Human Needs[2]

That is, Maslow did not expect people to completely meet one need before pursuing the next, but that they would begin to pursue the next need after reaching a minimum level of satisfaction with the previous need in the hierarchy. However, he did not believe that individuals would skip levels in the hierarchy—from belonging to self-actualization without meeting minimum levels of self-esteem, for example. The minimum level required to satisfy each need var-

---

2. Adapted from Maslow (1987)

ies among individuals, cultures, and even sub-cultures. One soldier in combat might wish for the safety of a tank, while another might feel, "I'd ruther dig. A movin' foxhole attracks th' eye (Mauldin, 1945)." An individual achieving an initial goal of becoming a millionaire often raises his sights to a ten million dollar goal. An individual elected mayor may develop a desire to become a member of Congress. Satisfaction may prove, like a tank, to be a moving target.

Maslow felt that humans were not violent by nature but tended toward growth and love. However, preventing people from meeting their minimum needs can result in aggression, crime, and war. This view is consistent with frustration-aggression theory. Integration of the two theories has the potential for eliminating the tautological aspects of the original.

Psychiatric Theories

From psychology, we turn to psychoanalysis: to Freud, Erikson, Fromm, and Fanon. Freud's answer as to why people are aggressive came in a response to a 1932 letter from Einstein. In it, he discussed how the "pleasure principle," mediated through the "death instinct" and its opposite Eros leads to aggression. This is murky at best but more important, Freud blames aggression on opposite causes, making it impossible to falsify, so unscientific. Unfortunately, much of psychoanalytic theory suffers from the same problem.

Freud's major legacy is the search for the "unconscious." He theorized that by identifying and exploring repressed memories, a person could gain relief from a wide range of emotional problems. This led in turn to psychoanalysis as a means of treatment and later as a basis for prosecution, one reason it is relevant to conflict theory.[3] Sixty years of research has failed to confirm the existence of repressed memory. Elizabeth Loftus (1997) has demonstrated how easily false memories are formed, particularly under the suggestion of therapists asking the same leading question as few as three times. The principal psychoanalytic techniques cause false or grossly inaccurate memories. Children are even more open to this sort of thing as they tend to want to please adults so say what is desired as soon as they figure out what that is.

Many crimes appear connected to psychiatric illnesses, but the use of lithium, Prozac, and other chemicals by non-Freudian, scientific psychiatrists are forcing recognition that they result from physical causes rather than the "unconscious." Approximately two-thirds of patients receiving psychiatric treatment improve, but approximately one-half who receive no treatment improve just as much. A placebo effect might underlie many of the successes, making psychiatrists the modern equivalent of shamans.

---

3. Infamous cases include the Amiraults in Massachusetts, Grant Snowden in Florida, and the MacMartins in California, all of which depended on testimony from 4-6 year-old children who testified to abuse and to bizarre fantasies such as a system of tunnels under their school and witnessing acts of eating babies.

Freud's claims for originality are much exaggerated (Stannard, 1980). He reworked the traditional Greek idea of the animal body, the human mind, and the divinely inspired soul into conscious behavior (the "ego"), blind impulses (the "id") and moral imperatives (the "superego")." According to Freud, the conflict between them is irresolvable, insuring perpetual intra-personal conflict, which although incurable requires the expensive ministrations of psychotherapy to control. Interpretation of dreams? Joseph's interpretation of pharaoh's dreams has been part of our heritage for three millennia. Babylonians wrote books on interpreting dreams a millennium earlier than that. Alan Hobson (1988, 2003) argued that dreams were the result of random firings of the nerve cells in the sleeping brain, explaining why they sometimes are bizarre. Applying Occam's Razor (Chapter 1), there is no reason to believe that dreams have any significance or that anyone needs special training to decipher them.

Freud evolved the idea of oral, anal and genital phases from the work of Haeckel who thought that sexuality developed from saclike organisms called *gastraea*. He said they originally reproduced by division of cells like amoeba, but then evolved a joint gastro-intestinal tract as in reptiles, and subsequently evolved true genitalia. Subsequent biologists proved Haeckel wrong. Carpenter (Chapter 3) demolished the idea that primates are obsessed with sex. Invalidated biological concepts also underlie such fundamental Freudian concepts as latency, sublimation, fixation, regression, and repression (Sulloway, 1979). The Freudians have kept the conclusions despite the destruction of the biological foundations on which they rest, which of course makes no sense.

Freud claimed to be a scientist but many of his fundamental ideas have nothing to do with objective observation of clinical cases. An important example of how he reached conclusions occurs in a letter to Fliess in which he wrote, "A single idea of general value dawned on me. I have found, in my own case the phenomenon of being in love with my Mother and jealous of my Father, and I now consider it a universal event in early childhood." There are plenty of "Eureka" moments in science, but they must be verified, not simply taken on faith. The Oedipus complex became a cornerstone of psychoanalytic theory because Freud felt that what he experienced must be true of all mankind! The anecdote illustrates another important difficulty with psychoanalytic thought, the tendency to infer what is normal from the study of people who are not—a negative proof so invalid. As Maslow (1987) wrote, "The study of crippled, stunted, immature, and unhealthy specimens can yield only a crippled psychology and a crippled philosophy." Maslow studied normal and even accomplished people, a needed and useful change in focus. His hierarchy of needs (described above) is a welcome alternative to the pessimism of Freud.

Erik Erikson (1950) offered a sequence of eight developmental stages each associated with a crisis and a resulting pathology if it is not resolved correctly. Figure 4.2 summarizes the theory. Erikson argues that these stages are universal, that the crises must be resolved in the order and at the stage of life specified, and that mental health requires that they be resolved as he specifies.

Stage	Age	Crisis	Positive Outcome	Negative Outcome	Pathology	Societal Element
Infancy	0-1	Trust-Mistrust	Security	Insecurity, mistrust	Withdrawal	Religion
Childhood	1-2	Autonomy-Self doubt	Confidence	Shame, self-doubt	Compulsion	Law & order
Play	2-5	Initiative-Guilt	Imagination	Gult	Inhibition	Heroes
School Age	5-12	Industry-Inferiority	Competence	Inferiority	(blank)	Technology
Adolesence	12-18	Identity-Role Confusion	Strong Identity	Role in life*	Repudiation	(blank)
Young Adult	18-40	Intimacy-Isolation	Relationships	Isolation**	Exclusivity	Cooperate-Compete
Adult	40-65	Generativity-Stagnation	Nurturing	Stagnation	Rejectivity	Tradition
Old Age	65 up	Ego integrity-Despair	Fulfillment	Despair	Self-contempt	Wisdom

Figure 4.2

Erikson's Stages of Life Development

* Confusion about vocation, sexual orientation, and general role in life

**Fear of commitment and inability to depend on anybody in the world

At best, Erikson's theory explains some personal conflicts some people experience. More important, the pathologies exhibit systematic bias. For example, Erikson asserts that failing to trust is pathological, but trusting too much is not. Parents wiser than the esteemed Erikson, teach their children not to trust strangers. Similarly, Erikson advocates cooperation and condemns competition, but competition improves athletic performance and national economies. Erikson's explanations often are incomprehensible jargon, and each stage is briefer and less specific than the one before. Like Freud, Erikson seems to draw much from his own personal experience, admitting as much in the section on Old Age, which he writes that he cannot say much about because he "is only now experiencing it." Beyond that, he presents no supporting evidence of any kind.

Erich Fromm (1973) distinguishes two types of aggression based on his extensive review of the literature of anthropology, biology, ethology, and paleontology. His major contribution may be distinguishing two types of aggression. Benign aggression is defensive, contributory to species survival, and instinctive—that is, programmed into the brain of animals and humans alike. Malignant aggression is cruel, socially disruptive, deleterious to species survival, and found almost exclusively in Man. Fromm explains malignant aggression with a mix of philosophy and Freudian rhetoric that is neither clear nor convincing. That is, he resolves the nature-nurture dispute by creating two types of aggression, one of which he attributes to nature, the other to nurture. It is a clever but also a largely non-scientific effort at explaining a distinction that may not even exist.

Franz Fanon (1976) was both a psychoanalyst and a revolutionary involved in the Algerian war for independence against France—a war partly fought by urban terrorism that is a precursor of the Palestinian *Intifadah*. Fanon located the roots of anti-colonial violence in the disintegration of native society resulting from the policies of the colonial powers. He regarded the violence of national liberation movements as a "cleansing force [that] frees the native from his inferiority complex and from his despair and inaction [that] makes him fearless and restores his self-respect." That is, Fanon saw violence as therapy for colonized and oppressed peoples regardless of its military effectiveness in gaining independence. "Only in the 'mad fury' of the violent deed can the wretched of the earth be reborn as free men." At the same time, based on his own work in psychiatric hospitals, Fanon identified four types of mental disorder caused by war. Thus, he claimed that violence both cures and causes psychiatric illnesses!

Conclusion

Fighter pilot, prisoner of war, and US Senator, John McCain (2004), no stranger to aggression and conflict, makes a nice point about anger that provides a fitting close to this chapter:

Anger might stimulate an impetuous courage, but of all degrees of courage, that is the least effective. By outrage, I mean taking moral offense at something. . . .Outrage, which our sense of duty summons us to redress, on the other hand, can find expression in a wider range of behavior. We can use expressions that anger uses, or we can purposefully go about redressing the offense in quiet, civil, ways, our comportment no different from what it is in other endeavors. . . .Anger and the courage it can spark are depleted rather quickly. We blow up, speak our piece, swing our fist until retribution is accomplished, and then we move on. . . . Outrage, if we have 'a sense of duty, endures until the wrong is righted, as can the courage needed to accomplish the task.

Chapter 5
Interpersonal Conflict

'Twas brillig, and the slithy toves
Did gyre and gimble in the wabe;
All mimsy were the borogoves,
And the mom raths outgrabe...

"It seems very pretty," she said when she had finished it, "but its
rather hard to understand!" (You see, she didn't like to confess, even
to herself, that she couldn't make it out at all.). "Somehow it seems to
fill my head with ideas—only I don't exactly know what they are!"

—Lewis Carroll, *Through the Looking Glass*

We turn from the question of why individuals are aggressive to conflict between individuals—that is to interpersonal conflicts. This chapter focuses on
personality, on how interests and relationships interact, and on conflicts stemming from difficulties in communication.

Personality and Conflict

The ideal conflict manager has the faith of Joan of Arc, the determination
and will to win of Packer coach Vince Lombardi, the warmth and empathy of
television's Mr. Rogers, the practical creativity of Benjamin Franklin, and the
cold analytical skills of Startrek's Mr. Spock. There is no such person, but the
aphorism provides a parsimonious if not very scientific way to identify one's
weaknesses and strengths as a conflict manager.

Social psychologists give us a number of more scientifically derived propositions. One is that tolerance of ambiguity is important to understanding how
people will react to conflict. Those who can tolerate ambiguity are more likely
to see the world in shades of gray and thus to be willing to listen to the other
side in a dispute, and more willing to accept a problem-solving or negotiating
stance. On the other hand, authoritarian personalities tend to want rapid and ab-
solute solutions. Thus, for example, as the Vietnam War developed, we saw
authoritarian conservatives demanding a US victory: "bomb them back into the
stone age," in one infamous phrase. But, we saw equally authoritarian liberals
demanding that we "just declare victory and get out," in an equally famous
phrase.

Adorno and his co-authors (1950) studied the relationship between personality and aggression rooted in prejudice. Prejudice was defined as a judgment

reached without regard for facts, usually based on oversimplified generalizations or stereotypes. It often is rooted in displacement, the process of transferring one's anger or frustration to a scapegoat and it often is used to justify aggression, discrimination or oppression. In an approach rooted in Freud and Marx, Adorno wrote that:

> The authoritarian personality does not want to give orders; their personality type wants to take orders [later interpretation suggested that they also love to give orders particularly to people they regard as inferior]. People with this type of personality seek conformity, security, stability. . . .They tend to be very superstitious and lend credence to folk tales or interpretations of history that fit their preexisting definitions of reality. They think in extremely stereotyped ways. . . the world is conceived in terms of absolute right (their way) vs. absolute wrong (every other way).

Stanley Milgram (1963, 1983), inspired by the defense so many Nazi's mounted during the Nuremberg War Crimes Trials that they simply were obeying orders, designed research to determine the credibility of that defense. The experiment was made to look like a study of learning under negative reinforcement in the form of increasing electrical shocks. The apparent learner was in reality an actor strapped into what looked like an electric chair. The real subject of the experiment was the "teacher," who had responded to an advertisement calling for paid assistants. The "teacher" was instructed to administer an ever-increasing shock every time the "learner" made a mistake. The shocks were not real. The "learner" feigned mistakes and increasing pain and made increasingly desperate demands to stop the experiment. The experimenter who hired the "teachers" ordered continuation of the experiment each time the "teacher" hesitated. Sixty percent of the "teachers" obeyed orders to punish the learners to the maximum on the 450-volt scale. The Milgram experiment demonstrated that perfectly normal men and women from all social classes and backgrounds are willing to wreak immense pain on others if told to do so by someone in authority.

Even more frightening, Haritos-Fatouros (1988), focusing on torturers who worked for the notorious government of the Greek colonels from 1967–1974, found that the "best" torturers were not sadists, but perfectly normal men or women who were desensitized by grueling and degrading training. For these once-normal people, torture was a method to achieve an end, usually information, so they were less likely to go overboard and kill anyone—at least not prematurely.

Personality Types

Social Psychologists have developed a host of instruments to measure that often are used in counseling and as part of the employee selection process. The

Myers-Briggs Type Indicator is prominent and fairly typical. Four "personality dichotomies" based on Jung's theory of psychological types underlie the instrument. The "sensing-intuition" [S-I] scale describes how subjects perceive or acquire information. "Sensing" types tend to accept and work with what is given, so are realistic, practical, and good at remembering and working with a great number of facts. "Intuitive" types go beyond the information of the senses to look at the big picture, seeing new possibilities and ways of doing things. The "extroversion-introversion" [E-N] scale describes whether a respondent focuses primarily on others or his own "inner" world, whether you prefer to communicate by talking or by writing, and whether you learn more by experience or thinking things through. The "thinking-feeling [T-F] scale describes how information is used to make decisions. "Thinking" types rely on analysis while "feeling" types emphasize values. Finally, "judging-perceiving" [J-P] distinguishes a preference for control, planning and order as opposed to adaptability, flexibility and spontaneity.

Respondents are "typed" on the basis of 92 questions, 43 asking which of two words, "appeals to you more." The remaining 49 questions asks which of two, sometimes three choices describes how the subject "usually feels or acts." Each respondent is then scored and "typed," reducing the six billion members of the human race to exactly 16 personality types as shown in Figure 5.1, which is to say, you share your personality with 375,000,000 other living people.

The major use of the Myers-Briggs for conflict management undoubtedly is in team formation, the idea being to put people together so that problems can be solved efficiently. It also has been used to identify difficulties within existing work groups that stem from personality differences. Some hold that compatibility is the major requirement for such a team, others that it is diversity. Critics point out that other factors, such as skills or inclusion of opinion leaders, are much more important in team formation. Further criticism extends to the validity and reliability of the instrument itself.

	Sensing Types		Intuitive Types	
Introverts	ISTJ	ISFJ	INFJ	INTJ
	ISTP	ISFP	INFP	INTP
Extroverts	ESTP	ESFP	ENFP	ENTP
	ESTJ	ESFJ	ENFJ	ENTJ

Figure 5.1
Myers-Briggs Personality "Types"

The underlying theory is deduced from a hodgepodge of ideas borrowed from ancient philosophy and modern science. The model oversimplifies. For example, it assumes that extroverts have broader interests than introverts. Academics tend to score as introverts and salesmen as extroverts, yet interests tend to expand with education. Other likely contradictions can be identified with a little thought. A person scoring 24-0 on a particularly dichotomy will be "typed" the same as one scoring 13-11. Forming teams based only on compatibility as recommended by *Myers-Briggs* overlooks considerations such as needed skills or the need to include opinion leaders to "sell" decisions later.

It is considered fair in an interview or selection process to put your best foot forward, so long as you do not resort to outright lying. When tests like *Myers-Briggs* are used as part of a selection process, it seems ethical to do the same in answering. When asked whether "compassion" appeals to more than "fore-sight," or whether a friend who has "new ideas" is preferred to one with "both feet on the ground," it is easy to think of situations in which either answer is true. Knowing which characteristics the job requires determines which situation to apply in answering the question. You may not guess right all the time, but you can do so often enough to get the profile that that will get the job.

Generation Gap

The "generation gap" describes a special form of interpersonal conflict at-tributable to age alone that stems from differences in maturity, perspective and responsibility. The term apparently originated with German sociologist Karl Mannheim in the 1920s. He argued that critical events molded social and politi-cal outlook into a worldview distinct to each generation. The term became common to explain parental reaction to the counterculture of the sixties. The concept has led to identification of five twentieth century American generations based on shared attitudes and values (www.library.thinkquest.org/23440, www.theatlantic.com/issues/99aug).

The GI generation, born 1901–1924, is characterized as comprising high achievers, patriots, idealists, and team players. They are doers who exceeded their parents in education yet remained modest in their expectations, coura-geously met the challenge of World War II, and who had a strong sense of right and wrong.

The Silent Generation, born 1925–1942, was formed by the Cold War. It is characterized as cautious, unimaginative, withdrawn and security conscious. Its members wanted a lifetime job, an early marriage, and a stable home. They struggled through tough times, and radically increased their own and the na-tional wealth.

The Boomers, born 1943–1960, are characterized by high self-esteem and high self-indulgence. Taught to think critically but not necessarily rationally, they question rules that impose on their freedom to do as they please and want to overhaul the world to provide the pleasures they expect and think they deserve.

Generation X, born 1961–1981, is driven by economic insecurity. They are career obsessed, conformist, eager to do whatever is necessary to ascend the career ladder, and even more materialistic than the boomers. Politically apathetic, they have a weaker allegiance to both country and political party and a more negative attitude toward the United States than any previous generation.

The Millennial Generation, born 1982–2003, still is unformed. It is not yet possible to tell how much is generational characteristic and how much is teen rebelliousness. It seems formed more by computers than by television, perhaps the cause of astoundingly high levels of attention deficit disorder particularly in boys. It has its high-achievers, but many males seem to model their behavior on the dregs of society, so are ill mannered, irresponsible, undisciplined, uneducated, and violent. However, every previous generation overcame the negative characterizations of its parents, and this one probably will also.

Dual Concern Model

Park and Burgess (1921) saw accommodation, assimilation, competition, and conflict as the four possible relationships between two or more people. They saw competition as the most "elementary and fundamental" condition and competition and conflict evolving toward accommodation and assimilation. They defined accommodation as adjustments that do not resolve differences and assimilation as adjustments that do. These thoughts provide at least a first cut, from one perspective, of how social order is possible, a major concern of some sociologists. Two distinct perspectives, sociologists who see conflict as negative and those who see it as positive, may be distinguished.

Several theorists developed similar models proposing that only two variables are necessary to predict how two people will react to one another in a conflict (Figure 5.2). Hall (1993) labels the first variable "Concern for relationship, Rahim (1990) calls it "Concern for others, Thomas (January 1978) labels it "Party's desire to satisfy others concerns and Pruitt (1988) calls it "Concern about other's outcomes," Hall and Pruitt both label the second variable "Concern for own goals" while Rahim labels it "Concern for self" and Thomas labels it "Party's desire for own concerns."

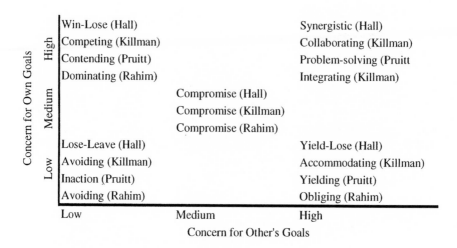

Figure 5.2
Dual Concern Models

The models predict the strategy individuals will pursue to resolve any conflict based on their positions on the two axes. Three are self-explanatory. The terms "win-win" and "win-lose" have become common in describing the remaining two. "Win-win," implies that the negotiators take a mutually beneficial, problem-solving approach on the assumption that creativity can enlarge the "pie" they are attempting to divide so as to meet the needs of both parties. "Win-lose" implies a competitive approach based on the assumption that the "pie" is fixed in size and the question is how big a slice each gets.

A person with a high concern for the outcome and little for the other person (a retail car salesman for example) will take a "win-lose" approach. Individuals with a high stake in the issues and in the relationship—a couple planning a honeymoon, for example—are more likely to want to find a solution both accept enthusiastically, so tend to pursue a "win-win" solution. An individual with little interest in the outcome of the negotiation tends to yield to the opponent's demands if the relationship is important (a "lose-win" result). If the individual does not want to waste time on either the issue or the relationship, the likely result is a deadlock or "lose-lose" outcome. Rahim has taken the model further by specifying the conditions under which each strategy is appropriate (Figure 5.3).

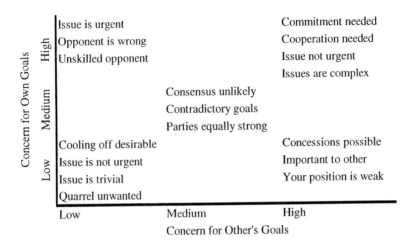

Figure 5.3
Conditions Affecting Strategic Choice

Some cautions are in order. First, you cannot assume two people in conflict assess the issues or their opponent in the same way. It is possible that one person is a lot more concerned with the relationship or the issue than the other. Therefore, it is possible each party will pursue a different strategy. In a multi-issue negotiation, some issues will be more important than others, and their relative importance may be the same or different for each. Thus, a negotiator may prove more cooperative on some issues than on others.

Second, there is a tendency among theorists to assume the superiority of the win-win over the win-lose strategy. They use terms for the former like "collaborative," "integrative," "principled," "problem-solving," or "synergistic," that imply moral superiority over win-lose, often labeled "competing," "contending," or "dominating." Theorists often assert that the former approach produces more creative, longer lasting agreements, while the latter tends to result in last minute, low-level compromise or even deadlock. Little evidence is offered to justify the conclusion, which seems to have more to do with how many wish the world to be rather than how it actually is. The indictment seems overdrawn if for no other reason than 98% or so of the world's negotiating is win-lose and has been for 5000 or more years,[1] which should cast some doubt on the deductions of academic theorists. Furthermore, it is possible to become too concerned with irrelevant interpersonal information or so concerned with the opponent that one sacrifices one's own goals in hope of making progress (Gilin and Mestdagh, 2004). Learning only win-win tactics is likely to prove disastrous, as its proponents

---

1. The statement is based on cuneiform descriptions of Sumerian, Babylonian and Assyrian merchants.

tend to make concessions in hope of inducing cooperation in tough opponents, who are more likely to simply pocket each concession and ask for more until they encounter resistance, then to finally begin negotiating.

The Dual Concern Model passes many of the tests of good theory. It is parsimonious, requiring only two variables to predict behavior. It applies to interpersonal, intra- and inter-organizational disputes, probably to social and community conflicts, and perhaps to international ones as well. It is logical. Conceptually, the model is empirical despite practical difficulties in reliably measuring disputants' concerns with reasonable validity across many types of dispute.

<u>Power</u>

Where there is conflict, people usually try to bring what power they have to bear. Power can be positive, the ability to do, or negative, the ability to prevent. Sometimes, the threat of using power is more effective than its actual use. Sometimes power increases when it is used, but sometimes it degrades. Power has many sources, some real, some perceived, some ephemeral. These sources include audacity, authority, charisma, image, knowledge, options, reputation, and time (Churchman, 1995). It is rare for one party to be utterly powerless, and common for parties in conflict to have different sorts of power. A boss may have more authority, but a subordinate more technical knowledge. A car buyer may need a car quickly, but usually has many dealers from which to choose. It is possible to adapt the idea behind the Dual Concern model to power (Figure 5.4) suggesting the tactic individuals are most likely to choose based on their power relative to their opponents.

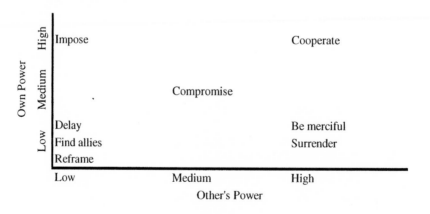

Figure 5.4
Power Tactics

System Models of Communication

System or feedback models of communication exist in almost as many variations as there are researchers studying them. They all have four major components: sender, transmitter, receiver, and feedback. Diagrams similar to Figure 5.5 portray these models. The components within this general model are supplemented by functions such as intended channels or medium (*e.g.*, in person, phone or letter), static or noise (anything that interferes with successful transmission), coding and decoding, receiving or listening, meaning and perceived meaning, and response. These vary from one theorist to the next.

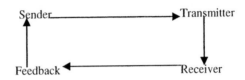

Figure 5.5
Generic System Model of Communication

One barrier to communication is simply the overwhelming amount of it. We are barraged with messages from people (family, friends, strangers, customers, salesmen, service providers, peers, subordinates, superiors...), newspapers, television, radio, the Internet, and mail. Senders compete to be noticed, but recipients must choose which messages to attend to, risking conflict by missing important information.

The greater the linguistic, class, and cultural differences are between sender and receiver, the greater the opportunity for misunderstanding and conflict. In a humorous but undoubtedly apocryphal story (Chernev and Reinfeld, 1948), a plumber passed on his discovery to the Bureau of Standards that hydrochloric acid was great for opening clogged drains. The Bureau replied, "The efficiency of hydrochloric acid is indisputable, but the corrosive residue is incompatible with metallic permanence." The plumber thanked the Bureau for its endorsement, leading to another letter saying, "We cannot assume responsibility for the production of toxic and noxious residue with hydrochloric acid and suggest you use an alternative procedure." The plumber again thanked the Bureau, which replied, "Don't use hydrochloric acid. It eats the hell out of the pipes." This the plumber finally understood.

In international conflicts where there is much dependence on translators, there are many opportunities for misunderstanding. Many words have multiple meanings and translators do not always get exactly the right sense of a word. Humor and word play seldom translate well. One example relevant to our topic is the oft-heard expression, "The exception proves the rule." It only takes a moment's thought to realize how absurd that is. In fact, it stems from a mistranslation of Latin verb "*probar*" as "prove" instead of "test," the meaning intended in the original Latin and one that makes sense, as argued above in addressing the importance of falsification as a means of testing the validity of a theory.

Many factors affect your ability to understand communication. Age, intelligence, and health have only academic interest because there is little each of us can do to change them. The major factor individuals can control stems from the "speech-thought differential." People can speak about 100 words a minute (a good number to keep in mind when asked to give a speech of a particular length) but think at 400-500 words a minute. That means they can simultaneously listen to a speaker and think about other things at a rate of 300-400 words a minute. It is why your attention drifts during lectures. If you train yourself to use the differential to evaluate and restate what your opponent is saying, you will listen more efficiently.

Active or vocalized listening, explaining what you understood your opponent to have opponent to have said before responding, is another time-tested device. It usually improves even the most antagonistic climate because it implies that you really want to understand the concerns of the people with whom you are talking. It helps prevent mistakes, because they can clarify anything you have misunderstood before you act on it. Finally, if you can get the other person to do the same, then you both will be listening to one another in the fullest sense of the word.

Empathic listening can be honest (when you really care about the other person) or tactical (when you are pretending to care so as to achieve an objective). Unfortunately, the literature on empathy is as ambiguous as it is extensive. The term is used with two distinct meanings. The first is viewing the world from the perspective of the other person, captured in the well-known folk saying about not judging anyone till you have walked a mile in his shoes.

Translated into a practical negotiating technique, try to imagine how an opponent could honestly believe a fact that you know to be false, and then to imagine how you could accept it. Imagine a union leader demanding a doubling of wages, an absurd departure from the usual demand for a 7% increase. Instead of exploding, which will only worsen the conflict, ask yourself what level of increased productivity it would take for such a proposal to be reasonable. Develop a counter-proposal accordingly, knowing that it will involve changes (such as replacing a large part of the work force with robots) that will be unacceptable to the union, but will establish a basis for continued negotiation and provide the union with a way to moderate its demand.

"Empathy" also is used, in fact probably most often is used, to mean sensitivity to emotional content. This is why Mr. Clinton's "I feel your pain" was so effective. It requires taking account of verbal, nonverbal, and situational clues to understand feelings. It also is useful because people often conceal as much as they reveal, or try to. Among the usually momentary clues that someone is being deceptive are a change in the rate or pitch of speech, a change in eye contact, a nervous movement of the feet, legs or hands (particularly the hand covering the mouth), turning away from the listener, or tensing of muscles in the face or hand. Because these signals can indicate stress instead of lying, suspicions should always be confirmed before acting on them. Of course, "white lies" intended to prevent hurt feelings ("You are a wonderful cook"), should not be probed, lest they result in hurt feelings or a completely unnecessary conflict (Nemko, 2004).

Linguistic Models of Communication

As most human conflict is expressed verbally, one would expect that the field of communications would contribute much to our understanding. Wilmot and Hocker (1997) tell us that from a communications perspective, "Conflict is an expressed struggle between at least two interdependent parties who perceive incompatible goals, scarce rewards, and interference from the other party in achieving their goals." The only thing in this definition specifically about communication is the word "expressed."

The most theoretical approach to the study of conflict is linguistic. In *Language and Disputing*, Brenneis writes, "Theoretical considerations of the language of dispute involve a number of issues. . . Participants in conflict talk have the same resources available for that interaction as do all conversationalists, and analysts have the same interpretive apparatuses." This suggests conflict talk is the same as all talk, which does not seem particularly interesting or useful to the student of conflict.

Discourse analysis is rooted in ethnomethology, which depends on participant and non-participant observation, verbatim recording of conversation, and interviews. It concentrates on how microelements such as turn-taking, pauses, paralingual variation (whatever that is—the word is not among the half-million in my *Oxford English Dictionary*), direct and indirect speech, address forms, silence, pronoun choice, and verbal static such as "you know," an expression used by people when they do not know what they mean and want you to figure it out for them. Grimshaw calls it "an extremely rich and varied conceptual apparatus." In *Conflict Talk*, he admits "there is obviously no such thing as a unified theory of sociolinguistic description of conflict talk. There are a variety of axiomatic orientations, proto-theoretic perspectives, and conceptual notions which are available for use in organizing the phenomenon for systematic analysis."

So, apparently linguists have several ways to study "conflict talk," or talk in general, and lots of variables to study, and no way to distinguish what is important from what is not, and no guidance in organizing or analyzing the data once it is collected. Edward Sapir foresaw the problem when he wrote in 1929:

One can only hope that linguists will become increasingly aware of the significance of their subject ...and will not stand aloof behind a tradition that threatens to become Scholastic when not vitalized by interests which lie beyond the formal interest in language itself.

Discourse analysts appear to have lost the forest for the trees in its obsession with minutiae and jargon. They apparently have no idea what data to collect or how to analyze or interpret what they do collect. This is a common problem among social scientists. They have emulated the natural sciences by relying on measurement and mathematics, but have not yet figured out what is important.

As Sapir predicted, the result frequently is reminiscent of the debates of the medieval Scholastics. St. Thomas's defined motion as "the act of that which is in potentiality and seeks to actualize itself." Rain "watered man's crops, which grew to feed man and man lived to serve and worship God." There were debates as to whether or not a spider (symbol of evil) could escape from a circle made of powdered unicorn horn (symbol of virginal innocence). Their debates sound remarkably like the convoluted rhetoric of many social scientists. The social sciences probably could do with a lot less of the trivial experiments, dubious measurements, obtuse mathematics, and incomprehensible verbiage that dominate their journals, and a lot more with speculation and debate on what should be studied and why.

As noted in the discussion of empiricism in the discussion on the nature of theory, the field of communications in particular and the social sciences in general need to figure out what is important. The failure, despite the enormous difficulties of doing so, is a major reason so much "theory" in the social sciences passes only technical requirements such as operational definitions, while failing important ones such as falsifiability, generalizability, parsimony and usability.

Social Models of Communication

Several social models of communication are relevant to conflict theory. They focus on individuals, organizations, culture and gender. We take up the first three of these below, reserving the fourth for the next chapter.

Deutsch (1973) has argued that the communication skills required for successful conflict management include ability to listen, assertiveness, clarity, credibility, empathy, flexibility, and openness. But, assertiveness and flexibility may be contradictory. Openness can give information away that leads to one-sided agreements. Ambiguous proposals make concessions easier, and euphemisms can make agreement possible (as when Cedras of Haiti refused to "quit" but agreed to "retire early.").

Communication sometimes is understood on the basis of the work of the Johari Window (Luft, 1969). It aims to increase self-awareness, gain greater self-control and help people to understand how others perceive them. The "Open" pane represents information that an individual knows about himself and is willing to share with others. It shows the extent to which two or more people can give and take, work together, and enjoy experiences together. Presumably, it gets larger as people become better acquainted. The "Hidden" pane represents information that an individual knows about himself but is unwilling to share. Presumably it gets smaller as people become better acquainted. The "Blind" pane represents information that an individual is unaware others have, the simplest illustration being speech mannerisms, the more important one being character traits. The "Unknown" pane represents untested characteristics, such as how a new soldier will react in combat.

	Information known to self	Information unknown to self
Information known to others	Open	Blind
Information unknown to others	Hidden	Unknown

Figure 5.5
The Johari Window

Hase (1999) proposed an extension (Figure 5.6) of the Johari Window he claims is applicable to power and control in the workplace and thus to organizational behavior and effectiveness.

	Things I know about myself and will disclose	Things I know about myself and will not disclose	Things I do not know about myself
Things others know about me and are prepared to disclose			
Things others know about me but are not prepared to disclose			
Things others do not know about me			

Figure 5.6
Modified Johari Window

Hase gives examples for each pane. For example, he places stereotyping and prejudice in the bottom left pane. But, it is perfectly plausible for others to know about your prejudices and to either keep the knowledge private or to use it against you. One can hold a belief that others regard as a prejudice but that others hold as a fundamental value or a simple matter of traditional definition (*e.g.*, that marriage must be between one man and one woman). That is, organizational communication is affected not only by what people know but also by their ethics, loyalties, and motives and by how they use knowledge. Hase further limits the utility of his model by limiting it to "dark" behaviors, such as blackmail, blind spots, collusion, desire for recognition, facades, glass ceilings, hidden agendas, lack of skill, nepotism and old-boy networks, powerlessness, prejudice, secrets, self-interest, stereotyping, threats, victimization, and whistle blowing.

Cross-cultural Communication

There are manuals aplenty for dealing with the cultural minutiae of international business, travel, and negotiation (*e.g.*, Axtell, 1985). Country guidebooks can help, as can the U.S. Chamber of Commerce. But, there are too many cultures and too many variations within them by age, class, religion, and sex for anyone who travels widely to get it right consistently. You must do the best you can, make sure others understand your good will, and rely on the tolerance of your hosts. Your opponents will not let small social errors stand in the way of an advantageous agreement. From the perspective of the theorist, these manuals lose the forest for the trees. A general approach identifying underlying dimensions of culture is required.

Gert Hofstede (2004) factor analyzed data on IBM employees in fifty countries and college students in 23 countries to identify key cultural variables. Results are impressive but one might ask just how typical of their cultures IBM employees and college students are? An immense amount of research in the social sciences is conducted on students who must serve as subjects as part of their own education. Depending on the purpose of the study, it may or may not be possible to extrapolate results on such subjects to a specific population of interest, or to the population at large, yet it is commonly done. Six cultural characteristics are particularly relevant to conflict theory.

Assertiveness, sometimes mistakenly called masculinity, often is contrasted with empathy, sometimes mistakenly called femininity. It is unlikely they lie at opposite ends of a single scale: one can be both empathic and assertive—particularly if one's empathy is purposive. Assertiveness is high in Japan, Germany, Austria and Switzerland, moderately high in Anglo countries; moderately low in France, Spain and Thailand, and low in Scandinavian countries and in the Netherlands. Assertiveness often also is a matter of education, authority, and social class.

Individualistic vs. collective cultures have quite different expectations for matters such as responsibility and assignment of credit and blame. Collective cultures tend to expect group loyalty in exchange for safety and security. Individualism prevails in Western countries, while collectivism prevails in less developed and Eastern countries; Japan takes a middle position on this dimension.

Power distance is the extent to which members of a culture accept unequal distribution of power. Latin, Asian, and African countries are more accepting than Anglo countries. It is important to understand the basis of authority, and to pick team members who will impress the opposition!

Risk orientation varies individually (Chapter 2), but culturally too. Some, people are raised to minimize uncertainty and risk by following strict laws and rules and believing in absolutes. Other cultures encourage risk acceptance by tolerating differences of opinion and minimizing rules. In general, the first creates a more bureaucratic, the latter a more entrepreneurial individual. Latin and Germanic countries avoid risk more than Anglo and Nordic ones.

Social distance takes four forms: intimate, personal, social and public social distances vary from one culture to another. For Americans these are 0-1.5, 1.5-4, 4-10, and over 10 feet (Hall, 1959). Americans have been seen at cocktail parties backing away to reach a comfortable personal distance while talking to Egyptians, who seem to prefer a personal distance of about six inches, only to be chased by the Egyptian trying to do the same. But, all anyone really has to do in such a situation is stand still and let the local citizen take up a comfortable distance for the situation. This automatically adjusts for all sorts of unknowns, such as sex and rank, without having to understand them.

Time has three dimensions important in conflict situations. Think of one as process—basically when things happen. North Americans and Northern Europeans tend be precise in business situations and fairly precise in social ones. Most cultures are considerably more relaxed, particularly in social situations—although their members remain perfectly capable of getting to planes and movies on time. Some people such as nomads and hunter-gatherers seem not even to conceive time in much more precise terms than seasons.

The second dimension is the time horizon. Americans are notoriously short-term, future-oriented thinkers. East Asian countries seem to look for results across a lifetime. Iranians still speak of Alexander the Great as if he marched through their country last year, and a Serb asked to explain why he killed a Muslim will trace every slight against his race since the battle of Kosovo in 1389. Hindus think in terms of cycles lasting tens of thousands of years.

The third dimension is the way time is distributed among the phases of a negotiation. Americans tend to move quickly through the exploration to concentrate on the bargaining phase during which they put considerable time into precise wording, reflecting the notorious litigousness of their culture. Many cultures, especially those in which relationships are important, spend more time on the exploratory phase, and once trust is established don't worry much about the details. The Japanese tend to close slowly, delaying to make sure that they can go ahead immediately once a deal is struck. Americans tend to close quickly and figure out later how to carry out the agreement later.

Conclusion

Given all the factors that affect personality, and the many different types of interpersonal conflict, some variation on the dual concern model seems to offer the most generalizable, parsimonious and usable approach to the study of interpersonal conflict. The Expected Utility Model (Chapter 12) can be interpreted as a variation applicable at the interstate level, so that the two have some potential for combination into a more general theory of conflict (Chapter 16).

Chapter 6
Gender Conflict

When the Himalayan peasant meets the he-bear in his pride,
He shouts to fool the monster, who will often turn aside.
But the she-bear thus accosted rends the peasant toot and nail,
For the female of the species is more deadly than the male.

. —Rudyard Kipling

Discrimination

Women were held in thrall through much of human history, and remain so in much of the world, due according to Hilary Lips (1981) to the "agonic power"[1] of men that derives from physical strength, education, money and status—all traditionally more accessible to men. The crusade to win equal rights for women began with Mary Wollstonecraft (1792) in her *Vindication of the Rights of Woman* at a time when revolutionary thoughts were common but did not yet extend to slaves or women.[2] Most men and many women opposed the fights for political, economic, and educational equality—in more or less that order.

New Zealand in 1893 was the first country to extend suffrage to women. Australia, Finland, Norway, Denmark, and Iceland followed. Most other countries finally did so in the years immediately after World War I. In some of these countries, including the United States and Norway, women had the right to run for office before they had the right to vote in them.

Elizabeth Stanton and Lucretia Mott initiated the suffrage movement in the United States at Seneca Falls in 1848. Wyoming gave women the right to vote when it became a territory in 1869 and when it became a state in 1890. Colorado and Utah followed in 1893 and 1896. Jeanette Rankin (R, Montana) served two terms in Congress before women could vote in federal elections, and again in 1940. A pacifist, she is famous for voting against declaring war both in 1918 (with 49 others) and in 1941 (alone) and, in 1967 at age 87, organizing a protest against the war in Vietnam. Congress passed and the states quickly ratified the Nineteenth Constitutional Amendment extending the vote to women in 1920.

---

1. The word is inexplicable here. Agonic means "Having or making no angle, having no inclination, as in 'agonic line,' the irregular line passing through the two magnetic poles of the earth along which the [compass] needle points directly north or south, the line of no magnetic variation." (*Oxford English Dictionary.*). Agonistic may be intended.

2. There were some isolated precursors, such as the fascinating and prolific Christine de Pizan (1365-1429).

Fourteen countries have constitutionally mandated quotas for women in parliament. Thirty-one have quotas in their election laws. Sixty require political parties to include some minimum percentage (usually about 30%) of women candidates in each election. In western democracies, the conflict over quotas pits two concepts of equality against one another (Chapter 2). One is the radical (now politically liberal) notion of equal result and compensation across generations for past ills. Defenders of quotas argue that they prevent tokenism and guarantee women their "fair share" of power. They argue that women bring valuable and unique perspectives to decision making. Finally, defenders of quotas argue that women are just as qualified as men, although in other contexts they argue that women do not have equal educational opportunity.

Opponents of quotas in western democracies take the classical liberal (now considered conservative) view that equality is limited to opportunity. In this view, society should remove the barriers, step aside, and let the chips fall where they may. Quotas are unfair, undemocratic, and imply that women need preferences because they are less competent (Dahlerup, n.d.; Hoffmann, 1994). Quotas for one type of under-represented group imply quotas for every under-represented group: religious, handicapped, occupation, sexual orientation, and so on *ad infinitum, ad nauseum, ad absurdum.* These arguments, pro and con, are almost identical to those made during the Civil Rights movement.

Women have served as prime minister, president or equivalent in Argentina, Bangladesh, Burundi, Central African Republic, England, Iceland, India, Indonesia, Israel, Latvia, Liberia, Nicaragua, Norway, Pakistan, the Philippines, and Sri Lanka (Inter-Parliamentary Union, 2000; Norris, 2000). Myanmar elected Aung San Suu Kyi, but the military junta prevented her taking office.

Women flooded into the factories in World War I, despite wages about half those men earned for the same work. The same thing happened in World War II, although the National War Labor Board ineffectually urged companies to voluntarily set equal pay scales. Newspapers listed jobs separately for men and women, with separate pay scales, until passage of the Equal Pay Act of 1963. The act required equal pay for equal work defined by skill, physical or mental effort, level of responsibility, and working conditions within each workplace.

American women have won the battle for equal pay despite statistics suggesting that they earn only about 75% of what men do. The statistic is true enough on average, but controlling for just three variables eliminates the difference and taking account of lifetime earnings and wealth may even reverses it! First, men tend to work from their first job till retirement, while women tend to drop out to raise children until they are school age, so that male workers average five to seven more years work experience than women.[3] Second, until recently, women had less education than men and had jobs requiring less skill, effort, and

---

3. Some homebound women have proved inventive and entrepreneurial especially when it comes to making life easier at home. A quarter of the sales of one catalog company are in such devices. *Wall Street Journal* 21 October 2004.

responsibility. Third, even among college graduates, women tended to major in fields that led to lesser paying jobs: in biology instead of physics, in sociology instead of economics, and so on. Regional differences in salaries and proportion of women in the work force may also help explain the apparent discrepancies. Finally, a lifetime view of income differences would adjust for the fewer years women pay into Social Security and pension funds and the greater number of years they collect, again on average.

Women were long denied equal education (one reason they had lesser jobs, of course), the third factor in pay equality, but this too is changing rapidly. Girls now are outperforming boys in high schools; and are more likely than boys to go to college. Girls are less likely to cheat on tests, wind up in detention, or drop out of school. Women have reached or are approaching parity with men even in high payoff graduate degrees including law, management, and medicine (Sommers 2000; Tiger 2000). Women increasingly are becoming presidents of major corporations and universities. By 2004, Hewlett-Packard, Avon, Travelocity, Xerox, eBay, Lucent Technologies, Ventas, and Young & Rubicam were among major corporations run by women, while women were "heirs apparent" at dozens more.[4]

Women and Peace

Many who are repelled by the argument that our genes determine our intelligence and abilities accept the argument that women are by nature more peace loving and gentle than men, and that the world would be more peaceful if it were run by women. Some radical feminists assert that patriarchal, god-worshipping nomads imposed war, conflict, and hierarchy on peaceful, matriarchal, goddess-worshipping agricultural societies. Finally, some argue that conflict between the sexes stems from differences in communication style. Do these ideas meet the tests of good theory?

Francis Fukuyama (1998) pointed to Norwegian Prime Minister Gro Bruntland as an example of the pacific woman leader the world should seek out. But, her pacifism is equally characteristic of male Norwegian prime ministers. Her nationality is more likely to explain her politics than her sex. Golda Meier, Indira Gandhi, and Sirima Bandarnaike are much more typical of the women who have led their countries. Margaret Thatcher insisted that a hesitant George Bush not "go wobbly" when Saddam Hussein invaded Kuwait. Hatshepsut of Egypt, Semiramis of Babylon, Cleopatra of Egypt, and Catherine the Great of Russia are among history's warrior queens. Tomyris, queen of the semi-nomadic Massagetae and a heroine of her Kazakh descendants, killed Cyrus, founder of the Achaemenid Persian Empire. England produced Boadicea, Matilda, Elizabeth I,

---

4. Through the Glass Ceiling. *Wall Street Journal.* 8 November 2004. A reported rapid increase in working mothers and "house husbands" may also be a sign of well-educated women getting better jobs than their husbands.

and Victoria (Fraser, 1980). Jinga in Angola, Rani in India, Soriyothai in Thailand, and the Trung sisters in Vietnam hardly fit the image of women as the peaceable sex.

Olympias probably murdered her husband Philip to insure the succession of Alexander the Great. Zenobia of Palymyra murdered her husband because he counseled negotiation with Rome, then led Palmyra to war and defeat. King Ferdinand of Spain was afraid that Queen Isabella wanted to murder him. One of the more famous events leading to the French Revolution was the March of the [8000] Parisian Women who pillaged and looted their way to Versailles—no peaceful demonstrations for them. When a man satirized the march, one of the women arranged his assassination. Later, she helped lead the assault on the Bastille. Madame Defarge may be fictional, but she is rooted in reality.[5]

One hundred thousand Russian women served in the front lines in World War II, many as snipers. Tito lost 25,000 women warriors killed and 40,000 wounded in his guerrilla war against Germany. Among 20,000 mainly Muslim soldiers in Bosnia, about 1000 were women, often serving as snipers. One of them, a 19-year old medical student, said, "When I liquidate an enemy soldier my heart swells. I only feel courage and the desire to kill another." In 1845, the King of Dahomey had an army of 12,000, of whom 5,000 were women. Women seem to have served as warriors in Albania, Arabia, Angola, Australia, the Canary Islands, Hawaii, Patagonia, Tasmania, and among the Ainu and Apache (Q.Wright, 1942).

Half the Red Army Faction in Germany were women. Maria Neyra succeeded Abimael Guzman as commander of the Shining Path in Peru. Women made up five percent of Kenya's Mau-Mau and a higher percentage of the officers. Arab women fought against the French in Algeria. A significant number of the ETA, the Intifada, the Red Brigade, and the Baader Meinhof Gang are or were women. There are 3000 or so Tamil Tigresses trained as suicide bombers.

More men are violent than women,[6] but the historical record does not substantiate the naive notion that turning the world over to women would insure peace. Would that it were that simple! It is no more than a fantasy intended to advance a contemporary social agenda,[7] as one early feminist finally recognized:

> . . . There is another thing that died for me in the last couple of weeks—a certain kind of feminist naiveté. It saw men as the perpetual perpetrators, women as the perpetual victims, and male sexual violence against women as the root of all injustice. Maybe this sort of feminism made more sense in the 1970s. There was a lot of talk about rape as an instrument of war and even war as an exten-

---

5. John Steinbeck observed that, "a thing could be true [illustratively or symbolically] even if it never happened." (*Log from the Sea of Cortez*).
6. Kerry Seagrave (1992) chronicles five centuries of women serial killers. Alix Kirsta (1994) among others provides a general record of women criminals.
7. Eller has since recanted, acknowledging that almost no serious archaeologist working today believes that ancient cultures were monotheist or matriarchal.

sion of rape. There seemed to be at least some reason to believe that male sexual sadism may somehow be deeply connected to our species' propensity for
violence.

. . . That was before we had seen female sexual sadism in action.[8] It is not just
the theory that was wrong. So was its strategy and vision for change. That strategy and vision for change rested on the assumption that women are morally superior to men. After all, women do most of the caring work in our culture, and
in polls are consistently less inclined to war than men.

. . . The implication of this assumption was that all we had to do to make the
world kinder, less violent, and more just was to become the CEOs, the senators,
the generals, the judges and opinion-makers. Once women gained power and
authority, they would naturally work for change. The most profound thing I
have to say to you today, as a group of brilliant young women poised to enter
the world, is that its just not true.

. . . What we have learned, once and for all, is that a uterus is not a substitute
for a conscience; menstrual periods are not the foundation of morality. Gender
equality cannot, all alone, bring about a just and peaceful world. What I have
finally come to understand, sadly and irreversibly, is that the kind of feminism
based on an assumption of moral superiority on the part of women is lazy and
self-indulgent. Self-indulgent because it assumes that a victory for a woman is
by its very nature a victory for humanity. Lazy because it assumes that we have
only one struggle—the struggle for gender equality—when in fact we have
many more. The struggles for peace, for social justice and against imperialist
and racist arrogance cannot, I am truly sorry to say, be folded into the struggle
for gender equality.[9]

The Matriarchal Past

Three claims about our prehistoric past provide the second pillar of the fantasy that women would create a more peaceful world. Radical feminists commonly claim that man's first deity was a "universally" worshipped goddess. Second, they claim this goddess is associated with a peaceful, matriarchal,
agricultural society. Third, they claim that patriarchal Indo-European invaders
destroyed this pacific world.

Marija Gimbutas (1989) claimed that hundreds of Paleolithic "Venus figurines" prove that Man's first deities were goddesses. Cynthia Eller (1993)
claimed that by the Neolithic a *single* goddess inspired a peaceful, matriarchal,
agricultural:

> There was no war, people lived in harmony with nature, women and men
> lived in harmony with one another, children were loved and nurtured, there was

---

8. She refers to the abuse of male Iraqi prisoners by female American guards. In fact
there is nothing new about it—the critics of feminism often pointed to women murderers,
serial murderers, and torturers, including two of Hitler's worst, but the criticism was dismissed as more sexism, so sure were radical feminists of their superiority.

9. Barbara Ehrenreich, Barnard Commencement Address 2004.

food and shelter for all, and everyone was playful, spontaneous, creative and sexually free under the loving gaze of the goddess. People were in touch with their bodies and the seasons, there were no rich or poor, and homosexuality (particularly lesbianism) was as valid or more so than heterosexuality.

There are many problems with all this. It is not possible to determine the sex of the majority of the "Venus" figurines. Among the remaining ones, there are as many males as females. There is no evidence that the figurines represent gods or goddesses, as opposed to dolls, fertility figures, healing talismans, boundary markers, erotica or simple decorative figures to name some of the equally plausible suggestions made based on the contexts in which they were found.

To the best of our knowledge, agriculture evolved in the Fertile Crescent, the Nile Valley and the Indus Valley, but the figurines are found primarily from Spain through Western and Central Europe to Siberia in areas inhabited by hunter-gatherers, including the original homeland of the Indo-Europeans whom feminists say are patriarchal. There is one clear case of an invading Indo-European tribe destroying an agricultural one. They devastated Anatolia, settled down, and became known to history as the Phrygians. Unfortunately for feminist theory, these aggressors worshipped a goddess.

Hunter-gatherer societies tend to be egalitarian. The nomadic case is more difficult because so many today also are Muslim. Mongolians are among the few remaining non-Muslim nomads, and they are egalitarian. We know from archaeological excavations and thousands of ancient documents that hierarchy and patriarchy developed in agricultural, not nomadic, societies. This is not particularly surprising, as they alone had the surplus that allows craft specialization, a prerequisite for hierarchy.

Few ancient goddesses are mothers. For example, Cybele is the goddess of the mountains and forests, Ninurta of creation, Demeter of agriculture, Diana of the hunt, and Ishtar of war. Kali wears a necklace of skulls and a dress of severed arms, and carries swords in her several hands. Thugee (assassination), sati (immolation of widows), and the Hindu caste system arose from her cult, none of which does much for the idea that goddess religions fostered peace or high status for women. Philip Davis (1998) has examined the archaeological, historical, and literary evidence of goddess spirituality and concluded that its roots lie with male authors of the 19th century Romantic movement in Western Europe.

We have no evidence of prehistoric monotheism. Pharaoh Akhenaten (14th C. BC) is the world's first known monotheist, or something very close to it.

It is not possible to deduce sexual practices from the skeletons, tools, potsherds, and artifacts that we have from the Neolithic period. When confronted on the point, Eller replied that, "even if these cultures cannot be proved to have existed, they at least are a possibility, and that is enough." But, of course, it is not enough. Almost anything anyone can imagine is "possible," but possibilities are neither probabilities nor evidence.

The existing "evidence" that patriarchal Indo-European nomads conquered goddess-worshipping agricultural matriarchal pacifists collapses under scrutiny. Virtually everything written about a matriarchal past is by non-archaeologists. It dismisses contrary evidence and distorts facts. It subjects credible archaeologists to personal attacks, such as "rigidity in the face of new ideas" that are no more than hopeful speculation. It dismisses or ignores plausible reconstructions of the past to create a mystery that seems to beg for explanation. Then, it combines conjecture, coincidence, and over-extrapolation to reach the desired conclusion. These are time-tested devices of ideological writing (Chapter 1). Wanting something to be true does not make it true.

Gender Differences in Communication Style

Deborah Tannen (1990) is a popular author who writes on gender differences in conversational style. She asserts that men cannot understand women, and women cannot understand men. Given her own assumptions, how can she write authoritatively about men?

Tannen makes much of her case by self-serving interpretation of small incidents. For example, she interprets men waving women ahead of them in traffic as "communicating" male dominance and female submissiveness. In fact, men wave both men and women ahead, and women do the same. Both cut each other off without checking the sex of the driver. Most of the time, they do neither, changing lanes based on safety and the rules of the road rather than the sex of other drivers. When they do otherwise, it is more likely that they are hurrying rather than "asserting dominance."

Tannen claims that American men get right to the heart of a matter in a conversation because they have not learned to engage in idle "chit-chat" the way women have. Although that is not the term that men would use to describe it, Tannen apparently has not spent much time listening to men in a bar "chit-chatting" about sports and women.

Tannen also claims that American men left home to find work, and to open the frontier, so became independent and left the responsibility for socializing to women. "Responsibility" for socializing? The three groups closest to Tannen's model were fur trappers, cowboys and miners. The fur trappers often married Indian women. The "wild west" of the cowboy lasted only about twenty years before the railroad brought law and stability. The mining era lasted longer, but the towns quickly went bust or became civilized. The three groups together represent a tiny percent of American men for a brief period in U.S. history. The actual experience of most pioneers was a lot closer to the family struggles described by Laura Ingalls in *Little House on the Prairie*.

Tannen claims that communication differences develop because boys and girls grow up separately. Boys and girls may play separately, but they are together in school and in family units. If they learn separate styles when separate, why can't they learn common styles when together? Tannen ignores mutually comprehensible male-female conversations, almost certainly the vast majority, and she does not recognize that the exceptions she mentions falsify her own conclusions. The differences Tannen describes between men and women can be found just as easily between two men and between two women.

Tannen attempts a cross-cultural spin by asserting that a divorce resulted because of differences in communicating style between a Greek man and an American woman. She asserts without evidence that communication problems caused the divorce. The characteristics of the Greek man are not characteristic of Greek culture, based on my own observations during several trips to Greece and eight months living in Cyprus. Further, she generalizes from the single case to all cross-cultural marriages, a ludicrous over-extrapolation.

Just as people often "prove" a point by some folk saying (Nearest is dearest, A stitch in time saves nine) but could just as easily "prove" the opposite with another saying (Distance makes the heart grow fonder, Haste makes waste), Tannen relies on anecdotes with equally plausible alternative interpretations. For *each* anecdote of conflict stemming from misunderstanding that she cites there are quite literally millions of successful conversations between men and women.

Tannen's work is typical of the way "pop psych" authors make their case. Facts are taken out of context, and then interpreted to support the theory. Anecdotes are heaped up. Remarkable cases are characterized as typical. Contrary evidence is ignored or dismissed. Possibility is sufficient for acceptance of favorable ideas, while certainty is demanded for competing ones. As Michael Crichton (San Francisco, 15 September 2003) has said:

> The greatest challenge facing mankind is the challenge of *distinguishing reality from fantasy, truth from propaganda.* Perceiving the truth has always been a challenge to mankind, but in the Information Age it takes on a special urgency and importance. We must daily decide whether the threats we face are real, whether the solutions we are offered will do any good, whether the problems we're told exist are in fact real. Our struggle to determine what is true is the struggle to decide which of our perceptions are genuine, and which are false because they are handed down, or sold to us, or generated by our own hopes and fears (emphasis added).

Men and women may find themselves in conflict, but it seems unlikely that the cause lies in sex-specific forms of communication. Even if such forms exist, there must be a third form used when they talk to one another, as the simple fact is that despite occasional misunderstandings, men and women understand one another fairly well most of the time.

Sexual Harassment

Unwelcome sexual advances, requests for sexual favors, and "other verbal or physical conduct of a sexual nature" violate Title VII of the [United States] Civil Rights Act of 1964 when "submission to or rejection of this conduct

Civil Rights Act of 1964 when "submission to or rejection of this conduct explicitly or implicitly affects an individual's employment, unreasonably interferes with an individual's work performance or creates an intimidating, hostile or offensive work environment." Anyone—even a non-employer—can be a harasser and anyone affected by the offensive conduct, even if not the target of it, can be the victim. The conduct must be unwelcome, but, it is not enough that an employee was offended. The plaintiff must show that "an ordinary, reasonable, prudent person in like or similar circumstances" would have been similarly offended (EEOC, 27 June 2002).

Sexual harassment takes two main forms. The first, "quid pro quo," such as Hollywood's infamous casting couches, is inexcusable. It exists whenever hiring, retention, firing or promotion hinge on sexual favors. The second, "hostile working environment," is considerably more difficult to define. The Supreme Court (*Harris v. Forklift Systems, Inc.* 1993) found that the existence of a hostile working environment can only be determined by considering all the circumstances, including (1) frequency of conduct or speech (2) severity of conduct or speech (3) whether the conduct or speech is physically threatening or merely offensive and (4) whether it interferes unreasonably with the victim's work performance. Justices Scalia and Ginsburg wrote separate concurring opinions saying that only the last criterion is necessary, Scalia arguing that the first three along with the "reasonable person" standard are too ambiguous.

Our main purpose is to understand causes. The sociobiologists offer us the common sense proposition that men are genetically programmed to be sexual aggressors. There may be times when it is inappropriate, such as in the workplace, but the reality is that men and women meet in the workplace, and both still seek mates. Outlawing courtship in the workplace is likely to be as efficacious as prohibition was (Wyatt, 2000).

Some anthropologists hold that the root cause of sexual harassment is our patriarchal social structure. This structure gives men social, political, and economic power over women. Some men in positions of power assume that they have sexual access to the women working for them. Some traditional patriarchal cultures confine women to the home as wives and mothers and deny them formal education. In others, stereotypes about appropriate male and female behavior assign women a subordinate sexualized identity even in the workplace. Men do not see their overtures as harassment and many women either share the same assumptions or are too afraid to resist (Wyatt, 2000).

Children learn culturally appropriate sex-specific behaviors that become intimately involved with personality. In most cases, men learn to be adventurous, competitive, dominant, forceful, independent, logical, and strong-willed. Women learn to be caring, compliant, cooperative, dependent, emotional, sentimental, submissive, and superstitious. Women who violate these norms to achieve professional success jeopardize their femininity and risk pejorative labels (Putnam, 1983), but it also is true that men who violate their norms jeopardize their masculinity and risk pejorative labels. This may be changing in some societies. Current trends make the future look bleak for American men, with 73% of boys but only 27% of girls diagnosed with learning disabilities and 76% of boys but only 24% of girls diagnosed as emotionally disturbed. Girls are trouncing boys on reading tests, catching up in math, and are beginning to dominate extracurricular activities. Women are earning bachelors and masters degrees at a significantly higher rate than men, make up almost half of all law students and are rapidly closing the M.D. and PhD gap (*Business Week*, 26 May 2003).

Some sociologists hold that women and men are socialized into different cultures—different beliefs, values, and ways of communicating. The traditional workplace was male dominated, and characterized by competition, rude jokes, and disrespect for women (apparently in this view women spoke only in the most respectful terms about men). Women entering the workplace have had to adapt to its culture, while men have had to adapt to having women in it. Both are changing slowly (Taylor 1999). While we work to free our students from sexual harassment, we must also guard against a return to the crippling gender-based protectionism of a time gone by, when someone else made all women's choices for them (Veraldi, 1995).

Relational Aggression

"Relational aggression" develops as early as age three in approximately 20% of females but is rare in males. This distinctive form of aggression relies on destruction of relationships through exclusion, gossip, guilt trips, meanness, manipulation, and peer pressure. Current studies suggest that relationally aggressive children tend toward paranoid interpretation of events, peer rejection, and problematic friendships. Identification of the phenomenon is further evidence requiring that we rethink the erroneous stereotype that females are not aggressive because they do not rely on fighting physically (Crick, in press, and 1998).

Conclusion

There is good reason to believe that gender alone, or differences in communication style, are not major causes of conflict between men and women. Those that stem from discrimination against women are declining in the United States and most of Western Europe, but remain significant elsewhere. Perhaps some future research should be directed at determining the extent to which women who achieve authority, power, and responsibility do so by bringing a more nurturing and supportive role to their positions or by becoming more assertive and competitive.

Chapter 7
Community Conflict

You've got to be taught to hate and fear
You've got to be taught from year to year
It's got to be drummed in your dear little ear
You've got to be carefully taught.

You've got to be taught to be afraid
Of people whose eyes are oddly made
And people whose skin is a different shade
You've got to be carefully taught.

You've got to be taught before it's too late
Before you are six or seven or eight
To hate all the people your relatives hate
You've got to be carefully taught.
—Oscar Hammerstein, *South Pacific*

This chapter focuses on class, gang, and ethnic or racial conflict. It also deals with hostage situations because they usually fall to local police to resolve. It does not address squabbles between neighbors, best handled as interpersonal conflict by negotiation or mediation (Chapter 8). Nor does it address political disputes (Chapter 10), coups, civil wars, or revolution (Chapter 11).

Class Conflict

Plato saw things in threes. Just as individuals comprised the sensual body, the willful mind, and the divinely inspired soul, Plato thought societies were composed of workers who devoted themselves to sensual gratification, soldiers who sought honor and prestige, and intellectuals who pursued reason and truth. Plato believed there were natural tensions between these groups that made conflict inevitable—an idea that inspired Marx, although he saw only two classes.

Marx popularized the idea of the irreconcilable conflict of social classes that would end only with the advent of socialism. In Marx's view, one's occupation determines one's class. In his view, an individual is an owner and a member of the bourgeoisie or a worker and a member of the proletariat. The bourgeoisie control the means of production, explaining its domination of society. They manipulate everything in society, such as education, family, law, and religion, to insure their control of the means of production, such as farming, herding, manufacture, trading. Wealth is the basis of political power.

Marx maintained that the transition from feudalism to capitalism merely changed peasants who toiled for noblemen into workers exploited by the bourgeoisie. The "iron law of wages" held: owners paid workers just enough to survive and reproduce themselves. The "labor theory of value" also held: the workers alone were responsible for profit. Owners were mere parasites.

Marx did not originate the iron law of wages, the labor theory of value, or the idea of socialism. His contribution was the inevitability of socialist revolution. With what he thought was impeccable logic he argued that the owners who controlled both economic and political power never would permit reforms that would reduce their profits. Workers would sink deeper and deeper into poverty until their suffering became unbearable and they revolted to replace capitalism with socialism, which with classes eliminated would put an end to conflict. Much of what Marx wrote had been refuted by the time he wrote it, and most of his predictions have since been proven false (Chapter 11).

Max Weber probably is the best known of all sociologists and almost as influential as Marx. Both believed that social change grew out of social conflict. However, where Marx saw just one basis for conflict, Weber (1968) saw three: (1) economic wealth or power which formed the basis of classes, (2) social reputation and prestige, which formed the basis of status groups, and (3) political power, which formed the basis of political parties and interest groups. Although there is a high correlation among the three, Weber thought them independent of one another, resulting in a much more complex class structure than is found in Marx.

Conflict theorists are most interested in Weber's employment of ideal types to study bureaucratic, charismatic, and traditional structures of authority. Reminiscent of Plato's allegory of the cave, Weber felt that understanding came about by comparing the "ideal" with the "real." According to Weber, an ideal captures the principal or essential features of some social phenomenon.

Ideal bureaucratic authority according to Weber is efficient, rational, and stultifying. He astutely and correctly predicted that socialist bureaucracies would be worse than capitalist ones, because in socialism, even the top-level leaders would be bureaucrats. The "ideal" bureaucracy has:

A permanent organization
Administrative decisions and actions based on written rules
Departments with specific functions arranged in a hierarchal system
Selection for positions based on announced qualifications
An educational system to qualify candidates for positions
Incumbents who do not own positions so cannot choose successors

Ideal traditional authority according to Weber takes three main forms. A gerontocracy involves rule by elders. Patriarchy involves male rule by inheritance. Patrimony involves personal rule backed by a military force. Weber saw all forms of traditional authority as essentially conservative and tending to prevent the rise of a rational social structure. The "ideal" traditional social system in all three cases involves:

Personal, often impulsive, rule limited only by tradition
Administration by loyal personal retainers
Lack of clearly defined departments
Lack of a rational hierarchy
Lack of training or specified qualifications for appointment
Lack of a regular system for selection, promotion, or compensation

Charismatic authority stems in Weber's view from the perception among followers of exceptional qualities in a leader. He viewed charismatic leadership as an important revolutionary force characterized by:

Personal rule
Lack of formal rules or precedents to guide decisions
Administration by disciples and believers
Lack of clearly defined departments
Lack of a rational hierarchy
Lack of training or specified qualifications for appointment
Lack of a regular system for selection, promotion, or compensation

A charismatic system is inherently fragile. Successors rarely succeed as charismatic leaders, so must find another basis for their authority. Failure to do so usually means failure of the society itself (Ritzer, 1983).

Ralf Dahrendorf, (1959, 1968) saw authority, not property and not class, as the key to understanding conflict. Positions vary in authority, which always involves superiors and subordinates who hold contradictory interests. Superiors always strive to maintain, and subordinates to change, the status quo.

Randall Collins (1975) focused on small-scale social conflict. He followed Merton (1968) in advocating theory development through the study of real life situations using empirical methods, ideally in a comparative fashion. He assumed that people are naturally social but turn easily to conflict if that is necessary to achieve their goals. He worked within the Marxist context of occupation as the major determinant of one's lifestyle, economic situation, and social groups. It follows that everyone brings different resources to bear in achieving his goals. Some are articulate, some are rich, some are smart, some are strong, and so on. Power stems from control of resources and will be used by those who have it to exploit those who have less.

Talcott Parsons (1951, 1966, 1971) was concerned with how social order, integration, and equilibrium are possible. He thought in terms of social levels (behavioral, personal, social and cultural) that are similar to the arrangement in this book. He also made much of biological and evolutionary analogies, although he did not see any general process that affected all societies equally and felt that individual societies could advance, stagnate, or regress. As his thoughts developed, he identified four imperatives for social order and survival, identified by the mnemonic acronym AGIL:

> Adaptation to the inevitability of change: Social subsystems of successful societies evolve in the direction of improved function and greater distinctiveness.
> Goal attainment: Societies must achieve their primary goals, which requires cooperation among its members to insure completion and coordination of primary tasks.
> Integration: Channels of communication and a common language are required to regulate the relationship among adaptation, goal attainment, and latency.
> Latency: A stable, meaningful and predictable society requires teaching a cultural value system to its members. However, as a society's subsystems adapt, the value system itself, despite the difficulty of doing so, must become more general and tolerant if it is to legitimize the wider variety among its subunits.

Parsons, following his proclivity for biological analogies, thought of conflict as akin to disease. Conflict threatened the health of the community. It had to be prevented or cured by social controls or force. The latter was itself dangerous, as Parsons did not think societies that depended on imposed order would survive for long. Parsons saw little that was good in conflict.

Georg Simmel (1955) and his disciple Lewis Coser (1956) took the opposite view from Parsons, emphasizing many positive effects of conflict. Among them, conflict established and maintained identity and boundaries, reduced social isolation, increased group cohesion, and energized group members. War and negotiation determined the boundaries of many nations, and colonial powers imposed many of the rest with a view to keeping the indigenous population divided and conquered. Similarly, gang wars establish "turf" and fans are intensely loyal to their teams. However, patriotism can become xenophobic, and war can divide as well as unite societies, as happened in the United States during Viet Nam and both parts of the Gulf War. Similarly, gangs seldom have a very positive effect on society and sports fans often take games too seriously.

Conflict can warn of growing problems within a society. In this view the lawsuits, bus boycotts, sit-ins, and protest marches of the early 1960s warned of the need to eliminate segregation in the United States. The riots and protests of the late 1960s warned of the need to end the war in Vietnam and solve the problem of poverty in the inner cities. A responsive society addressed the problems with Civil Rights and Great Society legislation in the mid-1960s and admitted defeat in Vietnam in the early 1970s.

Coser asserts that conflict can help to maintain relationships and allows consensus to develop. Echoing catharsis, he argued that demonstrations provide a safety valve that reduce frustration and allow consensus to develop. One reason we are interested in the size of demonstrations and counter-demonstration is that it helps decide "which way the wind is blowing." Elections and opinion polls do the same, of course. However, conflict does not always allow consensus to develop, as Simmel realized in pointing out that ending the relationship is a possibility too. Witness the countless religious conflicts that have led to schism (Chapter 11) and disputes such as abortion in the United States that have not been resolved by endless demonstrations or for that matter by the courts or legislation

Finally, Simmel and Coser saw conflict as a way of readjusting power within a group. If there is no tradition of a peaceful means of doing so, such as elections, then less peaceful ones, such as coups or revolutions, will take place. Either way, changes in political strength eventually will be reflected in the leadership of a group. When coalitions form to overthrow the existing leadership, success often leads to a power struggle within the successful coalition. Caesar emerged triumphant from the coalition that took power in Rome, the Federalists defeated the Anti-federalists in the American Revolution, and the Ayatollahs appear to have triumphed over the merchant and student allies in Iran.

Gangs

Urban youth gangs have been a problem in the United States since the mid-nineteenth century. They now are so large and numerous that they are likely to remain a pervasive source of community conflict for a long time to come. Criminologists, psychologists, and sociologists provide most suggestions for reducing the problem, but Leng and Henderson (1996) make an interesting case for looking instead to international relations for an analogy useful in finding a solution. Gangs are like nations in having recognizable territory that they control internally (with varying success) and protect externally. Like the state system, gangs assume sovereignty over their own members and do not brook interference in their internal affairs. Members identify with their gangs (nationalism) and accept their values (patriotism). Life is a constant struggle, there are few restraints on behavior toward other gangs, and an unstable balance of power provides what little order exists. There is a rough parallel between the UN and international treaties in the state system and that of the police and the churches in the gang world in providing higher authorities that are widely ignored in practice.

Despite these similarities, there are some important differences between the international and the urban gang systems. Gangs lag the interstate system with regard to human rights, sexism, racism, and religious tolerance. There is no expectation of seeking peaceful settlements before resorting to violence, which remains an accepted means of demonstrating power. Gangs have shown little concern for noncombatants and have become notorious for indiscriminant killing of innocent bystanders. In these characteristics, gangs are closer to terrorists than states.

The international model leads logically to mediation (Chapter 8) as the best method to minimize gang conflict. Respected community leaders drawn from the same culture and locale have proven able to exert influence. However, unlike the usual international situation, the mediation problem is not a matter of finding common ground but of persuading gang members that it is in their mutual interest to assume responsibility for the violence and its consequences in their territories and help them change existing behavioral norms. Getting leaders to apologize to innocent victims and surviving family members of gang violence has been an effective starting point, as even hardened gang leaders usually recognize the immorality of killing children.

Mediation is of course treatment of symptoms rather than a cure for the disease. The usual prescription for a long-term solution is to eliminate the roots of the problem, commonly said to be child abuse and neglect, drugs, poverty, and racism. The attitude of inner city youth to education, responsibility, and morality may be even more basic. Which to focus on, and what to do about each, seems more a matter of belief than of science, liberals focusing on the first and conservatives on the second set.

Ethnic or Racial Conflict

An ethnic minority is a social group that is set apart or sets itself apart from the rest of the community based on race, language, nationality, or culture.[1] Sometimes it entails official recognition, such as the Nazi requirement that Jews wear a distinctive armband or the affirmative action program intended to help American blacks. The Alawites, members of a Shi'a sect consisting of about 10% of the population, control Syria: in some cases minorities rule and not always gently. The Tutsi, about 15% of the population, long controlled Rwanda. Many of the world's conflicts since the end of the Cold War have been ethnic, religious, or both. Ethnic conflicts are not new, but their prominence seems a throwback to an earlier era many thought never would recur.[2]

Many cases of ethnic conflict originate in past conquests and migrations. The Welsh and Scots maintain a sense of identity in the UK, as do (to cite just a few examples) the Basques in Spain, Biafrans in Nigeria, Kurds in Iraq, Uighurs in China, and Xingu in Brazil. In the United States, ethnic diversity is the result of voluntary immigration, conquered indigenous peoples, and the descendants of slaves brought from Africa against their will.

States have tried six major strategies for solving the apparent contradiction between ethnicity and the nation state. The first is genocide.[3] There have been

---

1. Adapted from the *Oxford English Dictionary* and *Encyclopedia Britannica*
2. The reversion of once communist states of the former Soviet Union to ethnic conflict is impossible under Marxist theory, one of the facts that falsify it.
3. Ralph Lemkin coined the term (1944) in *Axis Rule in Occupied Europe* (*Oxford English Dictionary* and *Wikipedia Encyclopedia* online).

military campaigns that approach genocide, including Scipio's destruction of Carthage (salting the fields so that crops could not grow to prevent rebuilding the city). Additional examples are Julius Caesar's campaigns against the Gauls and Helveti, the Albigensian Crusade against the Cathars, the campaigns of Timurlane (marked by the towers of skulls he left behind), and the Jacobin campaign against the Royalists in the Vendee (Secher, 2003). Lord Amherst's effort to spread smallpox among American Indians during Pontiac's rebellion and the highland clearances following the battle of Culloden were genocidal in intent. The twentieth century saw too much genocide and mass killing, and the twenty-first century has started poorly.[4]

Acts of war such as the bombing of Dresden or Hiroshima do not qualify as genocide simply because many were killed or because years later armchair strategists judge them to have been militarily unnecessary.[5] On the other hand, killing just a few hundred people can be genocide if the victims are members of a small tribal group. In its narrowest sense, genocide is an effort to destroy an ethnic group regardless of numbers. International conventions specifically list as genocidal deprivation of food, medical services, shelter, or water, environmental destruction, forced sterilization, and forced transfer of children so as to bring them up divorced from their native culture.

The second method nations have used to deal with unwanted minorities is expulsion, which the Spaniards tried with the Jews and Muslims in the 15th century, the Americans tried in the 19th century for dealing with ex-slaves and several African nations tried in the 20th century for dealing with East Indians. The American effort was unusual in being voluntary and in helping the emigrants to establish their own country, Liberia.

The third method is segregation. It has taken many forms, from the ghettos of Eastern Europe through the apartheid of South Africa, unusual in that it was the majority that was held in thrall. Many immigrant groups have suffered it in varying forms in the United States (Myrdal, 1944). Sometimes, it is a matter of government policy, sometimes as in the case of the treatment of early Irish immigrants to America, a matter of social pressure without legal sanction.

The fourth method is internal migration. Stalin and the czars before him moved whole populations[6] away from their homelands to make revolt less likely or to provide needed labor in under- populated areas. American Indians were

---

4. Genocides in the Congo (1880-1920), Namibia (1904-1907), Turkey (1908), and Ukraine (1932-1933) preceded the Holocaust. Subsequent cases include Bangladesh, Cambodia, East Timor, Iraq, Kosovo, Rwanda, Sierra Leone, and Sudan.

5. The use of atomic bombs to end World War II is particularly interesting. For the case against, see Gar Alperowtiz (1995) *The Decision to Use the Atomic Bomb*, published by Alfred A. Knopf. Thomas Allen and Norman Polmar (1995), *Code Name Downfall*, published by Simon and Schuster, make the much stronger case for using it.

6. Chechens, Crimean Tatars, Don Cossacks, Estonians, Latvians, Lithuanians, Poles, Russians, and Volga Germans

forced onto reservations. The method hardly is new: the Babylonian exile of the Jews probably is history's most famous instance, although the Assyrians practiced the method even earlier.[7] China currently practices a variation. Instead of moving the target group out, they are moving millions of Han into regions such as Tibet and Xinjiang to overwhelm national minorities who were regional majorities. Indonesia has done the same, moving Javanese into Irian Jaya and Borneo.

Switzerland's three major ethnic groups are concentrated in separate cantons enjoying considerable autonomy. Bretons, Welsh, Scots, and Lapps are among groups that are similarly concentrated and exhibit considerable cultural pride but little serious interest in separatism. Many Quebecois seem to want independence in their hearts, but know in their minds that it will not work, so the issue festers without resolution but without violence either. Many immigrants to the United States concentrated by ethnicity, often where the climate and terrain were similar to their homelands. The Basques came with their sheep and dogs to the mountains of Oregon and California. The Scandinavians chose the upper Mississippi. The Germans settled Pennsylvania and Missouri. Those who stayed in the cities formed ethnic neighborhoods, which soon had names like Chinatown or "Little Saigon."

The fifth method is assimilation, its metaphor the melting pot. Roman citizenship was desired and extended regardless of ethnicity. British passports were available to its colonials. The French practiced forced assimilation in Langue d'oc after the Albigensian Crusade and centuries later in their African colonies where John Dewey observed black children chanting, "All of our ancestors were Gauls" in French. Traditionally, immigrants to the United States, although they might live in ethnic neighborhoods or even regions and maintain much of their old culture, tried to assimilate. The Civil Rights movement and the resulting legislation and court decisions was an overdue effort to assimilate black Americans into the majority culture.

The sixth method is pluralism, its metaphor the salad bowl in which each ingredient maintains its own identity. It rests on a combination of toleration, interdependence, and separatism. In part, it was a reaction to the difficulties encountered in achieving the dreams of the Civil Rights movement. Some blacks initially demanded integration but now demand separation. The charge that assimilation requires extinguishing cultures is largely untrue. Millions of Americans maintain ties to their original countries—it is in fact a national strength. The American approach at its best always has been a combination of assimila-

---

7. It is much more likely that the Colchians described by Herodotus as descended from Egyptians after an imagined invasion of Anatolia during the Middle Kingdom actually were descended from Egypto-Kushites deported by Esarhaddon in the seventh century BC. See Frank Yurco, Black Athena: An Egyptological Review, in M. Lefkowitz and G. Rogers, eds (1996), *Black Athena Revisited*. Chapel Hill: University of North Carolina Press.

tion and pluralism. No social scientist has put it as well as novelist John Steinbeck (1966):

> Our land is of every kind geologically and climatically, and our people are of every kind also—of every race, of every ethnic category—and yet our land is one nation, and our people are Americans. The motto of the United States, "*E Pluribus Unum*," is a fact...In the beginning, we crept, scuttled, escaped, were driven out of the safe and settled corners of the earth to the fringes of a strange and hostile wilderness...Many others were sent as punishment for penal offenses. Far from welcoming us, this continent resisted us...America did not exist. Four centuries of work, of bloodshed, of loneliness and fear created this land. We built America and the process made us Americans—a new breed, rooted in all races, stained and tinted with all colors, a seeming ethnic anarchy. Then, in a little, little time, we became more alike than we were different—a new society; not great, but fitted by our very faults for greatness, *E Pluribus Unum*...The surges of the new restless, needy, and strong—grudgingly brought in for purposes of hard labor and cheap wages—were resisted, resented, and accepted only when a new and different wave came in. Consider how the Germans clotted for self-defense, until the Irish took the resented place: how the Irish became "Americans" against the Poles, the Slavs against the Italians. On the West Coast the Chinese ceased to be enemies only when the Japanese arrived, and they in the face of the invasions of Hindus, Filipinos, and Mexicans...All this has been true, and yet in one or two, certainly not more than three generations, each ethnic group has clicked into place in the union without losing the *pluribus*.

Hostage Crises[8]

Although hostage crises occasionally are political and sometimes occur in prisons, most involve domestic incidents, suicide attempts, and barricaded suspects. They occur almost daily in large urban areas such as New York or Chicago. Incidents in which the FBI is involved occur about once a week. Incidents involving US diplomats have occurred about every two months between 1989 and 2002. Wealthy businessmen are perpetually at risk in some countries, and hostage taking and murder were common features of the war in Iraq in late 2004 and early 2005, but declined and became more sporadic as the new Iraqi government began to take shape.

Negotiation is possible only if the hostage taker has some demands and wants to survive, not always the case. The perpetrator must see the negotiator as someone who can hurt but is willing to help him, and as the only possible alternative to a police assault. The authorities must isolate the incident physically

---

8. This section draws primarily on McMains and Mullins (1996) and on conversations with Dr. Barry Perrou, lieutenant in charge of the Los Angeles County Hostage Negotiation unit.

and must control all communication with the hostage taker. Finally, there must be time to negotiate (FBI, 1985).

Hostages can go through five distinct psychological stages beginning with fear. Those who survive this stage, which passes fairly quickly, enter a second stage characterized by disbelief akin to that of the bride who spills red wine on her dress fifteen minutes before the ceremony. The third stage is characterized by acceptance of the situation combined with hope for quick resolution. Defense mechanisms begin to emerge that vary with the personality of the hostage. Arguing, complaining, threatening, and resisting are not conducive to survival. Withdrawal can be: one elderly woman caught in a 20-day hostage incident on a commuter train in Holland awoke periodically to comment that the train seemed unusually slow "today." Successful defense mechanisms include humor (if kept to oneself), fantasy (writing a book or planning a house in one's head), observing with a view toward later testimony, and rational analysis of the predicament. In general, age, education, spiritual outlook, daily experience of stress, and ability to socialize are positively correlated with survival.

If the crisis drags on, hostages enter a fourth stage in which they tend to become angry, not at their captors, but at the authorities for failing to rescue them. This drives the hostages and hostage takers together, sometimes leading to the "Stockholm Syndrome." It takes its name from a 1973 incident after which a hostage married a hostage taker. Patty Hearst is perhaps a double victim in that she not only seems to have joined the SLA that took her hostage, but married the bodyguard assigned to protect her afterwards. Hostage negotiators have evolved a number of devices to elicit the Stockholm Syndrome, as it reduces dangers to hostages. Sophisticated hostage takers have devised counter-tactics, such as putting bags over the heads of hostages.

Successful resolution and survival often leads to a fifth stage akin to post-trauma anxiety, manifesting itself in nightmares, gastrointestinal disorders, depression, survivor guilt if a hostage died in the incident, and paranoia. A 1979 ABC-TV special on hostage-taking ended dramatically with Gerard Vaders, a hostage in one of the train hijackings in the Netherlands in which his seatmate was murdered, saying, "Once you are an hostage, you always are an hostage."

Police crisis teams for dealing with hostage situations have three main elements. Regular police isolate and contain the incident site. The SWAT team posts snipers and prepares an assault should it become necessary. The negotiation team consists, minimally, of a spokesman and a supervisor. In large cities, hostage teams consist of around two-dozen specialists as representative as possible of the larger population.

The overriding goal is to save the hostages, but the usual practice is to downplay their importance so that threatening or harming them is less advantageous. All those yellow ribbons tied on trees to show community support almost certainly do nothing to shorten, and probably serve to lengthen captivity. One of President Carter's big mistakes in handling the hostage crisis in Iran was promising not to leave the White House until it was resolved, in effect making his presidency a hostage as well. This contrasts strongly with George Schultz's handling of the arrest by Iran of *Wall Street Journal* correspondent Gerald Seib as an Israeli spy although the Iranian government had invited him to Teheran.

Schultz advised that "making a gigantic public issue just raises the value of the hostage in the eyes of the terrorists...[who] take hostages so they can, in effect, sell them for changes in US policy, for changes in American behavior, for arms, for money, for the release of terrorists in prison on the west. If we make such deals, or if we convey an attitude that there's nothing in this world we won't do to see that he is free, we will only prolong his captivity by raising his value...The right strategy is first to avoid giving the impression that Seib is a valuable property and second to make clear that this action is going to cost Iran more than it can possibly hope to gain." This strategy resulted in Seib's release two days later.

Hostage negotiators concentrate on calming things down and building relationships. They speak quietly and stay positive and upbeat. Negotiators never set deadlines and ignore or divert attention from those given by the hostage taker. They usually portray themselves as someone with links to authority but unable to make final decisions, so that no demand can be satisfied instantly. The negotiator is likely to portray the person in authority as favoring an immediate assault and himself as the only one preventing it to head off demands to talk to someone who can make decisions.

Negotiators rarely make offers or ask hostage takers what they want. They wait for the hostage taker to make a demand because having to ask for something implies someone else is in control. Every demand is taken seriously no matter how silly or trivial it might seem. Among the reasons for doing so are the hypersensitivity of many hostage takers and the opportunity each demand gives to develop a relationship. Demands are negotiated to obtain something in return—even a promise to calm down—before they are satisfied. Concession timing is an effective device for gaining control of a negotiation and for preventing perpetrators carrying out threats.

Negotiators must respond to demands quickly without refusing or denigrating them, and must not say no directly. This often is possible by reiterating the demand in more ambiguous terms (*e.g.*, the hostage taker asks for a million dollars by noon; the negotiator responds by saying "you need some money soon") or breaking it down into components and focusing on just one component for discussion. This helps turn the demand toward negotiation and conveys the message that the hostage taker needs to reduce his demand.

Food, drinks and cigarettes are the most common demands. Perpetrators and hostages are given the same food, in equal portions or in bulk to reduce chances of argument and to promote cooperation. The ideal drink is cold, bland, decaffeinated, non-alcoholic, low in sugar, and slightly salty. Food, drinks, and cigarettes are provided in the smallest possible quantities, to reduce the time before they must be negotiated again. Nothing ever is drugged, the likelihood being that the hostage taker will first try everything out on his victims.

It is desirable to keep the hostage taker in place, but demand for an escape vehicle of some sort is a common element of hostage negotiation. Hostage negotiators will try to use it to open other issues, and often will go into details intended primarily to draw out the negotiation and wear down the hostage-taker. Reduced charges, a fair trial and legal representation can be negotiated. Although legally unenforceable,[9] agreements made with hostages probably should be adhered to. Failure to do so makes future negotiations almost impossible because there is an effective underworld grapevine, and a growing number of repeat offenders. Media coverage can be negotiated and can and can be helpful or harmful in resolving incidents

Weapons, release of prisoners, and exchange of hostages are nonnegotiable. Even talking about weapons gives the hostage taker a feeling of power that is undesirable. Drug addicts tend to use substances that produce paranoia, psychotic episodes, reduced rationality, and violence, all undesirable. Exchanging hostages interrupts the development of the Stockholm syndrome and enhances the hostage-takers feeling of power. Replacing hostages with a police officer tends to involve the police emotionally in the problem, also counterproductive.

One of the tasks of the incident supervisor is to monitor the negotiation. Not being directly involved in the conversation, he is more able to accurately judge progress. Figure 7.1 lists some of the indicators that the situation is improving (Soskis and Van Zandt 1986) or deteriorating (Strentz 1994).

Hostage negotiations have come a long way since the mid-1970s when they were left to the officer on the scene and Special Weapons and Tactics [SWAT] teams. Eighty percent of hostage incidents ended with people wounded or killed, motivating a shift toward negotiation (Schlossberg, 1979). Doctrine, practice, training, research, and theory have all evolved rapidly since then. Training now includes analysis of suspect needs and personality, communication and listening skills, criteria for assault, critical distinctions by type of incident, handling suspect demands, policy and warranted deviations, progress indicators, special equipment, stress management, and team formation and management (FBI, 1992). Although still dangerous, negotiation has proved a successful approach to such crises

---

9. Basically, such agreements have been ruled unenforceable because they were made under duress. Other rulings have found that hostage takers are not considered to be in custody during negotiations, that it is not necessary to inform them of their rights before negotiations, and their statements during negotiation are admissible evidence. *United States v. Mesa,* 1980; *United States v. Crosby,* 1983; *New York v. Quarles,* 1984; *People v. Gantz,* 1984; *State v. Sands,* 1985

Positive Indicators:	Negative Indicators:
Deadline passes without incident	Demands become less reasonable
Demands become more reasonable	Language becomes angry
Hostage released	No clear demands are made
Language becomes less violent	No rapport develops with negoti-
Perpetrator talks more and longer	ator
Perpetrator speaks more slowly or	Perpetrator has history of violence
calmly.	Perpetrator wants face-to-face
Perpetrator speaks in lower pitch	talks (sets up "suicide-by-cop[10]")
Perpetrator speaks in lower pitch	Perpetrator sets deadline for
Perpetrator talks of personal issues	own death
Threats decrease	Weapon tied to hostage

Figure 7.1
Progress Indicators in Hostage Negotiations

Conflict and Stress

While few of us are likely ever to be in a situation as stressful as a hostage negotiation, we all experience stress. Hostage negotiators have learned and can teach us a lot about handling it. Creativity and problem solving are most efficient at relatively low levels, while physical performance is highest at moderate levels. Both decline quickly at extremely low or high levels. Acute stress leads to impulsivity, excitability, and proneness to accident. People under stress experience aggressiveness, anxiety, boredom, fatigue, frustration, loneliness, moodiness and tension. They have difficulty concentrating and making decisions, and are forgetful and over-sensitive to criticism (Quick and Quick, 1984; Hart, 1991)

It is useful for a negotiator to monitor both his and his opponent's stress levels. A negotiator has several tactics to reduce them. Speaking quietly and slowly is calming and reassuring. Allowing opponents to vent their anger and describe their problems often defuses tension. Active and empathic listening (Chapter 5) reduces stress. Argument, condescension, moralizing and passing judgment, increase it; respect, sympathy and understanding reduce it. Deep breathing and progressive relaxation help.[11] Those who are frequently in stressful situations make such exercises part of their daily routine. Diet is a factor in stress. Small meals and avoidance of caffeine, fat, fried foods and sugar are equally important.

---

10. That is, putting the police in a situation where they must kill or be killed.
11. The usual progressive relaxation exercise is to tense all one's muscles then concentrating on relaxing them in groups, beginning with the feet and legs and working up through each muscle group. Some hostage negotiators keep a deck of cards handy for a quick game of solitaire. Doodling and eating are other common ways to relax.

Chapter 8
Dispute Resolution

The first thing we do, let's kill all the lawyers
—William Shakespeare, *Henry VI, Part II*

This chapter focuses on three methods of peaceful dispute resolution. Each has its strengths and weaknesses, its advantages and disadvantages.

<u>Torts</u>

Tort is the technical name for a lawsuit. It is a demand for redress, usually money, for a wrongful act that results in injury. Torts provide a remedy for damages caused by defendants unwilling to compensate victims for injuries they have caused. The redress can be compensatory, punitive, or both. Torts are based on specific liability (*e.g.*, manufacturing or selling defective products), intent, or negligence.

The American system is badly broken. It takes too long to settle claims while encouraging highly speculative class action suits brought by lawyers on behalf of individuals who have not suffered any real injury. Often, these result in ludicrous awards to plaintiffs and great wealth for lawyers. In a typical case, Ford settled a class action suit claiming that the Bronco II was prone to roll-overs by mailing safety stickers to the owners and paying four million dollars to the lawyers. Speculative lawsuits do more harm than good. Any of the reforms described below (Bernstein, 1997) would improve the tort system in the United States. Combined, they would provide a rational tort system similar to other common law countries that also will increases productivity by 7-8%, and employment by 11-12% (Campbell, 1995).

On average, litigation in the United States returns less than twenty-five percent of actual economic loss to claimants. It is a significant drag on the economy, absorbing over two percent of GDP, double the average in the industrialized world. Many states spend more on direct tort costs than on all other state expenditures combined except education (Ward 1993). Litigation has driven up insurance costs and thus the cost of virtually all products and services in the United States. Doctors can pay $1000-4000 per day in malpractice insurance, a cost they must pass on to patients. Every driver in the country pays $250-$350 per year in insurance due to the cost of litigation. This may not seem like much, but invested tax free annually at 5% interest over a 40-year driving career, it would grow to over $37,936.

Lawsuits blaming companies for unsafe products can discourage them from making safer ones. Liability concerns led two companies to delay, and one to abandon, promising research on AIDS vaccines (*Science Magazine*, 1992). Risk of litigation has led twenty of twenty-five US manufacturers to stop making vaccines, resulting in periodic shortages and reducing research just as the threat of bio-terrorism grows (Wood, n.d.). Thirteen of fifteen companies stopped research on contraception for fear of litigation. The same fear keeps the only FDA-approved anti-nausea drug for use during pregnancy off the market. Plaintiffs' attorneys' coerced a multibillion-dollar settlement in breast-implant litigation despite an utter lack of scientific evidence supporting their claims. Litigation has the similar effects on many other industries in the US (Committee on Commerce, Science, and Transportation, 1997).

Plaintiff's lawyers sue, often on behalf of individuals who do not even know they are plaintiffs, in numerous courts knowing that juries are unpredictable and that they only have to win once. Juries, unlike judges, do not have to explain their decisions. The American Bar Association and Britain's Royal Commission on Criminal Justice concur that juries frequently do not understand much of the evidence put before them or ignore it out of sympathy for the plaintiff. These factors encourage speculative litigation.

The Seventh Amendment to the Constitution precludes eliminating juries in civil trials in the United States, as has been done in every other common law country. However, improvements are possible. Some states have placed caps on awards for pain and suffering (but not on economic loss) and in others require judicial review of punitive damages. In three states, juries decide whether to award punitive damages, but judges determine the amount. This parallels the criminal trial system in which juries determine guilt and judges determine punishment.

The current system is unfair in that it requires the defendant to pay for his defense win or lose, whereas the plaintiff pays only if he wins. Shifting to a loser pays rule in which the loser pays the expenses of the winner would encourage plaintiffs to focus on strong claims instead of pursuing far-fetched complaints as they do today. It is in effect in almost every common-law country other than the US. and in the US for sexual harassment complaints. Actual experience refutes the assumed danger that it might reduce access to the civil justice system. This is because courts set fees conservatively to protect plaintiffs from excessive defense costs and delays intended to coerce settlements. Such a rule probably would create a market for insurance with fees that would help plaintiffs to judge whether to continue their complaints.

Two additional reforms would further reduce the problems of speculative litigation and greedy attorneys. First, require attorneys to have the active prior consent of each individual they claim to represent as a member of a class. That is, attorneys cannot create an imagined "class" of unknown size and anonymous membership made up of people who do not even know that someone claiming to represent them is requesting damages they never noticed they had suffered. Second, tighten standards and impose pretrial hearings to screen out junk science and ersatz experts.

Companies could help as well, by fighting speculative law suits despite the short term costs, by itemizing a fair share of their litigation insurance on all bills to educate consumers as to litigation costs, and by quitting business in states where litigation is out of hand. Doctors already are doing so, but if companies facing frivolous lawsuits did the same, reform would follow quickly in states where citizens could no longer get medical care, service their cars, or find jobs.

The 2004 election included propositions on tort reform implementing some of these ideas that succeeded at the polls, suggesting the people finally are beginning to connect runaway lawsuits to rising consumer costs. Nevada capped non-economic damages in medical malpractice cases. Similar propositions failed narrowly in Oregon and Wyoming. Florida limited amounts and increased transparency in setting contingency fees. California limited suits against businesses to people who have suffered an actual injury or loss in an effort that Governor Arnold Schwarzenegger says "will end the legal practice of shakedown lawsuits, in which private lawyers file suits without any client or any evidence of harm."

Negotiation

Negotiation is appropriate when disputants can directly settle disputes that involve exchanges or relationships. It is not particularly useful in settling difference in belief, as the history of both theological disputes (Chapter 11) and terrorism (Chapter 14) demonstrate. Methods such as voting, representative government (Chapter 8), or unions (Chapter 9) may work better when large unorganized groups are involved.

"Negotiation is a process in which explicit proposals are put forward for the ostensible purposes of resolving specific disagreements among two or parties with both conflict and common interests (Ikle, 1964)." The heart of the definition is in the requirement that the parties involved have both conflicting and common interests. Employees depend on their jobs to make their living and employers need workers if they are to receive a return on their investment. However, employees want the highest possible wage while employers want to pay the lowest one possible. Without conflicting interests, there is no dispute to be resolved; without common ones, there is no motivation to resolve the dispute.

Each word in the definition is important. Negotiation can resolve specific disagreements but is unlikely to solve disagreements in belief. Negotiators do not always want to reach agreement, so may engage in "bad faith" or "surface bargaining" only *ostensibly* aimed at resolving a dispute. To this end they may use tactics such as "poison pills," issues they know that the opponent never will accept (such as the Palestinian demand for "right of return" to Israel). Negotiations are not limited to two-party disputes, although at some point that varies with circumstance the number of parties can become unmanageable and other methods become more practicable (Churchman, 1995).

Distributive Negotiation

Negotiation theorists distinguish two basic approaches to negotiation. The vast majority of negotiations are "distributive." That is, they focus on how to distribute or divide resources among parties. They divide into phases, although theorists differ as to what and how many there are. One useful formulation specifies the phases as preparing, exploring, bargaining, and closing (Churchman, 1995).

Preparing for a negotiation includes identifying issues, identifying one's own needs and setting goals, and learning as much as possible about opponents. It may include selecting and training a negotiating team. Figure 8.1 illustrates the simplest and most normal bargaining situation. Those who start high and concede downward, including a student trying for a higher grade and a prosecutor working on a plea bargain, are "Sellers." Those who start low and concede upward, including a professor defending a low grade and a defendant trying to get a short sentence, are "Buyers." The "bargaining range" defines all offers a negotiator will make. If buyer and seller bargaining ranges overlap, a "settlement range" exists. Any agreement within the settlement range is fair (Chapter 2) in the sense of being acceptable to both.

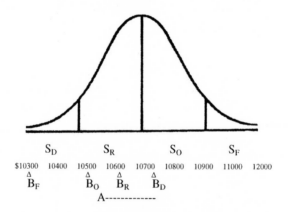

Figure 8.1
Buyer's View of the Bargaining Situation

The most crucial planning decision negotiators make is setting their "Deadlock" or "reserve" price, sometimes called the Best Alternative to Negotiated Agreement [BATNA] (Fisher, Ury, and Patton, 1980). Deadlock is the point above which the buyers will not go (designated B_D), and below which the sellers will not go (designated S_D). The concept of a BATNA has the advantage of requiring the negotiator to consider what his options are if he does not reach agreement at the deadlock price. It is useful as well for bargainers to pre-plan resistance points representing what they regard as "Realistic" and "Optimistic" settlements, as well as their "First," offer (such as the advertised price for a house, the sticker price for a car, or the salary range for a job). These points form the mnemonic "FORD." Phrasing such as "I would be happy to get W," "I hope to get X," "I must have Y," and "I will not go below Z" suggest the existence of these multiple resistance points. As each one is reached, bargainers slow down, take stock, change tactics, and tread carefully before resuming the pattern of concessions. Subjects in bargaining simulations did better when they were given such targets in addition to deadlock prices (Raiffa, 1982).

Usually, one knows one's own bargaining range and resistance points (perhaps only approximately) but can only estimate the opponents'. Figure 8.1 reflects this by indicating a precise bargaining range for the buyer. The probability curve (shown normal but it could be skewed) divided into four sections represents the buyers' estimate of the sellers' First, Optimistic, Realistic and Deadlock positions and the probability that each guess is correct. One function of bargaining is to refine the estimate of the opponents' bargaining range

The second, exploratory, phase focuses on establishing relationships, communicating one's needs to opponents, and learning opponents' needs. Culture, personality, past relationships and the issues at stake all play a factor in determining relationships, which can be formal or informal, friendly or hostile, businesslike or casual. If the negotiation is high profile, then both sides are likely to have a media strategy aimed at constituents, opponents, and the public.

The third, bargaining, phase consists of making and responding to specific proposals. Proposals always include an offer, however vague ("we might be able to pay a little more if you were able to deliver a lot sooner") and might include other components such as conditions, threats or ultimatums. Subsequent proposals often provide a face-saving rationale for making concessions, as the negotiations bring them closer together and finally either reach agreement or deadlock. Offers and counteroffers can be nearly instantaneous, but in important negotiations, there can be considerable time for study and reply. Although there were only three major issues to settle, the Korean War truce talks continued on-and-off for 103 weeks, beginning after 54 weeks of war.

The final, or closing phase becomes possible when all proposals meet the needs of all parties. The closing phase always will include terms and may include provisions for ratification, monitoring, insuring performance, and resolving disputes. Figure 8.1 indicates the Agreement [A] reached in a successful single-issue negotiation. Subtracting the value of the agreement, A, from B_D determines the buyers' "surplus," indicated by the dashed line, which is to say how much the buyers' improved on their deadlock prices. In practice, bargainers can calculate their own surplus but rarely can calculate that of their opponents, which is why that of the seller is not shown. Bargainers seldom reveal their deadlock price even after agreement, lest it affect future negotiations.[1]

Negotiation is not limited to two-person, one-issue situations. One party may consist of two or more people, there may be three or more parties, or both. Any of these situations complicates negotiation. A team can use classic tactics such as good cop/bad cop or can try to exhaust an outnumbered opponent. On the other hand, it can be the target of divide–and-conquer tactics. The possibility of alliances complicates multi-party negotiations. Shifting alliances are particularly common in legislatures, as individual representatives form temporary alliances on particular bills.

Negotiations usually involve more than one issue, each with its own bargaining range. If so, negotiations may go through each issue phase-by-phase, may go through all phases issue-by-issue or may follow some iterative process. The difference is important, as the second approach makes it easier to use linkage to reach agreement. Consider the situation in Figure 8.2. If the negotiators use the common technique of splitting the difference, each will receive half the value of each item for a total value of $1.50. If instead Negotiator One concedes all of Item B to Negotiator Two in exchange for receiving all of Item A for himself, each negotiator receives $2 in value, a 33% increase for both parties. Total value has grown from $3 to $4.[2] More generally, whenever there are as many or more issues as there are negotiators, and the negotiators differ as to the relative importance of the issues, linkage provides a way to "enlarge the pie." The most common tradeoffs involve the impact of quality, quantity, and time on price. It is exactly what happens when one gets a discounted demonstrator, a quantity discount, or pays extra for early delivery. This suggests that increasing the number of issues improves the odds of developing a mutually advantageous agreement.

	Item A	Item B
Value to Negotiator One	1	2
Value to Negotiator Two	2	1
Total	3	3

Figure 8.2
The Linkage Principle

Time is important to negotiation in many ways. Some situations impose real deadlines that give one side or another real power. A simple example is the preference of farm workers for negotiation at harvest time. The importance, and thus the time devoted to each phase of a negotiation vary by culture. For example,

---

1. Poker players do not reveal their hand after all opponents fold for the same reason, as it would let opponents know how much the player had been bluffing.
2. This explains the increase in value of the deal involving the diamond and the chess set in the example in Chapter 2.

relationship-prone Middle Easterners tend to spend more time on the exploration phase, and reach general agreement quickly once trust is established. By contrast, business-like but litigious-prone Americans move relatively quickly through the exploratory phase and spend more time "dotting the i's and crossing the t's" in the bargaining phase. The negotiator with the shorter deadline usually is in the weaker position, particularly if the opponent knows what it is. Finally, time affects value. Some investments or products decline with age, while some increase. Knowing which, and at what rate, is of obvious importance to any negotiator.

Power seldom is equally distributed among parties. It comes in many forms. Context is one source of power. For example, we speak of a buyers' or a sellers' market, meaning one has an advantage depending on economic conditions. Knowledge—financial, legal or technical for example—often is an important source of negotiating power. Knowledge of precedents or of opponents' tastes and ambitions can be important. Control of resources—in the form of equipment, money, skilled personnel, supplies and the like—often is an important source of power in negotiation. Authority—the ability to make and keep agreements—is a source of negotiating power that usually stems from one's position in an organization. Personal characteristics such as charisma, integrity, persistence, and ruthlessness are additional sources of power.

The weaker negotiator sometimes can level the playing field—or at least make the hill less steep. First, the weaker party can try to increase its power by manipulating the sources listed above or in Chapter 5. Try to bring more knowledge to the table, or try to delay the negotiation until relative power has changed, or send in a negotiator with more charisma. Second, find allies: sellers form cartels, buyers form cooperatives. Third, look for or create divisions such as the natural one between marketing and engineering within the opponent's organization. Fourth, use negotiating tactics well (Churchman, 1995; Lewicki, 1997). Fifth, try flattery or beg for mercy. Sixth, present a draft agreement that will shape the situation to your advantage. Seventh, reluctantly volunteer to take meeting minutes, gaining control of the record. Eighth, recognize that the more powerful party often is the busier party, less able to prepare fully or send its best people to deal with a weak opponent. Ninth, improve the bargaining climate by improving the relationship, emphasizing the long-term, or switching from distributive to integrative bargaining.

Integrative Negotiation

Integrative negotiation is the theoretical alternative to "distributive bargaining." Much of the literature is less analysis than advocacy of the assumed superiority of integrative over distributive bargaining (*e.g.* Fisher, 1980). More balanced views recognize the need to be prepared for both approaches (Churchman, 1995; Lewicki, 1997; Raiffa, 1982). Win-win advocates often make dubious distinctions, claiming for example that distributive bargainers assume fixed resources despite their use of linkage to increase them. The criticisms explain everything except why distributive bargaining has been successful for five thousand years or so.

Integrative bargaining becomes possible when the parties have high regard for one another and high concern for the issues at stake (Chapter 5). It requires that the parties are motivated to work together, willing to share real needs and objectives honestly and completely, and experienced at problem solving. The number of times all these conditions are met partially explains why the approach is so prominent in classrooms and so unusual in the real world.

Despite its rarity, integrative bargaining has been successful in bringing hostile opponents to successful agreements in a significant number of situations, particularly labor-management as practiced by the U.S. government's Federal Mediation and Conciliation Service [FMCS]. Before acting as mediators, FMCS requires joint training of the parties to the dispute. The training is designed not just to teach the method but also to reduce tensions, improve relationships, and accustom members of the opposing teams to working together. While nobody can argue with the success achieved, the approach raises the question of whether it is the integrative bargaining, the training and improved relationship that results, or the combination that explains the success.

Integrative bargaining as taught by FMCS progresses in five stages. The first stage focuses on defining the problem. The goal is a mutually acceptable definition, so the parties complete this stage jointly. The model calls for depersonalizing issues and focusing on "the primary problems" while identifying and keeping "less-important" issues out of the picture.

The second stage focuses on identifying and exploring the interests of the parties. Disputes can involve more than one interest and parties can differ as to the interests at stake (Lax and Sebenius, 1986). The model demands that the parties avoid taking positions (possible solutions to a problem) at this stage of the negotiation process.

The third stage focuses on finding as many options as possible that might meet the needs identified in stage two. The major technique at this stage is collective brainstorming involving all parties to the dispute. Neale and Bazerman (1991) suggest linkage, but it is just as common in distributive bargaining. Lewicki (1997) suggests increasing resources, "nonspecific compensation," and cutting the costs of compliance, but these hardly are specific to integrative bargaining nor do they seem particularly clear or practical.

The fourth stage requires the parties to develop criteria for assessing options. Typical criteria include cost, legality, and technical feasibility. There are likely to be additional criteria specific to the situation. For example, in labor negotiations, likelihood of approval by union members, directors, or stockholders may be an important criterion, as might be impact on competitiveness or retention of workforce.

The fifth stage applies the criteria of stage four to the options of stage three to select the option with the best payoffs for all parties. Usually, the negotiators vote as to whether each option meets each criterion. Sometimes there is a third choice, referral to committee for evaluation. The result of the survey presented in a simple grid often makes the best resolution of the issue obvious. Even when this does not happen, the process usually narrows the choices sufficiently that agreement can be reached quickly.

Third-Party Intervention

When people cannot resolve or manage their own conflicts, they often resort to third-party intervention. Arbitration is a quasi-judicial process in which a neutral third-party decides how to resolve a dispute based on evidence presented by the disputants. It is useful in disputes that involve large non-political stakes, when relatively speedy solutions are desirable, and where confidential or proprietary information is relevant to making a decision. It can be compulsory or not. Professional baseball developed an interesting version for salary disputes. The arbitrator must choose either the position of management or the position of the player without modification after taking account of the arguments presented by each side. The system drives the disputants toward moderation, as the arbitrator is likely to take the less extreme of the two positions.

Mediation is a non-judicial, usually voluntary, process in which a third party neutral helps disputants who retain the power of decision to reach an accord. Because of these characteristics, mediation frequently has resulted in innovative resolutions with higher satisfaction and compliance than more compulsory methods. It works best in relatively small-scale conflicts where there have been close relationships between two more-or-less equal disputants. It is potentially more confidential than arbitration (although in some cases mediators can be compelled to testify if the dispute is taken to court). Alternatives to mediation include conciliation, consultation, facilitation, imposition, intervention, and "rent-a-judge." We are less interested here in the differences among these methods than in how and why third-party intervention works to resolve disputes.

Third-party intervention varies in invasiveness. At the least invasive, neutrals act simply bring the parties together. Somewhat more invasive, they can facilitate the process but avoid all involvement in the substance. They might suggest cooling off periods, enforce procedural rules to keep tempers under control, suggest face-saving ways to make concessions, or help disputants distinguish positions and interests.

Neutrals can suggest contingency agreements when disputants cannot agree on future facts (the tactic also works in direct negotiations). These usually convert fixed payments into percentages, a simple and obvious case being the author's royalty rate of, say, 10% per book sold instead $100,000 that would leave the publisher unhappy if sales were low and the author unhappy if they were spectacular. Neutrals can prepare a draft agreement, submit it in turn to the disputants for changes, revise it, and resubmit it for further changes. This process can continue until the disputants are satisfied and the draft becomes the final agreement. It is a variation on the "Delphi Procedure" that negotiators usually call the "one text procedure."

A neutral can help each side to estimate optimistic, realistic and deadlock agreements, the likelihood of achieving each, and the opportunity costs of delay. Helping each side to combine this information so that they fully understood their needs, perceptions, values, aspirations, beliefs, and constraints provides both sides with more rational assessments that can narrow the gap between the parties.

Most invasive of all, Raiffa (1982) suggested a "contract embellisher" who would interview all disputants confidentially and in depth after a tentative agreement had been reached. The "contract embellisher" would then write a single proposal to discuss privately with each side. If both sides thought it an improvement on the tentative agreement, it would replace the tentative one without change. The goal is to reach an optimal agreement.

The idea is similar to the way the US House of Representatives and Senate reconcile their versions of a bill based on a committee report that both Houses vote up-or-down without amendment. It is based in turn on a seventeenth century proposal for a bicameral legislature, one house of which could debate and revise a bill, while the other could only vote on it without debate.

Consider a buyer and seller trying to reach agreement on a sale involving three issues that determine price, specifically quality, quantity, and delivery time. For purposes of illustration, assume there are only three possible discrete positions for each issue.

During confidential interviews with each, the contract embellisher begins by having the seller and buyer divide 100 points to indicate the relative importance they attach to the three issues (Figure 8.3). Cells A3-A5 represent the value the seller attaches to selling the product in three available qualities (basic, standard and deluxe), while cells A15-A17 represent the value the buyer attaches to having the product in each of those qualities. The same system is true for quantity and delivery time.

The contract embellisher then asks each to assign the maximum number of points for each issue to the preferred solution, and any lesser number of points to the remaining possible resolutions. This places the contract embellisher in the omnipotent position envisioned by Raiffa of knowing how the buyer and seller value every possible resolution to the dispute. Cell D3 represents the total value of the deal A3B3C3 to the seller.

The contract embellisher can calculate the joint gains of all possible resolutions (The final section of Figure 8.3). Cell E7 is the total gain of for the deal that the seller would identify as A4B4C2 or the buyer would identify A16B16C16. The omnipotent contract embellisher can identify three improvements on this deal, which is the one that splits the difference between buyer and seller. A4B5C1 gives the seller 86 and the buyer 75 for a joint gain of 161. A3B5C4 gives the seller 83 and the buyer 80 for a joint gain of 163. A3B5C5 gives the seller 81 and the buyer 85 for a joint gain of 166.

	A	B	C	D	E	F
1	Seller Values					
2	Quality	Quantity	Delivery			
3	10	45	10	65	70	75
4	15	55	3	58	63	68
5	20	70	1	56	61	65
6				75	80	76
7				68	73	85
8				66	71	78
9				90	95	100
10				83	88	93
11				81	86	91
13	Buyer Values					
14	Quality	Quantity	Delivery			
15	40	25	0	65	55	40
16	30	15	30	95	85	70
17	15	10	35	100	90	40
18				55	45	65
19				85	75	30
20				90	80	60
21				50	40	25
22				80	70	55
23				85	75	60
25	Joint Values					
26				130	125	115
27				153	148	138
28				156	151	105
29				130	125	141
30				153	148	115
31				156	151	138
32				140	135	125
33				163	158	148
34				166	161	151

Figure 8.3
Analysis of Seller and Buyer Utilities

The first of these three is a big improvement for the seller but not for the buyer. An unbiased contract embellisher would reject this solution. Of the remaining choices, A3B5C5 creates larger joint gains but divides them less evenly than A3B5C1. The contract embellisher would have to choose one or the other. Giving the disputants a choice risks a stalemate.

Two astute negotiators could have found these solutions *without* the help of a third party or knowing the opponent's valuations. One negotiator need simply offer a combination that improves the deal for himself and without saying so ask if it improves things for his opponent. Regardless of the answer, he can then work through other possibilities, always asking if the new one improves on the best one found so far. In this tedious fashion, negotiators can find the optimal deal without anyone having to reveal anything important.

Conclusion

Torts, negotiation, and third-party intervention, primarily by arbitrators or mediators, are the major tools by which disputes are resolved across every level of conflict from interpersonal to international. The stakes, rather than the level, in most cases determine the training and experience of those involved in such disputes.

Chapter 9
Organizational Conflict

If anything can go wrong, it will.

—Murphy's Law sometimes known as
Finagle's Law of Dynamic Negatives

Some of the theories and models treated earlier, such as negotiation and gender conflict, are relevant to but not limited to organizational conflicts. This chapter focuses on labor-management negotiations, competitive strategy, and crisis management, although the latter two along with the Law of Unintended Consequences have wider application.

The Law of Unintended Consequences

Man proposes, God disposes.[1] The Versailles Treaty created the conditions that led to World War II. "Three strikes" sentencing may motivate criminals with two convictions to kill rather than leave witnesses. Gun control has increased rather than decreased crime (Chapter 15). Pubic housing makes poverty worse by concentrating people with low skills in areas with few jobs. Rent control reduces the amount of housing for the poor because landlords cannot make a profit. Prohibition increased crime without reducing alcohol consumption. The "war on drugs" repeated the mistake. The reporting requirements of Sarbanes-Oxley increased unemployment by discouraging corporations from registering in the US. Medicines have side effects—usually but not always harmful. Civilization was the unintended consequence of agriculture. These are examples of what the CIA calls "blowback" and Merton (1936) calls the "Law of Unintended Consequences." He defined five sources that should concern every crisis manager.

First, managers seldom have all the information they would like by the time they have to make a decision. Many products require long lead times during which tastes and economic conditions can change. It is difficult to know what qualities—elegance, innovation, price, reliability, service, or something else—will be most important to consumers by the time a product is designed, engineered, produced, and on the market. Raw material prices, labor costs, and interest rates are among other factors that are difficult to forecast accurately.

---

1. Thomas A Kempis (1418), *Imitation of Christ* (Book I, Chapter 19)

Second, managers can err in appraising situations, in selecting a course of action, or in implementing one. American, British, French, Russian and other intelligence agencies concurred that Saddam Hussein was hiding weapons of mass destruction in 2003—but apparently he was bluffing. Something that worked in the past may not work again. Generals, they say, plan for the last war, although it is perhaps more accurate to say that winning generals stick with the old while losing generals may try something new.

Third, managers often put immediate before long-term concerns. Business executives plan for short-term profits rather than long-term growth. School heads facing budget problems often defer maintenance. In 1944, the D-Day planners focused so much energy on just getting the troops ashore that they had only a vague plan for to what to do next.

Fourth, some decisions are self-defeating. New York raised cigarette taxes for the [contradictory] purposes of raising revenue and reducing smoking, which led to massive cigarette smuggling that reduced revenue without reducing smoking. George W. Bush raised tariffs to protect steel industry jobs, destroying even more jobs in steel-using industries than he saved in steel making ones, a typical outcome of protectionism., without winning the labor vote that motivated him in the first place.

Fifth, the more ambiguous or complex a situation, the more likely people are to rely on their basic values (Chapter 11) than on available information. People seem to reach judgments on many issues more on philosophical than on cost-benefit grounds. The less information there is about political candidates the more likely voters are to vote along party lines. The IRS determines whom to audit based on departures from expected spending by income group.

Unintended consequences are not the same as unforeseeable ones. Managers can assess plans in light of the five main unintended types to determine the most likely ones in their circumstances, and then can devise contingency plans to address them. The energy devoted to doing so will vary by the importance and complexity of the decision and the time available to make it. They can withhold decisions until the last possible minute—but not beyond what subordinates need to implement them

Labor-Management Conflict

The labor-management relationship is the classic illustration of Ikle's (1964) point that bargaining requires both a cooperative and competitive relationship. Employees and employers must cooperate if the former are to have an income and the latter are to obtain a return on investment. However, employees want to maximize wages and benefits, while employers want to minimize them. Usually, each understands the other and the situation well enough to keep the bargaining within a narrow range. Most labor-management disputes involve salaries and benefits, rights and obligations, and responsibilities and relationships. Distributive bargaining usually dominates the relationship.

It is customary for the union to start with an unrealistically but not insultingly high demand and for the company to make a comparably low initial offer. The "negotiating dance" that follows consists primarily of justifications and adjustments in which opponents attempt to convince one another of their inability to compromise further and the reason the other should do so. Theatrics are common on both sides. Concessions are made gradually and reluctantly to imply approaching deadlock.

While this is the most common pattern, an alternative sometimes seen (but no longer in American labor-management negotiations) is "final-first" or Boulwarism. It takes its name from the strategy developed by GE negotiator Lemuel Boulware. Despite its current reputation as an unfair bargaining tactic, it began when Boulware was ordered to restore GE's traditionally excellent employee relations[2] following a vicious seven-week strike in 1946. He was a critic of the bargaining pattern that had developed after World War II. He thought it absurd for employers to go through the motions of offering much less than they expected to pay, then concede slowly "under public strike-threat pressure (Boulware, 1969)." Worse, he thought it discredited both capitalism and GE, allowed unions to take the credit for improvements that the company had planned to give from the outset, fomented employee resentment, and reduced productivity.

Instead, Boulware held that it was essential to "do right by employees," which he did by applying GE's consumer research techniques to learn employee needs. He then developed carefully researched opening offers that he thought would be attractive to employees while keeping the company competitive with customers. He presented the offers directly to employees, which co-opted and not surprisingly angered the main bargaining unit, the International Union of Electricians [IUE].

Commonly portrayed as take-it-or-leave-it, in reality Boulware (1969) maintained that he always was open to "any old or new information proving changes would be in the balanced best interests of all." Nevertheless, in 1969 the U.S. Second Circuit Court of Appeals upheld a National Labor Relations Board ruling in favor of the IUE against the practice. The court found GE guilty of surface bargaining and union busting, faulting GE for "sham discussions" and for portraying itself rather than the union as "the true defender" of employee interests.

Walton and McKersey (1965, 1991) developed a behavioral model of labor negotiation that integrates its distributive and integrative aspects (Chapter 8). Their model "abstract[s] and analyzes four sets of activities which account for *almost all* behavior in negotiation [emphasis added]." Competitive behaviors attempt to influence the division of limited resources, and result in "distributive negotiation." It is applicable when one side's can achieve its objectives only at the expense of the other side. That is, it assumes a conflict of interest, so is simi-

---

2. GE implemented a suggestion system in 1906, a pension system in 1912 and an insurance system in 1920, in each case well ahead of most US companies.

lar to what game theorists call a fixed- or zero-sum game. In practice, it involves selective trading and withholding of information and uses many tactics to manipulate, deceive, and coerce opponents.

In contrast, problem-solving behaviors seek to increase the joint gains that are available to the parties, and are termed "integrative negotiation." It is applicable when objectives are not in fundamental conflict but instead are areas of common concern. It is a joint rather than an adversarial decision-making process. Integrative potential exists when the nature of a problem permits solutions that benefit both parties, so is close to what game theorists call a variable-sum game. Early commitment to positions directly conflicts with this approach. Its potential for joint gains increases when more rather than fewer agenda items are under consideration and when trust is high (both are equally true of distributive negotiation). It is rare because it requires sufficient trust to discuss concerns accurately, completely, and openly. Boulwarism was an early but one-sided attempt to develop a more integrative approach. The 1969 court ruling against it enforced a superficial type of fairness based on incremental concessions that forced labor and management back into distributive bargaining.

In labor-management negotiations, the negotiators usually represent others who must ratify any agreement they make. This requires "intra-organizational negotiation" and "attitudinal structuring (Walton and McKersey, 1965, 1991)." Both negotiating teams must understand the goals and the level of commitment of those they represent. They also must convey what they learn about their opponents to those they represent, so that everyone becomes more realistic.

Union negotiators usually feel they must improve on the *status quo* to justify their existence. The main disutility is the cost of a strike, which for labor includes lost wages and union dues and the possibility of lost members, goodwill and public image and the possibility of retaliation by management. For management, the usual costs are lost profits and market share. Possible additional costs are public image, reduced employee morale and productivity, and damage to plant and equipment due to idleness.

Competitive Strategy

Competitive strategy is "a comprehensive framework of analytical techniques to help a firm analyze its industry as a whole and predict the industry's future evolution, to understand its competitors and its own position, and to translate this analysis into a competitive strategy for a particular business (Porter, 1980)." Competition is a permanent feature of sports, business and international life. Teams, corporations and countries must envision the future they wish and pit their strengths against the weaknesses of opponents. The offensive coach of a football team will use scouting reports to determine what sort of defense an opponent uses most and develop a game plan to exploit its weaknesses in tactics and personnel. Defensive coaches understand this, of course, so change their own game plan to try to catch the offense off guard.

Competitive strategy takes the opponent's likely reaction into account in the same way a chess player thinks to himself, "If I move my knight there, my opponent could put his bishop there, pinning it, so I should move my pawn there first to prevent the pin." However, surprised competitors sometimes come up with a surprise counterattack. In 2004, Miller Beer came up with a humorous ad campaign to run during the football season, in which football referees and umpires interrupted social situations and called fouls on the hosts for serving Budweiser. It succeeded brilliantly, increasing Miller's sales at Budweiser's expense, until Budweiser came up with look-a-like ads in which the umpires were portrayed as substituting Miller beer so that they could steal the Budweiser for themselves.

Competitive strategy requires identifying factors such as existing competitors, potential new ones, possible substitute products and bargaining power of buyers and suppliers that can affect achievement of goals. Information can come from annual and government reports, customers and suppliers, patent records, press reports, testing of competitor products, speeches by management, trade shows, and want ads. The result should be a profile that leads to methods such as advertising, customer service, distribution channels, economies of scale, market share, price competition, product differentiation and innovation, and warranties for dealing with each competitor (Porter, 1980).

Competitive strategy postulates three generic means for coping with competitors (Porter, 1980). The first, cost leadership, requires a constant focus on cost reduction by such means as efficiencies of scale, aggressive negotiation with suppliers, and avoidance of marginal accounts. Wal-Mart is an obvious example of the successful pursuit of this strategy. The second strategy, differentiation, requires identifying some quality customers will pay extra for, such as dependability (Fed Ex, Maytag), elegance (James Purdey, Limoges), innovation (Apple, Nokia), design (Eames, Escada), quality (Rolex, Oregon Shakespeare Festival), performance (Bose, Calumet Farm), romance (Carnival Cruises, diamonds), service (Lexus, Nordstrom), status (Harvard, Rolls Royce), technology (GE, Tempurpedic), or vulgarity (Hustler, almost any rap "musician"). The third strategy assumes that generic competitors (residential real estate) are not adapted to the needs of a particular buyer (empty nesters), region (northwest), or segment (mobile homes) of the product line.

Low-cost insulates against competition by making it difficult for new competitors to enter the market or for customers to switch to substitutes, but is at risk to technological change, product obsolescence, and imitation. Differentiation insulates against competition by creating brand loyalty and desensitizing customers to price. It risks imitation, differentiation based on increasingly minor features, and economic downturns. Focus seeks either low-cost, high differentiation or both for its specific target. It risks too narrow a target to sustain sales, too great a cost differential for the product's advantages, and even more specialized targeting (Porter 1980).

The basic principle in competitive strategy is to identify and align your strengths against or even create weaknesses in the competitor. The corollary is to anticipate the opponent's probable responses to one's own tactics. The strategy is identical to the war planner's principle that forces should be massed at the decisive point, which requires economizing (and thus taking risks) at less important ones. The idea dates at least to the Hittite tactics at the Battle of Kadesh (1295 BC) when Rameses II was lured into dividing his forces so they could be attacked piecemeal. Epaminondas reversed custom by placing his best men and greatest numbers on his left instead of on the customary right wing and held back his weak center and right. Frederick the Great rediscovered this "oblique order," and Schlieffen applied it on the grand scale against France in 1914 (Hart, 1954). The German plan in 1940 looked like a repeat of the Schlieffen Plan to lure the British and French into advancing into Belgium where they could be cut off by a drive on the English Channel. It succeeded spectacularly, although it was a closer run thing than usually is described (May, 2000).

An important recent example is Ronald Reagan's destruction of the Soviet Union. Ambassador Vernon Walters recounts a conversation he had with President Reagan, who was seeking some US advantage against the Soviet Union. Walters answered every suggestion Reagan made by pointing out that it was not the US but the Soviets who had more tanks, more submarines, more planes, more nuclear weapons than the US. Frustrated, Reagan finally asked Walters what the US had more of than the Soviets. Walters answered, "Money!" Reagan shot back, "Then, that is what we will use."

Reagan instructed his CIA chief to stop studying Soviet strengths so that the US would know how to counter them as all previous CIA chiefs had done. Instead, in a classic case of competitive strategy, he was to identify and exploit weaknesses. Reagan implemented National Security directives that:

1. Provided financial, intelligence and logistical support to Lech Walesa's Solidarity in Poland and Vaclev Havel's "Velvet Revolution" in Czechoslovakia.
2. Provided financial and military support to the Afghan resistance, including training of mujahedin to take the war into the USSR itself.
3. Obtained Saudi cooperation in reducing oil prices to reduce the hard currency available to the Soviets, 80% of which came from oil.
4. Sabotaged the Soviet pipeline to Europe by diplomatic, financial and covert means.
5. Reduced Soviet access to Western technology.
6. What technology was sold was designed to backfire. For example, equipment design software they Soviets bought was modified so that the resulting equipment used more raw materials than necessary, or would break down frequently!
7. Implemented a psychological operation playing up Reagan's cowboy image to fuel Soviet indecision.
8. Shifted the arms race from quantity (the Soviet strength) to quality (the American strength) with an aggressive high-tech buildup that the Soviets could not match (Schweizer, 1994).

Reagan's competitive strategy proved victorious in the penultimate year of his presidency. He had stretched the Soviets past the breaking point predicted in the famous *Foreign Affairs* article that recommended containment, deterrence, intervention, and development of the international economic system until the Soviet system collapsed of its own contradictions and weaknesses (X, 1947).

Jack Matlock (2004), who was US Ambassador to Moscow during the Gorbachev era, and was present at all the Gorbachev-Reagan negotiations, gives a more nuanced picture. Both Reagan and Gorbachev saw beyond the narrow vision of their advisors and made up their own minds on critical issues. Suspicion melted gradually through direct meetings. Unlike previous Soviet leaders, Gorbachev questioned Communist theory when the facts and his own experienced proved it wrong. He put the interests of his country above the interests of his political party, principle above personal power.

Reagan's competitive strategy convinced Gorbachev that the fragile Soviet economy could not win if it got into an arms race with the US. Gorbachev learned during his visit to the United States that the American people were not hostile to the Soviet Union as his propaganda taught. He understood the need for fundamental reform in the Soviet Union, and Reagan had the wisdom to support it as best it could. Reagan and Gorbachev both possessed the necessary political stature at home to win domestic acceptance for their agreements. Shultz and Shevardnadze helped their leaders keep priorities straight and overcame opposition within their own governments.

Reagan understood that the Cold War was ideological: that arms races and geopolitical competition were not causes but symptoms. He believed that an open and informed Soviet population would see that the United States did not threaten them and that they in turn would not be a threat to the United States. His greatest asset was his character. He was willing to learn, and he dealt with everyone, friend or foe, equal or subordinate, honestly and without guile.

Who won? Who lost? Matlock's answer, along with Reagan's and Gorbachev's, is that everyone won by the end of the Cold War. It was the Communist system and ideology that lost, not the countries it had victimized for seventy years.

Crisis Management

Business crises take many forms, including accident, accounting fraud, adverse international events, cash flow, hostile takeover, labor unrest, litigation, management succession, natural disaster, product failure, obsolescence or recall, regulatory intervention, rumors, scandals, slanders, strikes, stock decline, terrorist attacks, and violent protest. The Oregon School Boards Association Crisis Management Manual (2004) covers assault, bomb threat, child abuse, disturbances, earthquake, electrical storms, emergency release of students, explosion, extortion, fire, hazardous material spills, inclement weather, power failure, serious illness or injury, shooting, suicide, trespass, tsunamis, unauthorized visitors, volcanic activity and weapons.[3] While we focus in this discussion on businesses, the principles for dealing with crises at other levels from that of the family to that of the nation are much the same.

At the national level, the stakes are high and the planning is extended and elaborate. During the 1930s, the United States developed a series of "Color Plans" in the event of war. Among them was Plan Orange for war with Japan and even Plan Red in the unlikely event of war with Britain. There also were "Rainbow Plans" for wars against two or more countries, such as Red-Orange for war with Britain and Japan. There was no plan for war with Germany, which the terms of the Versailles Treaty made an unlikely threat—until Hitler ignored the treaty. Plan Red-Orange, which envisioned defeat of the European enemy first, was adapted to the changing situation, and guided US war plans for World War II. Similar plans for all sorts of contingencies were in place throughout the Cold War and following it, including one that conspiratorially-minded people see as evidence that the United States was determined to find an excuse to attack Iraq in 2003. Merely having a contingency plan does not signal intent! Predetermined plans are vital to rapid response in emergencies.

Three events in the 1980s gave impetus to corporate crisis management plans. The first was Johnson and Johnson's brilliant handling of the 1982 incident in which a terrorist poisoned a few Tylenol bottles. The second was the disastrous handling by Union Carbide of the 1984 Bhopal disaster and the third was the equally poor handling by Exxon of the 1989 Valdez incident.[4] The contrast in the way they were handled made clear how important it was to plan ahead for crises.

The key factors to take into account in developing a crisis management plan are the (1) possible types of crisis, (2) threat each type poses to organizational survival, (3) required response time, (4) ability to control events and (5) range of possible responses. Anticipating the types of crises requires thinking about everything that might go wrong, so is a matter of imagination applied to detailed knowledge of what an organization does and how. Figure 9.1 provides a general list of common crises that organizations face.

The first task in developing a crisis plan is to adapt the general list to the specific organization. The second task is to identify the specific ways these general crises could affect it. Burnett (2002) recommends quantifying the severity and probability of each, and multiplying the two together then factoring in control and response time to determine planning priorities. The difficulty of doing

---

3. Designed for adaptation by specific school districts, it includes space to write in emergency phone numbers, evacuation routes, etc. It and similar manuals provide an excellent and inexpensive starting point for any organization needing such a plan.
4. The author's partner in Wildlife on Wheels was in charge of the effort to rescue and rehabilitate the birds caught in the spill. Exxon actually was doing all it could to support the workers cleaning up the spill but failed to get the story out.

these things with reasonable reliability and validity suggests that simply di- or tri-chotomizing each is sufficient to establish priorities in all but the largest organizations. Figure 9.2 excerpts the crisis analysis for Wildlife on Wheels [WOW], which brings 100,000 Los Angeles basin children each year into "up-close and personal contact" with wild animals.

Boycotts	New competition
Death of a senior executive	Negative media or rumors
Embezzlement	New competition
Employee layoff	On-the-job incidents
Financial performance	Product failure
Government probes or fines	Product obsolescence
Lawsuits	Security breakdown
Loss of major customer or donor	Strike
Natural disasters	Technological failure

Figure 9.1
Common Organizational Crises

Threat	Time	Control	Options	Description
High	Low	Low	Few	Fire
High	Med	Med	Few	Loss of major donor
Med	Low	High	Med	Animal injures child
Med	Med	High	Many	Power failure
Med	Med	High	Few	Animal escape
Med	High	Low	Few	Changed regulations
Low	Low	Low	Many	Earthquake
Low	High	Med	Few	Zoning complaint
Low	Med	Med	Many	Volunteer shortage
Low	High	High	Many	Product obsolescence

Figure 9.2
Potential Crises Analysis for
Wildlife on Wheels

At the risk of stating the obvious, the best way to manage a crisis is to prevent it. Prevention planning led WOW to identify and purchase the emergency equipment needed in the event of animal bites, earthquake, fire, or power failure. A plan was developed to evacuate animals to the facility of a studio trainer, and in exchange to house their animals in case they needed to evacuate. An emergency off-site meeting point was established for staff. Animal enclosures were double fenced and a perimeter fence added to prevent and limit animal escape. The risk of injury was reduced by criteria for selecting and training animals and staff. Rules were established for public and volunteer contact with each animal.

The second step in crisis management is to spell out the immediate and fol-low-up actions that each staff member must take in each circumstance. Phone trees insure that everyone can be contacted quickly in an emergency. WOW designates a single individual to deal with the media and all staff members know to refer inquiries to that individual. Vehicles carry first aid kits, accident reports, and emergency phone numbers. Management updates the plan—especially the phone numbers—annually.

The final step in crisis management is training to make sure that each staff member knows what to do and why. Equipment is useless unless people know how to use it. Plans are useless unless everyone knows their primary and backup assignments. Fire drills complete with traps such as trying to get staff to talk to reporters test the plan.

While the particulars of the WOW Crisis Management plan are unlikely to be very helpful, the underlying principles should be. Every organization should have such a plan tailored to its own situation.

<u>Conclusion</u>

Conflict takes many forms within and between organizations. Personnel fight with subordinates, peers and superiors over things that matter and things that do not, and compete with one another for credit and promotions. Depart-ments compete with one another for resources and credit. Management contends with other organizations, including labor unions. Non-profit organizations com-pete with one another for grants and donations. Corporations compete with one another for business. Organizations contend with one another and with local and national governments over legislation and regulations, and frequently find them-selves in arbitration, mediation, or the courts. Conflict will remain a primary concern and responsibility of organizational managers and executives at every level.

Chapter 10
Political Conflict

Politics is not an end, but a means. It is not a product, but a process. It is the art of government. Like other values it has its counterfeits. So much emphasis has been placed upon the false that the significance of the true has been obscured and politics has come to convey the meaning of crafty and cunning selfishness, instead of candid and sincere service.

—Calvin Coolidge

Politics from a conflict perspective is a method for resolving differences as to what government should do and how it should do it. Political conflicts are pervasive: we continually contend over such issues as abortion, art, crime, defense, education, environment, foreign policy, guns, health care, immigration, poverty, taxation and transportation. We seldom settle anything permanently because the circumstances surrounding each problem seldom remain the same.

Deliberative Assemblies

Many political conflicts are resolved in what *Robert's Rules of Order* (1876) calls "deliberative assemblies." Each body follows its own procedures, intended to provide an orderly way to present views and make decisions. Successful rules for orderly meetings[1] develop from just four principles. First, the body must be a free agent limited by its constitution, bylaws and the laws of any state under which it operates. Second, the will of the majority must be respected. Third, everyone must have equal rights to present their views. Fourth, the body itself must be protected against precipitous or repeated action. These simple principles have guided the evolution of meeting procedures, which have evolved as people devise ways to subvert their intent. For example, the requirement for super-majorities to change the constitution or to repeal a previous action derives from the last principle.

Rules of order—*Robert's* or some other—keep disputes civil and thus resolvable. They help people to control their emotions—or provide a basis for controlling those who cannot. They keep the focus on the issues and interests. This in turn makes it possible for people to oppose one another on some issues but to work together on others.

---

1. Also usually included are rules for resolving such conflicts as impeachment, recall, and reprimand.

Voting Systems

Voting is a useful means of dispute resolution when substantial numbers of people have to choose among several alternatives. Voting is used to elect officials such as presidents, prime ministers, governors, legislators, or school board members. Votes are held on matters such as bond issues, ballot initiatives, and constitutional amendments. Once selected, the legislators themselves vote to determine budgets and laws. The US Supreme Court makes judicial decisions by vote of its nine members, and the United Nations makes political decisions by majority vote in the General Assembly and by majority vote subject to veto by one of five permanent members in the Security Council. Owners of corporations or members of nonprofit organizations vote to select directors, approve auditors, and on board and stockholder proposals. Votes select Oscar and *Palme d'Or* winners. Votes choose athletes for members in the Halls of Fame of many sports.

Many different procedures have been devised for conducting these many different kinds of elections (Brams and Fishburn 1991; Nurmi, 1987). The most common and most familiar is plurality voting, used to select senators and congressman in the United States. In plurality voting, each voter has one vote for each contest. The candidate with the most votes wins. Some methods require a run-off with weaker candidates eliminated if no candidate achieves a majority. This can get expensive and time-consuming if each round eliminates only the single weakest candidate until a majority is achieved. Therefore, it is common to eliminate all but the top two choices, virtually guaranteeing a majority to one candidate in two rounds.

There are some unusual variations on plurality voting. The US system of primaries to select presidential candidates for the two major parties is in effect a system of successive plurality elections in which the candidates themselves decide when to drop out of the competition. The Electoral College that elects US presidents equals the total number of Senators (2 per state) and Congressmen (435) plus three from the District of Columbia, currently totaling 538. Its members are chosen by plurality vote in each jurisdiction. It was developed to prevent a few big states (originally New York, Pennsylvania, and Virginia) dominating elections, and it usually comes under fire whenever a candidate wins the popular but not the electoral vote, as happened in 1824, 1876, 1888 and 2000.

An alternative to plurality voting is attributed to French mathematician Marquis de Condorcet (1785), although a 13th century Catalan philosopher appears to have anticipated him. Any system that allows tallying of results to simulate the outcome of paired elections of all candidates against all other candidates is a Condorcet method. The "Condorcet winner" is the individual who would win *all* the pair-wise contests. But, it is possible for the first candidate to defeat the second, the second to defeat the third, and so on with the last candidate defeating the first. That is, the Condorcet method may not always produce a winner. Despite this, it does provide a method for judging fairness, as no method of aggregating votes and determining winners should result in the defeat of a Condorcet winner.

At least three systems seek to ensure proportional representation of groups within an electorate. Borda (1781) proposed each voter assigning 0 points to the candidate he ranks lowest, 1 to the second lowest and so on up to C-1 points for the top-ranked candidate, where C is the number of candidates. Each candidate's points are summed across all voters, and the candidate with the highest total wins. Unfortunately, voters are likely to rank candidates strategically to give their preferred candidate the best chance of winning by giving the lowest ranking to the most powerful rival regardless of actual preference. The effect is even greater if voters do not rate some of the candidates (Nurmi, 1987). This strategy is easy for every voter to carry out, making a Condorcet winner unlikely.

Single Transferable Vote or Instant Runoff improves Borda's method. Devised in the 1850s by Thomas Hare, it is used in Australia, Fiji, Malta, Nauru, Northern Ireland and the Republic of Ireland. The number of votes needed to win is determined after all votes have been cast using a predetermined formula. The most common, the Droop quota, is $1+ v/(s+1)$, which makes it impossible to elect more candidates by first-place votes in the first round than there are contested seats. An election run under the Droop quota in which 1000 votes were cast for 9 seats would require $1 + 1000/(9+1) = 101$ votes to win a seat.

All candidates receiving 101 or more votes would be declared winners. All votes over 101 received by the winning candidates are transferred to the remaining candidates, either randomly or proportionately depending again on predetermined rules. All candidates who now have 101 votes are elected and the process is repeated until the nine seats are filled. Under this system, the first choice candidate can never be hurt by ranking a second choice, a second choice by ranking a third choice, and so on. Strategic voting is possible but the calculations required are so complex, and the control of voters needed is so complete, that it is extremely unlikely.

Cumulative voting gives each voter a fixed number of votes, usually equal to the number of seats at stake, to distribute among one or more candidates in any way desired, including giving all of one's votes to a single candidate. Such a system ensures minorities (however defined) can elect representatives approximately equal to their proportion of the community. Assume a population divided between minority Greens and majority Blues. Assume an election to select a city council, with each voter having as many votes as there are contested seats on the city council. The optimal strategy for the minority Greens is to run candidates approximately equal to their proportion of the electorate, and to concentrate all of their votes on those candidates. This will insure that the majority Blues will not have enough votes to prevent the election of those candidates. If the Greens dilute their vote across a larger number of candidates, they risk losing all seats. Conversely, despite their advantage in numbers, if the Blues dilute their votes to try to shut out the Greens, they risk losing control of the council. For both sides, putting up a full slate of candidates for all seats risks losing all races.

Cumulative voting offers the potential for proportional representation, but the complexities of real life do not insure that result, primarily because everyone is the member not of one but of many groups (*e.g.*, age, ethnicity, occupation, political viewpoint, religion, socio-economic class, sexual orientation). Therefore, even if party leaders could control the candidates, the electorate itself is very hard to control in practice.

Approval voting allows voters to rate each candidate as "acceptable" or "unacceptable." The candidate with the most votes wins. Its most prominent use is the selection of the United Nations Secretary General. It is more likely than even plurality voting with a run-off to select the Condorcet winner. Voters can cast a protest vote without losing the opportunity to affect the result by voting for the most preferred of the viable candidates. It is a clear improvement on street demonstrations as a means of sending a message to governments as to what opinions they can and cannot ignore safely, although it might also generate candidates who "triangulate" (in the phrase made famous by President Clinton's White House) to win elections. It is simple for people to understand and use, and can be implemented easily on existing voting machines.

Some claims for approval voting are speculative. One is that it will reduce negative campaigning. Another is that it will increase voter turnout. In both cases, the opposite seems equally plausible. In the 2003 recall election for governor of California nearly 200 candidates ran for the office, primarily, it seemed, in hope of gaining a little publicity and ego-gratification. This could become the norm under approval voting.

<u>Redistricting</u>

Redistricting of the U.S. House of Representatives and many elective offices in the states is a quintessentially American dispute in which political parties attempt to gain advantage over one another by winning more legislative seats than warranted by the vote. Popularly known in the United States as "gerrymandering," it long predates Elbridge Gerry's early 19th century efforts in Massachusetts from which it takes its name. It has parallels with England's "rotten boroughs" and is found in one form or another in other democracies as well. As John Steele Gordon[2] put it:

> Gerrymandering is altogether evil. It effectively disenfranchises millions of voters by dumping them in districts where the results are foregone conclusions. It makes incumbents arrogant and unresponsive because they do not need to fear the voters. And it polarizes American politics because the important elections tend to be primaries, where the party bases rule rather than the less politically motivated middle.

---

2. *Wall Street Journal*, 11 November 2004

Two basic techniques are used to create advantage in the United States. "Cracking" aims to waste the other party's vote by dividing it among several districts. "Packing" aims to waste the other party's votes by putting most of their voters into the smallest possible number of districts, so that they win those districts by great margins but lose everywhere else. The basic data used is voter turnout by party at the precinct level, with allowances made for factors such as changing party registration, migration, and turnout rates.

In most but not all states the legislature redistricts itself, almost inevitably colluding with the minority party to provide safe districts for as many incumbents as possible. This is the main reason that incumbents win 98% of the time in House races. US Senate races are statewide, so are more competitive.

The Constitution requires redistricting after each decennial census. But, when Republicans defeated hitherto dominant Democrats in the 2002 mid-term elections in Colorado and Texas, they attempted to redistrict immediately rather than wait for the 2010 census. Such a precedent, of redistricting after any election that reverses control of the executive and legislative branches, threatens chaos, particularly as it can take two to three election cycles before all the court challenges are resolved. That is, a bad system threatens to become worse.

Criticism of gerrymandering is as old as the practice itself and has led to four widely accepted "good government criteria" for reform. The first is "one-man, one-vote," established in principle if not in practice by three Supreme Court cases (Baker v. Carr 1962, Reynolds v. Simms 1964 and Wesberry v. Sanders 1964). If district "A" has twice as many people as district "B," then in effect everyone in district "B" has two votes compared to the people in district "A." Thus, districts should be equal in population. This is easier said than done. The census counts people without distinguishing citizens entitled to vote from legal aliens and illegal immigrants who are not. The proportion of registered voters and of registered voters who actually vote varies widely among districts. Americans are quite mobile, although more so in some parts of the country than others. Finally, the Supreme Court has demanded only "substantial equality" without ever defining how much variation is permitted

The second criterion is that all seats should be competitive. In practice, this means that both major parties should have at least a theoretical chance to win every seat. The best that has been done seems to have been the redistricting in California under Governor Reagan that made about a quarter of the districts competitive.

Rural districts have to cover a larger area than urban ones to encompass the same population, but all districts should be "contiguous and compact," the third criterion. Fourth, "communities with common interests" should be preserved. In California, these include people who live in the deserts or the cities and need water, those who live in the mountains who have water, farmers in the Central Valley who make their living exploiting the environment, and people who live along the coast who tend to prefer a pristine environment.

Implementing the criteria is difficult because they often prove contradictory. For example, combining people in California from the coast and the San Joaquin Valley in east-west districts would achieve compact districts at the expense of representing the views of people who live along the coast. The alternative is the existing long, thin, contiguous but non-compact coastal district. Our geographically based system under-represents dispersed minorities (*e.g.*, Armenians, Libertarians and gays) while giving undue power to concentrated ones (*e.g.*, Blacks in South Central Los Angeles or the wealthy liberals of Bel Air, Beverly Hills, Brentwood, Malibu, and Westwood). A third complaint is the exclusion from the process of minority parties, although it is not clear that this is a problem that can be solved without destabilization. The major role of third parties in the United States seems less to effect change by winning seats than to develop new ideas which, if they gain significant adherents, are taken over by one of the two major parties.

Reforms to implement these criteria have been proposed. One is a variant of the old standby for dividing candy between two children (Chapter 2). One party is allowed to redistrict the state (or city or whatever else is involved). The other party can select and freeze the boundaries of one district, then redraw the remaining districts, and submit it to the first party, which can select and freeze the boundaries of one district. The process continues until redistricting is complete. Another idea is eliminating districts and choosing representatives at large. Everyone would have as many votes as there are seats (see cumulative voting, above). This might work at the city level, but probably would be disastrous at higher levels. First, voters are unlikely to follow 50, 100 or more races closely. Second, representation is likely to become geographically concentrated and to leave some people without representation.

A third approach is to take redistricting out of the hands of the legislature. The most common proposal is to turn the task over to an independent panel, such as one made up of retired judges who are naively assumed to be nonpartisan. Some have proposed programming a computer to implement the good government criteria. Clark (2004) carried out one such effort for California using data on party voting by census tract. Figure 10.1 compares actual and theoretical districts for 1992 using his algorithm. Clark reports, "Maximally compact districts produced more districts with the party votes within one or two percent than the actual 1992 districts. At three percent difference, the two sets of districts were equal. For differences up to ten percent, there were more in the 1992 set, but for differences of thirteen, fourteen, or fifteen percent, there were more in the compact set...Another surprise was that maximally compact districts would not have changed the outcome of the election. There were still thirty-three Democrat to nineteen Republican districts. My conclusion is that maximally compact districts are not a threat to either party. We can eliminate gerrymandering without a political upheaval (Clark, personal correspondence)." But, this conclusion is based on a single state at a single point in time, so requires considerably more experimentation along the lines carried out by Clark.

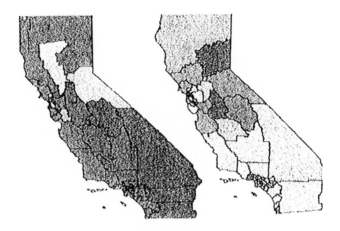

Figure 10.1
Actual (left) and Theoretical (right) 1992
California Congressional Districts

The Tragedy of the Commons and the Free Rider Problem

The related concepts of the "tragedy of the commons" and the "free rider problem" explain why government programs are wasteful. The idea can be traced to Aristotle, who noted, "what is common to the greatest number has the least care bestowed upon it."

In 1833, William Forster Lloyd observed that shepherds in England who had the right to use the village commons in an emergency reversed the formula, grazing their sheep on the commons until it was exhausted, only then using their own land. This led to the general idea, expressed in the phrase "Tragedy of the Commons," that all resources owned in common—air, oceans, fish, grasslands, for example—will be exploited to the point of destruction because nobody is motivated to care for them (Hardin, 1968). The concept also explains such phenomena as the use of tenement stairwells as toilets and the litter in public streets and parks.

In much of Europe, bus and tram riders buy and cancel their own tickets. Inspectors who find riders without tickets fine them several times the normal price. This "Free Rider Problem" is a form of Prisoners' Dilemma (Chapter 2). Riders compare the price of a ticket with the amount of the fine and decide whether or not to buy a ticket. Bus companies make a similar calculation to decide how high to set the fines and how many inspectors to hire. Overtime parkers, speeders, and tax avoiders are among those playing the same game.

Consider a hypothetical example. You eat lunch with three friends and spend about six dollars, the average in the restaurant.[3] Over time, the habit develops of simply splitting the tab for lunch—in other words, lunch becomes common rather than private property. You would enjoy having desert and coffee for four dollars more, but do not do so because it would cost your friends a dollar each. Suppose instead that all 100 diners in the restaurant split the tab. Adding desert and coffee now will only cost you four cents, with 96 strangers picking up the remaining $3.84. In fact, believing that the strangers all are richer and cannot possibly need all their money, you will upgrade to steak and wine. Your tab now comes to $40, but you only have to pay forty cents. Unfortunately, everyone soon will come to the same conclusion, and the average lunch bill will jump to $40 from $6. If you try to save money by returning to your traditional lunch, your tab will be $39.66 for your $6 meal.

This is of course a parable explaining why government programs become wasteful and cost more than they should. There are only three serious possible solutions. The first is to hope individuals will work a sensible solution out among themselves. That worked so long as four friends split the tab just as it has worked in rare cases such as Swiss hamlets where social networks are strong and populations are small. However, it breaks very quickly as the group gets larger. When a Vermont town of only 4000 made school taxes voluntary, many stopped contributing. Residents divided into two bitterly opposed factions, leaving, as the *Wall Street Journal* headline put it, "Manchester Disunited," a pun English football fans are more likely to enjoy than Americans.

The second possible solution is government regulation. Americans live in a pervasive regulatory regime that touches almost every aspect of life but most affects agriculture, consumer goods, environment, and industry. Examples of regulations that have saved lives are not difficult to find: seat belt laws and fire-retardant child pajamas come immediately to mind. In other cases, the impact has been perverse. Regulations requiring particular systems to limit pollution discourage development of better ones. The seventeen regional gasoline formulas required during the summer increases prices and create shortages because refineries cannot estimate regional as accurately as national demand. Subsidized sugar production encourages farmers to produce more than we need and keeps more wetlands in production than necessary.

Regulation has real benefits, but also has real costs, many hidden and hard to assess. Regulatory paperwork in the US costs an estimated five billion dollars a year. People ignore manuals and warning labels because the print is too small, and the warnings are long and often just plain silly.[4] Environmental regulations

---

3. Abridged from an example by Russell Roberts in the *Wall Street Journal*.
4. Such as a warning not to use a hair dryer while sleeping, a warning not to turn a dessert upside down printed on the bottom of the package, a warning not to iron clothes while wearing them, a warning that a can of peanuts contains nuts. In Chicago, it is illegal to eat in a place that is on fire. In Indiana, it is illegal to go to a theater within four hours of

have proven particularly perverse, killing jobs to protect ecologically unimportant species instead of focusing on habitats, and preventing owners using their property while requiring them to pay taxes on it. Regulators tend to think the world needs more of what they do and apparently, some are not above distortion to prove the need. The US Forest Service used false data about spotted owls to block logging in California. The Fish and Wildlife Service distorted data to justify cutting water off Klamath River Basin farmers on behalf of suckerfish. In the first case, the government lost in court and had to pay the loggers $9.5 million in damages. In the second case, the Klamath basin lost 2000 jobs and $134 million in crops in a single season.

The third possible solution is the free market. The government could auction, assign, or sell permits to pollute after setting regional standards. Firms that produce less pollution than their permits allow could sell the excess to companies that cannot meet the limits. This gives a competitive edge to companies that pollute less by driving up the costs of those that pollute more, eventually driving the latter to reform or bankruptcy.

An unregulated free market poses its own dangers (Chapter 11). Undoubtedly, the most general and productive approach is to combine the regulatory and market approaches in a way that takes account of the circumstances of each industry. An example of a beneficial combination would be to transform the FDA from regulatory to information agency. Drug companies wanting approval of particular products could ask for it. Patients who wanted to be cautious could take only FDA-approved treatments. Others, especially those with terminal illnesses, could try experimental ones without breaking the law. The US "cap and trade" program takes a market approach to reducing sulfur dioxide. It has achieved the same result as the regulatory approach it replaced at a savings of two billion dollars a year. A purely regulatory approach remains available should nobody be able to devise a combined or purely market approach, but is best reserved as a last instead of first resort because it reduces freedom and usually is inefficient and wasteful.

---

eating garlic. There are hundreds of other examples that can be attributed to obsessed citizens, over-protective legislators, and greedy tort lawyers.

Chapter 11
Intellectual Conflict

Truth springs from argument among friends.

—David Hume

I wish I were as sure of anything as you seem to be of everything.

—Lord Melbourne to Thomas Macauley

Ideas are a major source of human conflict. They sometimes excite great passion, sometimes turn bloody, and often change our conceptions of the world and ourselves. This chapter focuses on ideas about Society, History, Nature, and God that have been at the heart of intellectual conflict throughout western history (Baumer, 1977).[1]

Society

Philosophers, political scientists, economists, anthropologists, and "just plain folks" have long debated the nature of human society. How do people manage to live together? What is the best way to organize society? Is it an organism whose growth cannot be controlled or a machine that Man can design to achieve some purpose and if so what?

There are hundreds of answers to these questions, but we can begin to make sense of them based on the underlying assumptions associated with conservative, liberal, or radical thought. These resemble a color wheel, progressing almost imperceptibly from one shade into the next. Just as we each have our favorite color, we each have our favorite philosophy. No color and no philosophy are demonstrably right or wrong and no amount of debate is likely to change individual preferences very much. Just as it sometimes is difficult to tell where one color ends and another begins, variations and borrowings make it hard to distinguish one philosophy from another. To further complicate matters, the terms vary in meaning across time and place. We define them below in the classical philosophical rather than the modern political sense.

Conservatism assumes mankind is fallible and morally suspect. Passion, materialism, and vanity overwhelm common sense, decency, and morality. Thomas Hobbes is the seminal conservative thinker. His *Leviathan*, one of the most impressive arguments ever made for strong central government, popularized a hypothetical "state of nature" as a starting point for analyzing society. His

---

1. The fifth, the nature-nurture controversy, was discussed in Chapters 3 and 4.

state of nature was one in which "life is solitary, poor, nasty, brutish and short." In these circumstances, men gave up some of their freedom to attain order and security. The sole task of government is to maintain order, which, Hobbes argues, will make it possible for private individuals to identify and provide all needed goods and services. If government fails to maintain order, Hobbes permits rebellion to install one that will.

Conservatives tend to see war as natural and peace as best insured by patriotism, strong government, and military preparedness. Pessimistic conservatives believe war is so rooted in human nature that it is ineradicable. Optimistic conservatives see war as caused by government error, so preventable. Conservatives tend to support war that advances the interests of the state and tend to oppose war fought for idealistic reasons.

Liberalism assumes man is intrinsically good and capable of continuous improvement. Enlightenment thinkers drew this conclusion, somewhat dubiously, from the incredible growth of scientific knowledge in the 17th and 18th centuries and the expectation that it would continue to grow until everything worth knowing was understood.

The seminal liberal thinker is John Locke, author of *The Second Treatise on Civil Government*. In his view, the purpose of government is to make "natural rights" more secure than they are in the hypothetical "state of nature," which Locke saw as one of imperfect harmony because it lacked a way to settle disputes over natural rights. Such a government should be limited. John Stuart Mill defined this limit by the "harm principle," by which government cannot prevent a person harming himself, but can prevent a person harming someone else. As Oliver Wendell Holmes put it, "Your rights end where my nose begins." Complementing limited government is the economic doctrine of *"laissez faire,"* minimum interference by the state in the marketplace. These ideals emerged primarily in Scotland and England and inspire American Republicans to this day. France took a different path, one in which the government was seen as the best way to protect the masses from an oppressive nobility. That is, continental liberalism, with its reliance on government to protect the individual, inspires modern American Democrats.

Liberal views as to the cause of war are diverse. Some blame it on the nation-state, some on the absence of peaceful alternatives for solving conflicts, both of which lead to calls for supra-national organizations such as the United Nations and the World Court. Some blame arms races, leading to such efforts at arms control as the Washington Naval Treaty and the Strategic Arms Limitation Talks (SALT). Liberals emphasize the costs of war and are particularly distressed at fighting for economic gain, as illustrated by the slogan "No blood for oil." Generally, they see wars of self-defense as justified, but differ as to which national interests warrant action.

Radicalism assumes Man was perfect while living in a state of nature, but was corrupted by civilization. Radicals tend to ignore what is good in and to focus on what is bad about their own civilization while romanticizing primitive ones. For example, it is reflected in the story of the Garden of Eden, in Tacitus' comparison of Roman immorality and corruption with German tribes that he saw as models of rectitude, and in Jefferson's notion that the farmer was more honest than the city dweller. It underlies the assumptions of many anthropological descriptions of primitive cultures and in the views of hippies and flower children in the 1960s.

The seminal radical thinker is Jean-Jacques Rousseau, whose *Discourses* and *Emile* are most relevant for our purposes. His state of nature, based on early reports of the idyllic life of South Pacific islanders, was Paradise. However, looking at France in the *ancien regime*, he concluded that the nobility lived well at the expense of the masses, or as he put it, "Man was born free and everywhere is in chains." By an inexplicable twist of logic, it led Rousseau to advocate totalitarian government in which the supreme leader interpreted the "general will." His ideal state as reflected in his proposed constitution for Corsica required complete loyalty, allowed no factions, no political parties, no religious groups, and no freedom of speech. It inspired the murderous ways of men such as Stalin and Pol Pot.

Radicalism is associated with two contradictory traditions about war. The first is pacifism (Chapter 15). Marxism (below) sees history moving inexorably from religious to ethnic to class conflict and finally international conflict as an extension of class warfare that develops after capitalism reached its monopoly stage.

Our preferences tend to change over time, the usual transition illustrated by the saying "If you are not liberal when you are 20, you have no heart; if you are not conservative by the time you are 40, you have no mind." As scholars, we must overcome our tendency to blindly accept as true those theories that reflect our prejudices of the moment and to instinctively reject as false those theories that do not. Wisdom begins by determining whether our agreement or disagreement with a theory stems merely from the way we wish the world to be.

History[2]

At one level, the Cold War that dominated the second half of the twentieth century was a conflict between two ideas of history implied by two distinct economic systems.

Capitalism's central tenet is private property that owners can exchange freely in competitive markets. According to capitalists, under these conditions society benefits from maximum productivity, optimal allocation of resources, lower prices, and greater choices. Adam Smith's *Wealth of Nations* is the first great analysis of capitalism. Smith's most fundamental belief was in the efficiency of market competition in optimizing resource use, described metaphori-

---

2. This section relies on R. Heilbroner (1962), P. Heyne (1973), and T. Sowell (1985).

cally as the "Invisible Hand." If there is an unmet need, someone will recognize it and seize the opportunity for profit. If successful, he will overcharge because, being human, he is greedy. The resulting wealth will draw competitors, driving prices down. If there are too many sellers, competition will eliminate the highest cost producers, bringing supply and demand into balance to the benefit of consumers.

Smith championed capitalism but not capitalists. He warned that they always advocate policies that benefit themselves at the expense of the general interest. Thus, at one point he famously wrote, "People of the same trade seldom meet together, even for merriment and diversion, but the conversation ends in a conspiracy against the public, or in some contrivance to raise prices. It is impossible indeed to prevent such meetings by any law which either could be executed, or would be consistent with liberty and justice."

Smith saved his greatest disgust for mercantilists who dominated economic theory in Smith's day and believed that the key to national prosperity was a favorable trade balance, so advocated state-sponsored monopolies, high tariffs on imports, and government subsidies for exports. Smith found that these policies promoted the interests of producers at the expense of consumers and distorted efficient allocation of capital. He argued for free trade, which he claimed increased prosperity by stimulating the division of labor. Today's mercantilists, now known as protectionists, want high tariffs and export subsidies, and bemoan trade deficits and competition from foreign workers. Free traders respond that the problems are high tariffs, high corporate and income tax rates, mandated employee benefits, undue risk from lawsuits, and excessive regulation.

Government had three main roles in Smith's view, starting with national defense. Second, it should protect property, enforce contracts, and ensure free trade. Finally, it should provide essential services that the market was unlikely to do, such as roads, harbors, mail, and education.

Charlie Chaplin satirized problems of the factory system in *Modern Times* that Smith foresaw and suggested public education as a cure. He understood that capitalism produces an unequal distribution of wealth, but argued that as long as there was economic growth, the poor would be better off than under other systems. He argued that the wealth of a nation stems from the productivity of its consumers. In all of this, he proved more prescient than Marx.

Communism according to Karl Marx would be the utopian "end of history." Its inevitable triumph would produce the "greatest good for the greatest number of people." Getting there was the result of class struggle, which was the history of all existing and past societies: "Freeman and slave, patrician and plebian, lord and serf, guild master and journeyman, in a word oppressor and oppressed, stood in sharp opposition to each other. They carried on perpetual warfare." Despite the centrality of class to his theory, he left *Capital* untouched for twelve years and unfinished because he could not define the term under capitalism, a system in which people can and do change class and status.

As far as we know, Marx never set foot in a factory or workplace. He never talked directly either to owners or to workers about working conditions. Rather, he searched books, newspapers, and government statistics for data to justify his preconceptions. When facts proved him wrong, he simply found more convenient ones. To prove that capitalism exploited workers, he had to prove that pre-capitalist workshops were better workplaces than capitalist factories. He did so by referring to a twenty-year-old book by Engels based on an even older government "white paper" that had led to The Factory Act of 1833 that corrected many of the conditions reported. Where abuses continued, they were in worker-intensive rather than capital-intensive industries, falsifying Marx's theory.

Marx predicted that capitalism would concentrate wealth in the hands of a few monopolists and that the middle class would shrink. Instead, small businesses proliferated, creating most of the jobs and vastly enlarging the middle class. His prediction that machinery would destroy jobs and profits was wrong. His asserted that ownership implies control. Instead, employees control bureaucratized modern corporations, while the stock market turned workers into owners who have little control.[3] The number of product and corporate failures refutes the claim that corporations can control our lives and sell consumers whatever they make. Thirty to ninety percent of all new products (varying by industry) fail. From 1955 when it first appeared through 2005, the Fortune 500 listed 1877 different companies, and only 71 of the original list remain.[4]

Marx's economic reasoning depends on the "labor theory of value" and the "iron law of wages." The first wrongly asserts that the prices of all things vary only according to the amount of labor required to produce them, adjusted in Marx's formulation for the skill required as measured by differences in pay rates. Unfortunately, the theory refutes itself as it leaves unanswered why one worker is paid more than another. Every effort to save the theory is easily rebutted by contrary real-world examples. The second declares that capitalist employers pay workers just enough to keep them alive and breed their replacements. Marx was wrong again, this time due to the rise in capitalist countries of labor unions and ever-wider suffrage that led in turn to reform legislation, pro-

---

3. Some believe that this prediction is coming true in 21st century America, pointing to data suggesting a declining middle class and a widening gap between the very rich and the very poor, outsourcing of jobs, and a shift to service work. The actual situation is considerably more complex and the outcome less certain given capitalism's historical record of adjustment to changing circumstances. Consider outsourcing, for example. New Jersey has banned all state contract work from being performed outside the US, inevitably increasing state procurement costs, which in turn means a higher burden on taxpayers or reduction of other benefits such as education. The law will drive state contractor costs up, which means some combination of lower profits, worker layoffs, and higher costs (even if they outsource to Nebraska instead of India which hardly is the result the legislators had in mind), all of which is bound to end up costing more local jobs than it protects (*Wall Street Journal*, 16 March 2005).

4. www.Fortune.com

gressive taxation, trust-busting, wider public ownership through sale of stock, prosecution of wrongdoing executives, more efficient competitors, incentives for product improvement, pension and retirement plans, and health benefits. In a word, Marx, like Smith before him but with much less excuse for doing so, overlooked the impact of democracy on capitalism. Marx was wrong a third time when he predicted that socialism would correct the problem. In fact, in the second half of the twentieth century, laborers in Marxist countries received a lower percentage of what they produced and a lower percentage of GDP than those in capitalist countries.

Marxists like to argue that capitalist systems must spend "excessively" on the military to counter economic stagnation. In fact, the 38 Marxist governments of the Cold War era put twice as high a percentage of GDP into the military than non-Marxist countries and maintained twice as many troops per 1000 people than non-Marxist ones (13.3 versus 6.1). Ten countries that became Marxist during the Cold War nearly tripled their military spending. Ironically, the Marxist countries are the ones that stagnated economically, partly in consequence of excessive spending on their militaries.

Marx predicted that workers in industrialized countries would lead communist revolutions. He was wrong again. In fact, they have taken place in agricultural societies such as China, Cuba, and Russia rather than industrialized ones such as England, Germany and the United States, and have been led by intellectual rather than workers. Marx posited a transitional period between capitalism and communism in which a dictatorship would confiscate private property to set up a system of communal ownership. He never explained how to select these dictators or why they ever would surrender power. In fact, every communist state became a police state in which dictators used secret police to exterminate opposition and hold on to power. They nationalized production, expected citizens to work in state enterprises, and set quotas and prices for all goods and services. It proved inefficient and impossible to get and keep right.

Despite the theoretical flaws and the disastrous historical record, some still see salvation in Marxism, blaming imperfect implementation for its failings, while pointing to the imperfections of real capitalism. In effect, they compare apples with oranges, an imagined Marxist utopia with the worst aspects of capitalism. The opposite, comparison of an idealized capitalist economy against the horrors of actual Marxist states, is equally disingenuous. This is an old debating trick, one to which anyone engaged in conflict of any kind should be alert. The only fair comparisons are equals with equals: ideal Marxists states with ideal capitalist ones, or real Marxist states with real capitalist states.

Nature

Our view of Nature reflects a long intellectual struggle that began with the efforts of the Sumerians and Egyptians to make some sense of human existence, and today focuses on whether Man is destroying the environment and if so what to do about it. The ancient approach was mythical, polytheistic and largely tolerant of other religions, unlike most monotheists. The Greek approach depended on logic and observation. Muslim Arabs preserved classical learning and contributed new mathematical tools and advances in scientific and medical knowledge.

Medieval European scholastics tried to demonstrate the compatibility of reason and Christian faith, which St. Thomas Aquinas codified into a logical, convincing, and coherent whole, resolving problems such as the relationship between reason and revelation that dominated western thought for about 400 years. In this model, the four elements of air, fire, water, and earth in varying proportions formed all things. The striving of the elements to reach their true order (earth, water, fire and air from lowest to highest) explained all phenomena. In humans, the elements expressed themselves as four humors (blood, choler, phlegm, and bile). The scholastics eschewed direct observation and conducted sophisticated criticism of Arab, Christian, Greek, Jewish, and Roman texts, gradually discovering and increasingly questioning the contradictions. As the Church became aware of the threat, it began to fight back

The overlapping lives of four men illustrate the course of the conflict. From 1543, the year Copernicus died and his *Revolution of the Heavenly Spheres* was published, it was a penal offense in Catholic states to print, sell, buy, or own any literature not sanctioned by the Inquisition.[5] Fifty-seven years later, the Catholic Church burned Giordano Bruno at the stake for advocating an infinite universe, an atomic basis for matter, the insignificance of man, and freedom of inquiry. Thirty-two years later, the Inquisition condemned but did not execute Galileo. Newton, born the year of the Catholic Church's pyrrhic condemnation of Galileo, experienced adulation instead of condemnation because the Church by then had lost the intellectual battle. In Newton's universe, God was the creator and the author of the laws discovered by science. "Nature and Nature's laws lay hid in night; God said 'let Newton be' and all was light [Alexander Pope]."

During the eighteenth and nineteenth centuries, new instruments with which to observe and measure combined with new mathematics completed the Newtonian revolution. The world was fashioned in accordance with mathematical laws. Man was part of, not superior to Nature. The heavens followed the same laws as earth and probably were made of the same stuff. Hume argued against the need even for a creator. The universe became an eternal, infinite, self-moving machine. God lost not only his home in the heavens but his importance. Mathematics explained everything.

---

5. Some historians use 1543 as a "marker date" dividing the medieval from the modern mind, as it also is the year in which Vesalius's *De Humani Corporis Fabrica* was published. Just as Copernicus changed our conception of the heavens, Vesalius reversed the conception of the human body in vogue since Galen and, along with Harvey, established sound principles for medical research.

Romanticism was from one perspective a radical reaction to the extreme determinism of this "Clockwork Universe." Edward Blake offered a toast, "To Newton's health, and a curse on mathematics" (Kline, 1953). The twentieth century introduced relativity and quantum mechanics, and along with fearsome wars made life seem uncertain again.

The conflict between science and religion continued over evolution with Darwin in the role of Copernicus delaying publication of his book for fear of church reaction, and Scopes in the role played Galileo. Scientific advances such as stem cell research raise ethical issues that make continued conflict likely. Christianity is even weaker and more divided than ever. However, as seems appropriate, religion (not just Christianity) provides a check on scientific excess by raising ethical questions.

Today's great intellectual conflict concerning Nature is over Man's relationship with the environment. There is abundant evidence of environmental change—but just how much is due to man is a matter of dispute. Four distinct strands underlie the environmental movement (or rather movements). The first, originating in transcendentalism, involves a radical rejection of industrialization and globalization. Thoreau (1854) wrote in this vein, saying in *Walden Pond* that, "I went to the woods because I wished to live deliberately, to front only the essential facts of life... to live deep and suck out all the marrow of life, to live so sturdily and Spartan-like as to put to rout all that was not life."

The second strand focuses on environmental destruction. Rachel Carson's (1962) *Silent Spring* described how DDT upset the balance of nature, entered the food chain, accumulated in animal and human tissues, and caused genetic damage and cancer. The chemical industry reacted with indignation, attacking Carson's integrity and sanity and painting a picture of a return to the Dark Ages in which diseases and vermin would destroy humanity. In the face of the conflict, President Kennedy ordered an investigation that led to banning DDT. The burden of proof shifted to the proponents from the opponents of pesticides. *Silent Spring* made the public aware that nature was vulnerable, and that technological progress entailed risk. Concern expanded from DDT to other forms of pollution, then to other forms of environmental damage.[6]

---

6. A partial list of the concerns begins with the possibility that global warming could force one billion people to move from existing seashores, while causing droughts in other parts of the world. Half the forests of 8000 years ago have disappeared, primarily in the tropics. Over 70% of the ocean's fisheries are depleted, over-exploited, or full-exploited. Nearly 25% of the world's coral reefs are degraded beyond recovery, and another 45% are threatened. The Gulf of Mexico contains a dead zone of 5000 miles due to runoff of agricultural chemicals from the Mississippi Basin, and China and India continue to use DDT, banned elsewhere because of its effects on wildlife. Automobiles contribute about 16% of CO_2 emissions in North America, the atmosphere's Ozone Hole appears to be enlarging (National Geographic, 2004) and species of animals and plants are disappearing at an alarming rate.

A third strand focuses on the consumption of nonrenewable and destruction of renewable resources. Schumacher's (1973) *Small is Beautiful* proposed human-scale, decentralized and appropriate technologies as an alternative to Western capitalism. The book called for community self-sufficiency and back-to-basics thinking. Schumacher maintained that man's current pursuit of profit and progress, which promotes giant organizations and increased specialization, has in fact resulted in gross economic inefficiency, environmental pollution, and inhumane working conditions. Schumacher challenged the doctrine of economic, technological, and scientific specialization and proposed a system for "Intermediate Technology," based on smaller working units, co-operative ownership, and regional workplaces using local labor and resources.

A fourth strand originates with Lovelock's (1979) idea that the earth is self-regulating:

> . . . the physical and chemical condition of the surface of the Earth, of the atmosphere, and of the oceans has been and is actively made fit and comfortable by the presence of life itself. This is in contrast to the conventional wisdom which held that life adapted to the planetary conditions as it and they evolved their separate ways.

Although Lovelock endorsed a mechanistic explanation,[7] some interpreted his ideas to imply that the Earth had a life force that was actively controlling the climate, and that the earth itself was alive. This gave a spiritual or mystical dimension to environmentalism.

Gore's (1992) *Earth in the Balance* pulled these strands together around the idea that global warming constitutes a widely agreed, desperate environmental crisis due to industrialization and our "pathological isolation" from nature. Gore argues that solving this crisis must be the "central organizing principle for civilization." He suggests a "Global Marshall Plan" controlled by international organizations, international summits, and spiritual values. He proposes a vast array of technological and regulatory fixes administered by government fiat.

Some critics question the science underlying these ideas (Ellsaesser, 1994; Lindzen, 1994). Other critics question the underlying philosophy of extending "rights" to elements of nature such as earth, water, forests, or animals and the supposed pathologies we suffer from living apart from nature (Lennox, 1994). Most critics acknowledge that there are environmental problems but focus on serious flaws in the economic (Lott, 1994) and political (Hahn, 1994) solutions that Gore proposes.

---

7. In 1991, Lovelock wrote that, "Neither Lynn Margulis nor I have ever proposed that planetary self-regulation is purposeful. . . Yet we have met persistent, almost dogmatic, criticism that our hypothesis is teleological."

Many environmental disasters, such as Chernobyl, the Aral Sea, and the Yangtze dam are excesses of centralized government but that is the solution many environmentalists propose. They dismiss, distrust, or seem unaware of alternatives to imposition. Tax incentives change behavior. Extending property rights can go a long way toward avoiding this "tragedy of the commons (Chapter 10)."

Environmentalists seem unaware of the practical difficulties and unintended consequences (Chapter 9) their proposals involve. Incorporation of resource destruction into national accounts such as GDP is a good idea, but harder than it seems with at least three theoretical approaches yielding entirely different results implying contradictory policies. Energy-efficient buildings tend to trap gasses and breed bacteria that make them less healthy. Old-growth trees remove much less CO_2 from the atmosphere than young ones. Global warming means longer growing seasons and less demand for heating fuel.

At times, environmentalists seem to have no sense of proportion, as when they advocate sacrificing the economy to restore a pristine environment, or when they equate failure to recycle with the Holocaust (Gore, 1992). However, environmentalists are right to insist upon the importance of the environment to our future. Neither government nor the market is likely to solve these problems alone. A wise effort combining the strengths and weaknesses of each is required.

God

From the perspective of the conflict theorist, theological history is the history of disputes over scripture, doctrine, and authority. Does God exist and how do we know? How many gods are there? What are the nature and attributes of God: should we be polytheists, dualists, henotheists, monotheists, agnostics, or atheists? How does God relate to Man and how must Man relate to God? How should we relate to people with different beliefs? Such questions are at the heart of hundreds of conflicts, some fought with words, some with swords.

Already by the end of the second century AD there were many forms of Christianity in conflict with one another. The question of authority was unsettled, with Christian communities organized in vastly different ways. Prelates of major Christian communities—primarily Alexandria, Antioch, Cairo, Constantinople, and Rome—struggled for primacy. The Bible did not exist as we know it till the end of the fourth century AD, the 27 books of the New Testament ultimately selected from nearly 70 candidates, including sixteen gospels in addition to Matthew, Mark, Luke, and John. *Ad hominem* attacks, forgeries, fabrications, and polemics flew back and forth along with learned argument (Ehrman, 2003).

The first general council of the Church met at Nicea in 325 AD, presided over by the Emperor Constantine, not yet officially a convert. The main question was the relationship among God, Jesus, and the Holy Spirit. The presbyter Arius admitted that a Holy Spirit became incarnate in Christ but insisted that it was a new, separately created being possessing a wholly different nature. To Bishop Athanasius this denied Christianity as a mystic religion of salvation.

We can imagine the bishops applying rhetorical skills and Greek logic to sacred texts in defense of their positions. We even can picture the ancient equivalent of smoke-filled back rooms in which some Cappadocian theologians mediated the dispute. They eventually worked out a compromise formula that the Council ratified in its formal sessions. This compromise was the doctrine of the Trinity to explain the relationship between God the Father, Christ the Son, and the Holy Spirit. It became the Nicene Creed, named after the location of the council. The Trinity was one substance of three persons. Most accepted the innovative but now orthodox formula, but there were exceptions. For example, Germanic tribes that converted to Christianity tended toward Arianism.

Settling one controversy merely opened another, specifically that of the relationship between Christ's human and divine nature. Doecetics, Ebionites, Marcionites, Monophysites, Nestorians, and Proto-orthodox contended between and among themselves as to whether and how Jesus combined the human and the divine. The Alexandrian theologians insisted that a single divine nature was required for salvation. Those of Constantinople, partly inspired by rivalry for precedence, insisted on Christ's human nature to emphasize the ethical challenges faced by humans. In much the same way as at Nicea, the bishops meeting at the Council of Chalcedon in 451 reached a compromise formula. "Jesus Christ, perfect in deity and perfect in humanity, God truly and man truly. [He is] of one substance with the Father in his deity and of one substance with us in his humanity. [We] acknowledge two natures without confusion, without change, without division, without separation; the distinction of the natures being by no means taken away because of the union but rather the property of each nature being preserved and concurring in one person" (Thompson and Johnson, 1937). This formula became orthodox east and west.

As in the previous and most subsequent cases, some refused the compromise. In this case, some adhered to the Alexandrian position, and formed the still extant Monophysite (*mono* = one, *physite* = being or nature) sect, while some adhered to the position of Constantinople and formed the still extant Nestorian (after Bishop Nestorius of Constantinople) sect. The people of the eastern empire remained much interested in theology, Gregory of Nyssa noting that you could hardly buy bread, change money, or go to the baths without getting into an esoteric theological discussion with a tradesman or even a slave.

Disputes in the declining western portion of the empire tended to be legalistic rather than metaphysical. Characteristic was the question of whether sacraments conducted by immoral priests were valid. The Donatists insisted they were not. Others including Augustine insisted that the character of the priest had nothing to do with the efficacy of the sacrament. The controversy echoes today whenever reformers are chided for being less than perfect human beings.

Augustine won the battle but not the war, which ultimately would give birth to Protestantism. The conflict resumed late in the twelfth century when laymen followers of Waldo took vows of poverty and inveighed against the immoral and worldly character of the clergy. At the Third Lateran council, Waldo obtained approval from the pope of their vow of poverty and permission to preach, provided they first got the consent of the local ecclesiastical authority. They largely ignored the provision and were condemned at the Council of Verona in 1184, along with the Cathars (or Albigensians).

The Albigensians dominated southwestern France from castles such as Montsegur and Puylaurens whose ruins remain tourist attractions today. Their heresy turned on another great conflict within Christianity, the problem of how evil could exist if the Creator was all knowing and all good. The orthodox explanation was a falling away from divine grace, as Satan, originally an angel, had done through pride, ambition, and disobedience. The Albigensian answer was an Evil God in opposition to the Good God. At the risk of simplification, this heretical dualism originated with Zoroaster and came west via the Manicheans of Iraq and Bogomils of the Balkans. The Albigensians predicted the ultimate victory of the Good but until then Evil would preside over the world of matter.

The Albigensians appeared early in the eleventh century and were condemned early in the twelfth. When Innocent III's efforts at conversion failed, he ordered a crusade in 1209 to stamp out the heresy. The crusade pitted the nobility of northern France against that of southern France and was as much political as religious. The resulting Treaty of Paris (1229) destroyed the independence of the southern princes. The Church initiated the Inquisition in 1233 to root out the surviving heretics, and backed it with a second crusade, led by Louis IX. The destruction of the fortress at Montsegur in 1244 drove what was left of the movement underground, and the Albigensians slowly dwindled, finally disappearing in the fifteenth century.

These few examples from among many theological conflicts illustrate the methods the Catholic church used to deal with intellectual conflicts. The primary tools for dealing with theological conflict have been the authority of the bishops (and later the pope) and debate in councils. Mediators among the participants often worked to find compromise formulas. A majority usually accepted the result but a few diehards usually refused to go along, leading to schism. For a brief period, the Church relied on force in the form of crusades and the Inquisition. The abstract and obscure theological arguments of the medieval scholastics no longer interest an increasingly secular world, but they are echoed in recent disputes such as the ordination of women, pedophile priests, and stem cell research.

The Importance of Dissent

As destructive as some of these intellectual conflicts were, repression of dissent is even more costly. We saw this in the spate of corporate corruption in the 1990s (*e.g.*, Adelphia, Enron, Tyco, WorldCom) when directors approved executive wishes with little or no discussion. We saw it in the planning for the Bay of Pigs from which the Postmaster General was excluded as irrelevant although he was the only Cabinet member with covert warfare experience during World War II and nobody else expressed any concerns for fear of being labeled "soft" on communism.[8] The same thing may have happened in assessing intelligence regarding Iraqi possession of weapons of mass destruction.

These "cascades" occur when larger and larger numbers of peoples follow the lead of a few early proponents. Christianity and Islam are examples but so are fascism, witch-hunts, and teen fads. That is, people can just as easily converge on harmful or erroneous instead of beneficial or correct decisions. When early leaders are articulate, charismatic, and confident, they frame and control the debate. Cascades begin when people are swept up by the momentum instead of exercising independent judgment (Sunstein, 2003). Sometimes, particularly when individuals can leave the group, schism occurs, as we have seen resulting from church councils.

We admire the lone dissenter who courageously stands up for what is right and gradually wins people to his side—the Henry Fonda part in *Twelve Angry Men*. Dissenters are not always right, but creating an atmosphere in which they feel comfortable speaking their minds is the best device we have to identify the flaws in any idea. GE president Jack Welch (*Wall Street Journal*, 28 October 2004) wrote that whenever he faced a crisis he made sure to assemble "a group of the smartest, gutsiest people I could find at any level from within the company and sometimes without [and] make sure everyone in the room came at the problem from a different angle." These sessions were contentious, but they surfaced meaningful questions, challenged assumptions, and led to better decisions. Objections can be major or minor, probable or improbable, fixable or fatal.

A surprisingly large proportion of the boards of corporations and the cabinets of prime ministers and presidents have 12-15 members. Teachers asked the best class size to promote discussion will come up with similar numbers. Smaller groups seem not to be diverse enough, and larger ones seem to promote conformity. Simplifying a task, assigning self-confident people with records of decisiveness and achievement, providing resources such as staff to thoroughly explore alternatives, and putting multiple teams to work on the same problem all encourage diversity and dissent. Strong norms against leaking encourage frank discussions. Making individual rewards, economic or otherwise, dependent on the success of a group decision can counteract social pressure to conform. Finally, dispensing with rank, as World War II British scientists and military did in "Sunday Soviets" to find quick fixes to problems faced by the troops, can contribute to successful problem solving (Jones, 1978).

---

8. Conversation with former Postmaster General Arthur Goldberg.

Conclusion

Ideas play a larger role in conflict than our theorists, with their roots in the social sciences and their tendencies toward positivistic or even ideological explanation of human behavior, tend to acknowledge. Some are resolved through research and improved understanding. Events resolve others. Still others seem unlikely of resolution beyond temporary accommodation. Conflict theory must accommodate this reality if it is to be comprehensive.

Chapter 12
Causes of War

Nations don't fear each other because they are armed.
They are armed because they fear each other.

—Ronald Reagan

Much of what we have said so far about the causes of aggression and conflict also applies to war. Beyond that, theorists have suggested eleven other explanations that we discuss in this chapter.

Ecological Equilibrium

Marvin Harris (1974) suggests that war maintains "ecological equilibrium" in primitive cultures. War, he says based on his study of highland tribes in New Guinea, is a method of bringing the population back into line with resources even if the participants do not understand that is what is going on. War breaks out whenever population size reaches the carrying capacity of the land. It both reduces the population and allows the land to lie fallow long enough to recover. Harris asserts that primitive war is adaptive, although he does not make the same claim for modern war. Ecological equilibrium may explain the origin of war, but not its continuance. Harris (1980) further suggests that Freud may have had it backwards: that the Oedipus complex, if it exists at all, is not an inevitable expression of human nature but a predictable outcome of training males to be combative and "masculine," whereas warfare is caused by ecological and political-economic stresses (Harris, 1980).

The low casualty rates in the battles, their short duration compared to the time required for land to recover its fertility, and the existence of war in primitive societies with no shortage of resources suggest that Harris's theory is at best incomplete and at worst invalid.

Reproductive Success

Some theorists explain primitive war by "reproductive success." The idea is consistent with Jane Goodall's report of "Chimpanzee War" and with sociobiological thinking (Chapter 3). Napoleon Chagnon (1990) notes that Yanomamo men who have killed at least one other person have twice as many wives and children as those who have not. In a sample of 87 hunter-gather wars, women were the direct cause in 39 and obtaining bride prices was the direct cause in 35 cases. The evidence supports Berndt & Berndt's (1951) view that "the majority of arguments in an aboriginal society are directly or indirectly brought about through trouble over women". If the evidence of living peoples can illuminate human evolution (Wright, 1942), it suggests that males regularly fought over females. This may be reduced to a syllogism:

> Organisms strive to pass on their own genes.
> The limiting resource for males is females (the opposite is not true)
> Male possessiveness insures that only some males mate.
> Consequently, there is fierce competition among males for females.

Such a milieu is unlikely to favor simple male belligerence. Accurate risk assessment and the ability to lead, and therefore oratorical, tactical and strategic skills undoubtedly were as important as courage and aggressiveness (van der Dennen, n.d.) in attracting females.

Territorial Imperative

A territory is an area that an animal guards against all members of its own kind except its mate as its exclusive possession. Dramatist and anthropologist Robert Ardrey (1966) combined this well-known concept with Maslow's needs theory (Chapter 4). Territory—a home—provides security, stimulation, and identity. Ardrey argues that the same is true for war, which gives everyone identity in the form of rank, stimulation ("moments of sheer terror amidst endless hours of sheer boredom" as soldiers put it), and security for one's family, tribe or country. As one can be killed providing security, it may be altruistic, which Ardrey asserts evolves from the existence of territory and a family to protect, a notion consistent with but predating sociobiology (Chapter 3).

Relative Deprivation

Gurr (1970) attributes civil and revolutionary wars to Relative Deprivation, a "perception of the discrepancy between value expectations and value capabilities." Expectations are the conditions of life to which people feel entitled. Capabilities are the goods and services people think their society can and should provide. Revolution occurs when a feeling of unjust deprivation spreads throughout society. In effect, the theory is a group version of frustration aggression influenced human needs theory and the hydraulic model (Chapter 4). The idea is not new. Aristotle held that democracies and oligarchies were prone to this sort of revolution because the common people aspired to economic or political equality while the ruling elite aspired to increase their advantage.

Over time expectations and capabilities in a society could improve, remain stable, or decline independently of one another, giving $3^2 = 9$ possible patterns. According to Gurr, three of them increase the likelihood of revolution. The first, "decremental deprivation," describes the situation in which group expectations remain constant but the productive capabilities of the society decline. The collapse of the Soviet Union seems to provide an example. Russian expectations did not seem to change much with the fall of communism, but the unexpected economic collapse did cause considerable discontent, many demanding a return to communism.

The second pattern, "aspirational deprivation," describes the situation in which capabilities remain relatively static while expectations increase. The twentieth century saw much of this, as people were disabused by reality of their naïve expectation that they automatically would become rich and free with the departure of their colonial masters.

The third pattern, "progressive deprivation," describes the situation in which capabilities decline and expectations increase. The US Civil Rights movement provides an example. Black income and education increased rapidly during the 1940s and 1950s, then began to decline, so that by 1960 half the gains had disappeared. That is, expectations were rising while capabilities were declining, leading to the relatively peaceful revolution of the Civil Rights movement.

While measures such as GDP work reasonably well in cash economies, measuring capability in economies that include a high proportion of non-cash transactions is difficult. Measuring expectations, which vary wildly both within and across cultures is even more difficult, despite several efforts to do so and to correlate results with the outbreak of revolution or civil war. The difficulty of effective measurement of one of its two independent variables leaves the theory supported by little more than anecdotal evidence such as that given above. There has been still less success in identifying how much of a decline in capabilities or rise in expectations must occur before unrest breaks out. Finally, Gurr acknowledges that other patterns may also lead to revolution. These problems seriously weaken the theory, however compelling it may otherwise be.

Nation-States

The United Nations was established in no small part on the assumption that nation states are the cause of war, and that an international body could help prevent wars between them. As Kenneth Waltz puts it, "With many sovereign states, with no system of law enforceable among them, with each state judging its grievances and ambitions according to its own reason or desire, conflict, sometimes leading to war, is bound to occur." But, it is possible to have strong nationalistic feelings and yet avoid war, Sweden and Switzerland being the usual examples.

War certainly dates from 3000 BC and probably is five millennia older than that (Chapter 13). This is long before the emergence of the modern nation-state system, which dates from 1648 in Europe and from 1945 in the rest of the world. Nation state wars are a minority of the nearly 300 wars fought from 1945–2000, many of which have been some combination of anti-colonial, civil, ethnic, Marxist, or religious wars.

Sometimes it even is difficult to know what is and is not a nation state. In the 1990s, Coca-Cola claimed sales in 195 countries excluding Iraq, Libya and Cuba, making a total of 198 nation states worldwide. The Statesman's Yearbook (2003) lists 191. The Universal Postal Union has 189 members in 2005 (www.upu.int) excluding Taiwan. The 2004 Olympics included 201 countries, including Hong Kong, up from the 197 that participated in 2000. The United Nations has 191 members, Switzerland finally having joined in 2002. Soviet satellites such as Kazakhstan were admitted as nations—not because anyone thought they really were independent at the time although they have become so since, but to "balance" western voting strength. Pinpoints such as Andorra and Saint Lucia are members; Taiwan, with the eleventh biggest economy in the world, is not.

The Turkish Republic of North Cyprus has many of the trappings of a state and claims to be one but is recognized only by Turkey. Nagorno-Karabakh and Abkhazia have claimed independence that is recognized by no other nation. The latter is unrecognized even by Russia, which both fomented its existence and blockades it. Sealand has its own constitution, currency, flag, passport, stamps, and website. Its passport, often forged, is much in demand, and it is doing a booming business licensing often dubious Internet companies. A *Monty Python* country if there ever was one, Sealand is six miles off the English coast, a steel and concrete WWII antiaircraft tower governed, since they "liberated" it in 1967, by Major and Mrs. Roy Bates. Even smaller but more widely recognized, the Sovereign Military Hospitaller Order of St. John of Jerusalem, Rhodes and Malta has diplomatic ties with 87 countries and hopes to become a UN member. It has its own license plates, issues postage stamps, passports and currency, and runs dozens of hospitals and clinics worldwide. Descended from a medieval order of crusaders, its sovereign territory is a second floor office suite in the Palazzo Malta at 68 *via de condotti* in Rome. It is unclear just what a country is, and equally unclear how many of them there really are.

The assertion that modern nationalism and the nation-state lead naturally to mass warfare is dubious. It now appears that mass warfare and its associated dogma of the "decisive battle" was a phase that lasted about two hundred years, from the French Revolution until the end of the Cold War. Popular sovereignty and the return to professional armies in recent years have mitigated the trend.

Characteristics of States

If the nation-state system does not provide much of an explanation for war, are there individual states that are particularly prone to war—the so-called "bad seed" idea. A few nations account for most of the wars in the 150 years following the defeat of Napoleon (Singer and Small, 1972). But, Naroll (1969), taking a much wider view, found that over a 2000 year period that states that took expressly defensive postures were involved in just as many wars as more war-like ones.

On the other side of the coin, some theorists argue democracies and republics are less prone to war, particularly against one another, than other forms of government. However, Athens and Sparta and Rome and Carthage, fought one another bitterly for years. Some phases of the on-again, off-again 1830–1999 war between Peru and Ecuador began when both had elected governments. The El Salvador-Honduran "Football War" of 1969 is another exception. Other militarized disputes between democracies, all in the 1990s, include Guatemala and Belize, Guyana and Suriname, Venezuela with Guyana, Trinidad-Tobago, and Colombia, Nicaragua with Colombia, Costa Rica, El Salvador and Honduras, and Honduras with El Salvador and Guatemala (Dominguez, 2003). Some might regard the wars between India and Pakistan as exceptions, although calling Pakistan a democracy is a stretch. Poland and Germany had democratically elected governments in the 1930s, although Hitler was ruling as a dictator by the time he invaded Poland. All-in-all, considering the small number of democracies and republics that existed simultaneously and within fighting distance of one another, there seem to be enough exceptions to falsify the claim that idea that democracies do not make war on one another.

Numerous studies have attempted to determine more generally whether there are characteristics that make a state prone to war. These studies focus on different periods or lengths of time and consider a vast number of different dependent and independent variables. Rummel (1968) is typical of such studies. He correlated 235 cultural, demographic, economic, geographic, political and sociological characteristics of nations and 13 measures of foreign conflict behavior. None of these studies identified any statistically significant relationship between characteristics of states and war proneness.

Polarity

Some theorists suggest that the stability of the "international system" is determined by the number of "great powers" or "poles" at any given time. A nonpolar system is logically possible but historically rare. Ferguson (2004) cites the ninth-tenth centuries AD as the only good historical example. Rome had collapsed, Byzantium had receded,[1] Viking raiders ranged widely, the Abbasid Empire was breaking up and China was in chaos. India was divided among several minor but well-run states, so is an exception to the chaos elsewhere. The end of Bronze age civilization around 1200 BC seems to qualify as well. Harrapan civilization had collapsed in India. The last vestiges of Egyptian power and achievement had ended with the twentieth dynasty. The Hittites had disappeared, Babylon had fallen and the Assyrians had not yet emerged as a major

---

1. Ferguson overlooks the Byzantine revival under the Macedonian dynasty.

power. Greece was entering its dark age, and the Canaanites and Israelis were competing in the Levant and the mysterious "Sea Peoples" raided widely.

The *Pax Romana* is the classic example of a uni-polar world. It is of particular interest because the post-Cold War period also is uni-polar, the United States being the only power with global reach. Rome emerged from its struggle with Carthage as the greatest power in the Mediterranean. It became an empire more by accident than design. When Augustus came to power, he halted the expansion of an empire that then extended from Spain to Iraq and from the Rhine to the Sahara and established a peace that lasted a century and a half.

A common language, a law code that is one of the great intellectual achievements of mankind, and unsurpassed engineering skills translated into a system of roads, aqueducts, and fortifications that combined to insure peace within the Roman empire. The elite enjoyed a common high culture. A highly trained professional army kept the peace—but was almost continually at war to do so. These were small wars fought by hardened professionals on the fringes of the empire, hardly noticed by the majority of the citizens. They were like the wars the British army fought in Asia and Africa during the nineteenth century or the American army fought in Central America and the Caribbean in the twentieth and the Middle East in the late twentieth and early twenty-first centuries.

The era of peace begun by Augustus collapsed with Marcus Aurelius. Caligula had exposed the flaw in the law: the emperors were above it. Claudius, Trajan, and Hadrian resumed expansion of the empire, requiring an expanded army that was beyond the capability of the Roman economy to sustain. Despite Roman engineering skills, industry remained primitive. Slavery kept wages low and high taxes drove free peasants off their lands and into the cities where there were no jobs. Commerce withered, cities decayed and civil unrest grew. Formidable barbarian armies began to appear along the Rhine and the Danube. Many have asked if current efforts to extend the *Pax Americana* to the Middle East will prove a similar over-reach.

Realist theory predicts that a uni-polar world is unstable, secondary powers uniting against the dominant one. There were no such other powers in Rome's day, but there are many today. China, India, Russia, and the European Union all are potential counterweights from which a new bi- or multi-polar balance of power might emerge.[2] The perception (true or false) that the United States acts unilaterally could hasten such a development. In other words, despite the absence of major inter-state wars, the international environment remains anarchic, and states will protect themselves as best as they can.

Intense rivalry characterizes bi-polar systems such as the Cold War era. The competition is not always direct: each power will seek allies through defections

2. Unity of policy among EU states may prove an elusive ideal. Early in the twenty-first century, former eastern block nations tended to follow the US lead, Mediterranean nations tended to take their cue from Britain, and Belgium, Germany and Russia often followed the French lead.

from the other camp while preventing defections from its own, and by drawing neutrals into its orbit. Intervention on opposite sides in internal crises is common, particularly in states that have important resources or are strategically located (Chapter 13).

Historical examples of bi-polar systems include the Egyptian-Hittite, Greek then Macedonian-Persian, Roman-Carthaginian, Sasanian-Byzantine, Ottoman-Byzantine, and US-USSR rivalries. Wars were frequent in all six periods. The first ended with the collapse of both rivals. The fourth ended with the collapse of one and the severely reduced power of the other before the rising tide of Islam. The second-named power was destroyed in the remaining four cases. Conflict theorists have given most attention to the rivalry between the United States and the USSR (1947–1989). The Cold War sometimes is called the "Long Peace" because the two major powers never fought one another directly. However, nearly 300 wars began during the Cold War, taking in total the same 50,000,000 lives as World War II itself. War was averted in about 250 additional cases, for an average of nearly a dozen new wars or crises for each year of the Cold War!

For some, US and Soviet restraint in crises that threatened escalation into direct hostilities is insufficient proof that nuclear deterrence kept the war "cold." These critics say that nuclear weapons are merely the last in a long line of inventions predicted to end war, none of which has ever done so. The best evidence that nuclear weapons did deter war may be the Cuban Missile Crisis. [3] Arbatov (1990) argued that nuclear weapons exacerbated tensions—but this is exactly how they keep the peace. None of these and similar arguments are very convincing. Every other bi-polar system in history saw direct conflict.

Some theorists have developed logical arguments as to why multi-polar systems are prone to war primarily because there are so many ways to miscalculate and so many ways for them to become imbalanced. Other theorists have replied with equal logic that the very difficulty of judging strength and reliability makes states less willing to risk war. Alliances change constantly in multi-polar systems, usually with no one change making a major difference in the overall balance. Rather, it is an indication of the ability of the system to maintain a balance and minimize the number and severity of wars. A third group maintains that multi-power periods are characterized by small wars among combinations of small states but that they usually are ended by the rise of a new great power (Figure 12.1).

No multi-polar systems were peaceful, although just how many wars there were for some of the earlier periods is not always clear. Of the first six systems identified, two ended with the rise to hegemony of local contenders and four ended by outside conquest. The Mayan system seems to have ended due to ecological collapse. Of the remaining six, one ended with a change in polarity, lead-

---

3. The Cuban Missile Crisis was by general consent the closest the US and USSR came to nuclear war with one another.

ing to the Cold War and a bipolar world. The other five ended with about thirty wars over 375 years that did not change the situation much.[4] That is, as Doran (1991) has argued, the hierarchy persists, but the rank order of states changes within it. The catastrophic wars that punctuate the system may reflect failure of the system to cope with this rise and decline.

System	Period	Minor States	Terminating Event
Sumer	3000—2350 BC	City states: Eridu, Kish, Lagash, Nippur, Umma, Ur	Akkadian Empire
Near East	1900—1200	Regional empires: Assyria, Babylon, Egypt, Hittites, Mitanni	Barbarian invasions
China	771—221	Warring states: Ch'u, Ch'in, Han, Wei, Ch'I, Yen,	Ch'in Empire
Greek nian Empire	700—338	City states: Athens, Corinth, Sparta, Syracuse, Thebes	Macedo-
India	232BC—320 AD	Regional empires: Gandhara, Surashtra, Mulaka	Gupta Empire
Maya collapse	300—900	City states: Copan, Palenque, Tikal, Uaxactum	Ecological
Italy	1300—1494	City states: Florence, Genoa, Milan, Naples, Papal States, Venice	French invasion
Europe	1495—1618	Regional kingdoms: Austria, England, France, Netherlands, Portugal, Spain	Thirty Years War
Europe	1648—1702	Early state system: Austria, England, France, Netherlands, Spain, Sweden	War of the Spanish Succession
Europe	1715—1792	Early state system: Austria, England, France, Prussia, Russia, Spain, Sweden	Napoleonic Wars
Europe	1815—1914	Modern states: Austria, France, England, Italy, Japan, Prussia, Russia, US	World War I
Europe	1919—1939	Modern states: France, England, Germany, Italy, Japan, USSR, US	World War II

Figure 12.1

---

4. Excluding wars fought by great powers against lesser ones, wars that lesser powers fought against one another, or wars of revolution and independence.

Multi-polar Periods in History[5]

Making allowance for differences in historical circumstances, polarity does not seem a particularly useful concept in understanding peace and war, even if it is dressed up with consideration of additional variables such as "tightness" of alliances at the expense of parsimony. War was common under all four possible types of polarity.

Number of Bordering States

In a similar vein to polarity theory, some theorists (*e.g.*, Midlarsky, 1975; Garnham, 1976) have suggested that the more neighbors a state has the more likely it is to find itself in a war. In pursuit of this concept or variations of it, researchers have tried to correlate wars with variables such as the distance between capitals, the length of the frontiers measured in population units, fuel consumption, and steel production.

The basic concept seems to state the obvious. States are more likely to find themselves in disputes with neighboring than with distant states and the more of them there are the more likely are the number of disputes. Devising additional measures seems more likely to produce spurious correlations than significant understanding.

Arms Races

Lewis Richardson's work on arms races has dominated serious discussion of the arms race theory since its publication in 1960 (although his research was done much earlier). He was a British patriot and conscientious objector who served in WW 1 as an ambulance driver. A brilliant scientist, he pursued work in physics and meteorology after the war and was elected a fellow of the Royal Society. He retired from these pursuits to study the cause of war.

Richardson brought the natural science model for theory building to his study of war. His four-step approach demonstrates a sophisticated, systematic approach to theory building and testing that is all too rare in the social sciences.

First, he identified key concepts to be used as the basic independent and dependent variables of his theory. Think of the former as inputs and the latter as outputs. The dependent variable is the concern, in the current case, quantities of armaments, and the independent variables are the factors to take into account in predicting it. Second, Richardson made specific assumptions about the relationships among the variables. For example, he assumed that the more difficult it was to produce a weapon, the fewer there would be of them, which makes general sense. In effect, this variable combines cost and technology. Third, he put these assumptions into mathematical form—that is, he attempted a parsimonious

---

5. Adapted from Kegley & Raymond, 1994

explanation of the phenomenon under study. This was a common practice in the physical sciences as early as Ptolemy but relatively new to social scientists when Richardson was doing his research. Fourth, he tested his model using data from real wars.

Richardson's conclusions were published in *Statistics of Deadly Quarrels,* in 1960, seven years after his death. He wrapped everything up in a formula for country x reacting to a potential enemy y:

$$dx/dt = ay - mx + g$$

That is, the *change* in armament levels of nation x (symbolized by *dx*) over a period of time (*dt*) is a function of three factors: the reaction to the threat of another country (*ay*), the difficulty of producing arms (*mx*) and the extent of accumulated grievances (*g*). A similar equation represents the changes of arms on the other side:

$$dy/dt = bx - nx + h$$

It now is a straightforward procedure to combine these two equations for analysis. We then can grind out the logical consequences using historical data on the independent variables (*ay, bx, mx, nx, g* and *h*), and compare the results (*dx/dt* and *dy/dt*) with what actually is happening in the world to see if the theory describes reality. It is exactly the same procedure that many first year physics students have experienced in testing the theory of gravity by timing the fall of objects from buildings or the periods of pendulums of various lengths. However, quantifying variables such as "accumulated grievances" is a lot more difficult and subjective than weighing objects and measuring length, opening the theory to *post hoc* "fudging" to make things come out right. This is why replication, particularly using arms races that took place after Richardson's book was published, is essential to testing the theory.

Richardson derived four possibilities from his analysis of arms races:

1. The two sides move quickly to a stable equilibrium. This happens when factors such as cost outweigh the accumulation of grievances.
2. The sides move quickly toward total disarmament. This happens when goodwill outweighs grievances: g and h are negative. Braking factors and costs outweigh reactivity.
3. The runaway arms race. This happens when we start with an accumulation of grievances and the reactivity (a and b) outweigh the braking factors (m and n).
4. Indeterminacy. The result could be either disarmament or runaway arms race depending on initial armaments levels.

Richardson predicts all three possible outcomes of an arms race and throws in a fourth to cover anything he might have missed, providing only ambiguous suggestions as to which is most likely in specific situations. In the subsequent debates, only one of the four possibilities is given any credence—that arms races lead to war. In this vein, the Fall 1960 *Canadian Army Journal* reported that:

> Computations made on an electronic computer by a former president of the Norwegian Academy of Sciences, aided by historians from England, Egypt, German and India, have produced some astounding figures on the frequency and severity of wars. Included in these findings is the fact that since 3600 B.C., the world has known only 292 years of peace. During this period there have been 14,531 wars, large and small, in which 3,640,000,000 people have been killed. The value of the destruction would pay for a golden belt around the earth 156 kilometers in width and 10 meters thick Since 650 B.C. there have been 1656 arms races, only 16 of which have not ended in war. The remainder have ended in economic collapse.

It may be true that there have only been 292 years (or some similar small number) of total peace—but most wars have been local and most of the world was at peace at any given time. Even World War II left South America, and most of Africa untouched (although some troops from both did participate). If instead one counted the number of states at peace each year, war would appear rare rather than common. For example, since 1815, approximately 150 states never experienced war and approximately 50 experienced only one or two brief ones. Only nine (Britain, Egypt, France, Germany, Greece, Italy, Russia, Turkey and the United States) were involved in ten or more, and even they experienced more years of peace than of war.

However, that is a quibble. The real interest of this article was in the way arms races were defined, identified, and assessed. An inquiry directed to the Norwegian Academy requesting a reprint or source for the original resulted in a handwritten reply eight weeks later on a post-it attached to the original letter:

Dear Professor Cherchman,

We return yr. letter of 21/3-88. No such study has taken place, as far as we know. The story must have been made up. We are sorry for the late answer, it took us some time to find this out.

24/5-88

Yours sincerely

Det Norske Videnskaps-Akademi

Anne S. Lind

No better reason for skeptical reading and replicating research and the importance of falsification emphasized in Chapter 1 could have come to light!

Third, as any first semester statistics student knows, correlation does not prove causation. There is, for example, a correlation between stock market prices and skirt lengths that leads to the adage, "Do not sell until you see the whites of their thighs," but it is unlikely that miniskirts are the cause of a rising Dow-Jones average or vice-versa. It is true that World War I was preceded by a vast increase in arms expenditures. French and British spending on armaments doubled, and German spending increased ten-fold. Inconveniently for the arms race thesis, non-defense spending increased even faster! Even more inconveniently, nations that never got into World War I, such as Sweden and Switzerland, also vastly increased their arms spending. Finally, we now have access to the minutes of German cabinet meetings leading up to World War I, and now know that Germany knowingly risked a general war but hoped for a limited one. The war was neither accidental nor unforeseen. In short, increased armaments did not change or drive policies of the regimes amassing them.

The Richardson model has been modified over the years. For example, Michael Intriligator (2000) proposed taking greater account of economies of scale and changes in technology. For, as Lewis Richardson wrote, "Another advantage of a mathematical statement is that it is so definite that it might be definitely wrong; and if it is found to be wrong, there is a plenteous choice of amendments ready in the mathematicians' stock of formulae. Some verbal statements have not this merit; they are so vague that they could hardly be wrong, and are correspondingly useless."

Correlates of War

David Singer and Melvin Small of the University of Michigan initiated the Correlates of War project in 1963. The basic strategy was to (1) define "war" operationally, (2) collect all sorts of statistical data about every war from the fall of Napoleon to the present, (3) and search the data for variables correlated with the outbreak of war. This is similar to the steps Richardson took (see above), except that Singer and Small did not assume, but sought to identify, causes of war. It was an incredibly bold undertaking at a time when the most advanced computers were about as capable as the computer chip in the average refrigerator forty years later. Yet the approach proved so fertile that it shaped much subsequent research generated dozens of books and hundreds of journal articles and book chapter, and created the possibility of making better decisions.

War was operationally defined as a military conflict waged between national entities, at least one of which is a state, which results in at least 1000 battle-deaths of military personnel. The original analyses were based on data covering wars taking place from 1816–1965. The time frame has since been extended at least for some analyses as far back as 1495 and as far forward as 1992). Data was recorded such as start and end dates, location, battle deaths, total deaths, pre-war population, pre-war armed forces, initiator, nature (interstate, colonial, or imperial war), and political status of combatants. Civil wars were coded separately with data including dates, location, intervention by outside powers, their political status and on what side they intervened, who won, battle deaths, total population, and total number of pre-war armed forces. These massive data were then explored to test virtually every hypothesis anyone could devise, even astrological ones. The unsurprising answer in that case was "no connection" but other questions produced more fruitful results.

That is, the Correlates of War Project is a search for consistent empirical patterns rather than an argument for some one particular explanation of war. It is inductive rather than deductive. That is, it collects data and searches for a pattern rather than imagines a pattern then searches for supporting data. Both methods are valid and necessary, and most researchers spend their careers, as Geller and Singer (1988) put it, working both sides of the street. "That is," they continue, "[sometimes] we get general ideas from all sorts of stimuli and try to think of examples that support or question them, and [sometimes] we encounter all sorts of facts and ask which generalizations can be drawn from or refuted by them." The resulting publications surrender this complexity for the sake of clarity. Or, as T. E. Lawrence put it, "These [thoughts about guerrilla strategy and tactics] would have been too long if written down; and the argument has been compressed into an abstract form in which it smells more of the lamp than the field. All military writing does, worse luck."

The major findings of the Correlates of War Project and the many research studies stemming from it may be divided into four main categories, beginning with those pertaining to individual states. The evidence reveals the lack of a connection between wars and business cycle, form of government, geographic size, population density, and total population. There is weak evidence of a link between domestic and foreign conflict, although there is no consistent cause for this from one case to another. Domestic violence may break out to protest a war but the government may try to divert domestic discontent by engaging in a foreign war.

There appears to be a strong relationship between war and both capabilities for war and number of alliances. Major powers are more likely to engage in war than are minor ones, and they are more likely to fight severe wars. Highly militarized societies (customarily measured by the ratios of military personnel to population and defense expenditures to GNP) lean toward aggressive foreign policy. Alliances probably are a result rather than a cause of war: that is, states logically enough seek alliances when they feel threatened.

The second major set of conclusions pertains to pairs of countries. At the economic level, there exists the long-standing idea that there is a positive correlation between peace and economic development, free trade and market economies. This idea is corroborated by a study of Correlation of War data in conjunction with trade data from sources such as the UN and IMF. At the political level, there are three long-standing but contradictory findings. First, balance of power theory (see below) maintains that relative parity deters war because victory becomes problematic. Second, power preponderance theory maintains that relative parity encourages war because both sides see a prospect for victory. Third, power transition theory maintains that war is more likely under conditions of changing capabilities—that is, the erosion of a dominant nation's capability or the rise of a new power. Researchers using the Correlates of War database found disputes more often led to war under the second condition. But, by incorporating such factors as attitude toward risk, Expected Utility Theory (see below) comes to a conclusion more nearly supportive of the first position using the same data. To thoroughly confuse the situation, proponents of the third position have used the same data to estimate that capability shifts within a rival dyad significantly increase the odds that a dispute will end in war.

The third major set of conclusions pertains to world regions, defined as the five most populated continents. Over the past two centuries, major rather than minor powers have been the most likely to be involved in military action, and those actions are more likely to be severe. In the decades since 1945, regional shifts in the frequencies of interstate conflict have become evident, with the newer regional subsystems of sub-Saharan Africa and Asia accounting for the majority of militarized interstate disputes. The thesis that wars occur in cycles of one sort or another has been tested primarily in Europe, where most evidence for them tends to disappear under careful scrutiny.

The fourth major set of conclusions takes a systems view of war. Since 1816 the number of wars has increased but so has the number of countries, the ratio remaining constant. With regard to great power wars, the tendency from the end of the fifteenth century to the last quarter of the twentieth century has reflected a decrease in the number of wars but an increase in their destructiveness. Some formal efforts, like the Peace of Westphalia and the Congress of Vienna, were very successful in resolving the issues that led to war and mitigating future conflict, but others such as the Versailles system have been disastrous, so that the prospects for keeping the peace through intergovernmental organizations are not hopeful.

As with any groundbreaking study, the Correlates of War project has been both damned and praised for its operational definitions, for the variables chosen for or omitted from the study, for the chronological framework, the analytical methods used and the hypotheses tested, which is to say just about every aspect of the study. These criticisms may be divided into technical and theoretical objections, the latter being the more important for our purposes.

The study can be viewed as a search for variables that are the most significant for a study of war. That is, it echoes Galileo's effort (Chapter 1) to identify a few key variables with great explanatory power. The Correlates of War project focused on states so is related to the research described above on characteristics of states. However, many wars since 1945 have involved non-state "actors." Even accepting the chronological framework of the project, the technology of war has changed radically over the last two hundred years. Its wars have been fought for many different purposes by many different kinds of forces. Finally, humans are likely to use anything science learns to their own advantage, making the object of study itself a variable. This is a significant problem for the study of all human behavior and for the social sciences in general.

Despite these difficulties, the Correlates of War meets three tests of good theory. It is falsifiable, parsimonious and usable. Whether or not it is generalizable remains to be seen. Regardless of the outcome of that debate, it changed the way we study war and provided a starting point for other thinkers.

Expected Utility

Bueno de Mesquita's (1981) "Expected Utility Theory" grew out of the Correlates of War project and like it has become required reading for anyone interested in international conflict. Expected Utility Theory assumes that leaders choose war only when they expect to gain more than they would by pursuing *any* alternative. Over time, it has become integrated with game-theoretic approaches (Bueno de Mesquita and Lalman, 1992). The core assumptions are:

1. Decision makers are instrumentally rational.[6] Given three choices and connectivity (A > B > C), transitivity implies that the decision maker will prefer A to C. That is, an instrumentally rational decision-makers can order or rank, but need not be able to rate, their preferences)
2. Decision makers consider options in terms of probabilities associated with possible outcomes multiplied by utilities associated with those outcomes.
3. Decision makers choose the option with the highest expected utility.

The equation for the expected utility of a challenge to the existing policy is:

$$E(U)_c = P_s (U_s) + (_1 - P_s)(U_f)$$

Where:

$E(U)_c$ = expected utility of challenging the policy
P_s = probability of successful challenge
U_s = utility of successful challenge
U_f = utility of failed challenge

The equation for the expected utility of *not* challenging the status quo is:

$$E(U)_{nc} = P_q U_q + (1 - P_q) [P_b U_b + (_1 - P_b)(U_w)$$

Where:

$E(U)_{nc}$ = expected utility of not challenging the policy
P_q = probability that the policy will not change
U_q = utility of the policy
P_b = probability that the policy will change with positive utility
U_b = utility of a positive policy change
U_w = utility of a negative policy change

The overall expected utility then becomes simply the difference between the two equations:

$$E(U) = E (U)_c - E (U)_{nc}$$

Which is to say, it is rational to initiate a war when the expected gains exceed the value of continuing the current peaceful policy. That is, a necessary, but

---

6. Instrumental rationality requires connectivity and transitivity. Connectivity implies that a decision maker can state whether he is indifferent to or prefers one alternative to another (that is A preferred to B, B preferred to A, or indifferent between A and B). Transitivity implies that a decision maker who prefers A to B and B to C prefers A to C.

not a sufficient condition for starting a war is that the expected utility of victory must be greater than the expected utility of defeat.

De Mesquita does *not* claim that leaders actually work through these equations in making decisions, any more than, say, a rock calculates how fast it should fall by consulting Newton's formula. Rather, he claims, the formula predicts how leaders will act regardless of what factors they actually consider. Most theories of human behavior have this characteristic: that is, they explain behavior rather than guide it.

De Mesquita tested his ideas by using the Correlates of War data for 251 conflicts and crises from 1816 to 1974 in which the aggressor was clear. He incorporated both attitude toward risk and relative power into the formula determining utility, after considerable work developing methods to measure each. Aggressors won 75% of the wars they started. The formula predicts most of the losses: that is, the leader made a mistake in choosing war. The most recent significant example of such a mistake was Saddam Hussein's invasion of Kuwait (with the threat of continuing into Saudi Arabia). He may have failed to understand how the end of the Cold War eliminated the risk of World War that he thought would protect him. Of the remaining cases, where the aggressor "should" have won but did not, the expected utility scores of the adversaries are so close as to lie within the margin of statistical error. None of this should come as much of a surprise. Leaders simply do not go to war lightly, although their reasons for accepting or avoiding the risk and the amount of risk they can tolerate may vary considerably.

Expected utility theory has been criticized both for improper application of rational choice assumptions in foreign policy and for the statistical evidence supporting the model. The criticism has been particularly pronounced with regard to some of the operational indicators used to measure elements in the model. Nevertheless, it remains one of the most important constructs in the analysis of war decisions (Geller and Singer, 1988). Further, it is not limited to foreign policy, but can be applied to corporate decision-making, choice of investment, and numerous other circumstances as well, so is generalizable to other levels of conflict already discussed

Conclusion

War has many causes, most contrary to much liberal opinion perfectly rational from the perspective of the initiator. The Expected Utility model meets more of the criteria for good theory than other formulations, and is in effect an extension of the dual concern model (Chapter 5) for explaining individual conflict. In fact, the approaches using proxy variables pioneered by Bueno de Mesquita for measuring the utilities of parties to a conflict and for extending study to additional parties might be applicable to studying conflicts at lower levels, including those between individuals.

Chapter 13
Interstate Conflict

War is an ugly thing, but not the ugliest of things. The decayed and degraded state of moral and patriotic feeling which thinks that nothing is worth war is much worse. The person who has nothing for which he is willing to fight, nothing which is more important than his own personal safety, is a miserable creature and has no chance of being free unless made and kept so by the exertions of better men than himself.

—John Stuart Mill

<u>Eight Types of War</u>

War predates civilization, has many causes (Chapter 12) and takes many forms. The eight types proposed below expand on Chaliand (1994). Actual wars may simultaneously be of more than one type.

<u>Mass wars</u> aim at the destruction by battle of the enemy's armed forces and of the civilian infrastructure that supports it. They now appear to have been no more than an aberrant phase of military history lasting from the French Revolution through World War II. Clausewitz's *On War* is the bible for this type of war, although it was an unfinished work published posthumously. Clausewitz did not understand sea power. His declaration of the superiority of numbers (although he understood qualitative elements such as morale) led to the mass armies of the nineteenth and twentieth centuries. Of the possible causes investigated in Chapter 12, arms races, expected utility, and the nation state best explain such wars

<u>Limited wars</u> are primarily associated with periods when diplomats sought to maintain a balance of power, such as the period between the Thirty Years War and the French Revolution. Dynastic disputes, limited aims, maneuver to avoid battle except with a high likelihood of victory, and a generally accepted code of behavior characterize these wars. Sun Tsu's *Art of War* is the bible for such wars. For him, war was an essential aspect of statecraft subject to rational analysis. He stressed adaptability, deception, intelligence, mobility, striking at enemy weaknesses, and surprise. However, Sun Tsu and Clausewitz were alike in linking strategy and policy, and in stressing psychological factors, loyalty, and morale. Of the possible causes investigated in Chapter 12, expected utility and polarity best explain such wars

<u>Imperial wars</u> began with the reign of Sargon of Akkad (c. 2350 BC). Many centuries later, Western imperialism advanced in three main phases, the first initiated by the Portuguese and taken up by the Spanish and Dutch in the six-

teenth and seventeenth centuries, the second by the English with some competition from the French in the seventeenth and eighteenth centuries, and the third by the English and Americans in the nineteenth centuries. Russian imperialism began in the sixteenth century and continued on-and-off through the twentieth century. Japan and Germany were latecomers. Of the possible causes investigated in Chapter 12, expected utility best explain such wars.

Anti-imperial wars in the modern era date primarily but not exclusively from, and were inspired by, the American and French Revolutions. They often exhibit characteristics and methods of asymmetric war (Chapter 14) such as guerrilla tactics and terrorism. Some, such as the 11th-15th century Spanish *reconquista* and the American, French, and Russian revolutions, evolved into imperial wars. Many colonies gained their freedom in anti-imperial wars following World War II. Of the probable causes investigated in Chapter 12, expected utility and territorial imperative best explain such wars

Wars without quarter have been the cruelest types historically. Civil wars[1] often are lengthy, bloody, and extend to civilians. Race wars[2] often have involved systematic extermination. Religious wars[3] often were civil or imperial as well. Of the possible causes of wars, Chapter 11's focus on ideas best explain such wars

Ritual wars usually occur within societies that are archaic or traditional. Little that we would recognize as important was at stake. Casualties were low and battles sometimes were settled by single combat between heroes from each side. However, this may be an incomplete picture, as students of these wars tended to focus on "formal" battles and ignore the raids and ambushes that caused most of the casualties. Of the possible causes investigated in Chapter 12, ecological equilibrium and reproductive success best explain such wars.

Private wars, fought primarily for loot, usually occur when and where central governments are too weak to maintain order. Bedouin raiders, sea borne pirates, and private or mercenary armies in early medieval Europe and some parts of today's Africa and Caucasus are among their many practioners. Soldiers tend to be brave individually but unskilled and undisciplined. Of the possible causes investigated in Chapter 12, expected utility and reproductive success best explain such wars.

Nomad wars were concentrated in time from about 400 BC to about 1400 AD and in space along the margins of the Asian and European steppes. The Arab Muslim conquests and the Viking conquests—nomads of the sea—are equally important cases that took place in the same timeframe but different ar-

---

1. *e.g.*, French Wars of Religion, US Civil War, Russian Revolution, Spanish Civil War.
2. *e.g.*, Armenian, Gypsy, and Jewish genocides and, within their technical limits, the wars of Cortez against the Aztecs and Pizarro against the Incas.
3. *e.g.*, Muslim conquests of the seventh century, the Crusades, the Hindu-Sikh and Hindu-Muslim conflicts, the Thirty Years War, and the current Islamic terrorist jihad.

eas. The brilliant fourteenth century historian Ibn Khaldun[4] (1969) observed that Arab nomad dynasties seemed to repeat five-stage cycles of a little more than a century based on the formation, climax, decline, decay, and disintegration of *aṣabiyah* (group feeling). Gunpowder was the key factor in ending the dominance of nomad warriors. Of the causes investigated in Chapter 12, territorial imperative and expected utility best explain such wars.

Archaeology of War

Many anthropologists argue that inter-tribal primitive war was ritualistic and that casualties were rare. In Shaka Zulu we have a historical case of the transition from ritual to mass war (Ritter, 1978). Brought up in the tradition of ritual war, Shaka developed a new weapon, new tactics, and trained his warriors to kill most of his opponents and incorporate the survivors into his armies and the women into the Zulu harems. The Zulus, until then a minor tribe, built a kingdom that was able a century later, still armed primarily with spears, to hand the British one of its worst defeats of the nineteenth century at Isandhlwanda in what now is South Africa. We would like to know how and how often this transition took place in other societies. Was it a gradual evolution, did a similarly charismatic leader work a revolution, or were there other ways the transition took place? The question suggests a new way to approach the study of the emergence of states (*e.g.*, the unification of Egypt) and the impact of leaders who emerged suddenly from obscurity whether they succeeded (Genghis Khan, Shaka) or failed (Tecumseh).

Some anthropologists dispute the model of ritual war. Keeley (1996) synthesized nearly 300 studies that point to a much different conclusion. Data on primitive war are scarce and non-random. Extrapolating from recent to ancient primitive warfare is dubious. However, Keeley suggests that all the data that we do have points in the same direction. The mean fatality rate among primitive warring populations is about 45%, compared to about 12% for modern interstate war—and fifty to seventy percent of the fatalities in interstate war are from disease rather than wounds.[5] The main difference is that primitive war is almost constant whereas interstate war is episodic. Almost all the comparisons suggest the same surprising conclusion: primitive war is more likely to destroy whole societies than is interstate war.

The earliest, admittedly ambiguous, evidence of warfare is from the proto-Neolithic (the period 12000–8000 BCE in which agriculture was beginning to

4. His *Muqaddimah* (prolegomena) is the earliest effort to discover a pattern to the changes that occur in social and political organization. In effect, he invented modern historiography and pioneered sociology.

5. Keeley is careful to limit his analysis to intertribal wars. He also points out that until the late nineteenth century, medical practices in western armies probably was no better than that provided by tribal medicine men.

emerge). There are four types of evidence. First, four new weapons date to this period. The bow and arrow, dagger, and sling are useful in hunting so inconclusive. However, the mace, is useful only for fighting. Second, Saharan rock paintings portray battles. Several Neolithic cliff and cave paintings show battles between archers. That in Figure 13.1 from a cave in Morella la Villa, Spain, shows an apparent flanking attack, suggesting tactics already had evolved. Third, all of the men in a Nubian cemetery had multiple wounds and several had broken left forearms apparently from warding off blows. Fourth, some of the earliest towns from the ninth millennium BC were fortified. The most impressive of several examples is a ten-foot thick wall incorporating a 25-foot high tower at Jericho. Some interpret the ruins to be a dam with a built in grain storage tower, but this seems an unlikely combination.

Figure 13.1
Cave painting of Neolithic battle (Keeley, 1996)

Sumer occupied an area about the size of modern Belgium in what now is southern Iraq. An incredibly inventive people, the Sumerians have left us cosmogonies, cosmologies, epics, essays, fables, farmer's almanacs, horticultural manuals, hymns, king lists, laments, legends, literary debates, love songs, morality tales, myths, pharmacopoeias, philosophies and poems. Many Biblical stories echo Sumerian literature, including those of the Flood and Job. They probably originated the plow, potters wheel, vehicular wheel, draft animals, irrigation, kiln-fired bricks, copper casting, sailboat, and sledge. They originated mathematics and developed maps and the first practical calendar. They standardized measures of weight, length, area, volume and time. Their social inventions included libraries, schools, written law, and law courts (with two levels of appeal).

In a word, the Sumerians invented civilization. They even had a deity, Sataran, dedicated to settling conflicts

Sumer like ancient Greece was a land of warring city-states. They used four- then two-wheeled chariots and their troops were equipped with helmets, body armor, and pikes. The earliest war we know of in any detail began about 2500 BC and continued on-and-off for nearly 150 years. One of the more famous works of Sumerian art, the Stele of the Vultures dates from this war. At one time or another this war involved alliances, foreign aid, hidden agendas, indemnities, negotiations, truces including one based on restoration of the *status quo ante bellum* and third party mediation. That is, the first war we know about exhibits virtually every known device of statecraft! The two Sumerian cities fought to exhaustion, creating an opportunity for Sargon of Akkad, who conquered both to found history's first empire, perhaps stretching from Bahrein to Syria.

Although historians know of earlier battles, the Egyptians and the Hittites fought the first one we know of in political, strategic, and tactical detail. The battle is variously dated between 1295 BC and 1274 BC. Egypt, facing threats to its trade with the Levant, had been attempting for several decades to secure the area by conquest. Kadesh, a town on the Orontes River in Syria, already had changed hands several times.

In the fifth year of his reign, Rameses II advanced north toward Kadesh with his army. The army was organized into four divisions of 5000 bowmen, spearmen, and 2-man chariots each. Each division could operate independently or as part of a larger force. Marches of half to a full day's march separated each division—too far apart to support one another in an emergency. There is considerable dispute as to the identity, size, composition, movements, and role of a fifth unit, the Ne'arin, although they probably marched independently along the coast to protect the Egyptian flank.

The Hittite King Muwattilis had more and heavier, but slower 3-man chariots supported by less reliable levies of infantry from the Syrian part of its empire. Two different systems would clash: an Egyptian army, primarily infantry but including highly mobile light chariots, that depended on firepower, and a Hittite army of heavy chariots that relied on shock, with heavy infantry in a defensive role.

Rameses II made camp west of Kadesh, unconcerned because he had learned from two captured Hittite soldiers that Muwatilis's army was still far to the north. Unfortunately, it was a ruse. The Hittite chariots ambushed and destroyed the trailing second division. They then swung in arc to attack Rameses II's fortified camp from the south or west. Thinking the battle won, they began looting the Egyptian camp. Rameses II organized and personally led a counterattack at the same time that the Ne'arin debouched from the Eleutheros Valley to attack the Hittites in their flank and rear, forcing them to retreat. The battle appears to have ended in an agreed stalemate, the exhausted Hittites worried about the two remaining Egyptian divisions, and the decimated Egyptians worried about the Hittite infantry that had not yet appeared.

The battle confirmed that Egypt at the height of its power could not control Syria, but that the Hittites at the height of theirs could not reach further south, stabilizing the boundary between them. This stability and the emergence of Assyria as a greater threat led the two enemies into an alliance confirmed by a treaty signed a dozen years later. Egypt temporarily lost control of Palestine, probably creating the opportunity for the Jews to establish their state in the hills above the coastal plain.

Strategic and Tactical Theory

Von Moltke (1909) defined strategy as "the practical adaptation of the means placed at a general's disposal to the attainment of the object in view." The important point is distinguishing the responsibility of the general as carrying out, but not making, policy. The government can legitimately interfere in the strategy of a campaign by modifying its object. The general cannot interfere in the government by trying to set its object. The principle explains the firing of General MacArthur, a general in the field improperly trying to force foreign policy on Harry Truman, constitutionally both the commander-in-chief and the elected head of state (Fehrenbach, 1963).

The best theories identify a few key variables that have general explanatory power. Archer Jones (1987) has done this for warfare as neatly as Galileo did it for physics, although he proposes different sets of variables for tactics and for strategy. Tactically, Jones parsimoniously distinguishes fighting forces using only two variables. Until World War I armies fought either on foot (whether they marched or rode into combat) or mounted (whether on chariots or horses). Second, they depended either on missile (javelins or arrows) or shock (spears or swords) weapons (Figure 13.2). Missile-wielding troops tended to be more lightly armored and more mobile than shock troops.

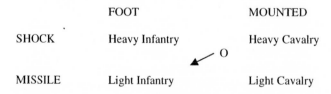

	FOOT	MOUNTED
SHOCK	Heavy Infantry	Heavy Cavalry
MISSILE	Light Infantry	Light Cavalry

Figure 13.2
Tactical Capabilities of Weapons Systems

Any number of horizontal, vertical, or diagonal arrows labeled either "D" for "Defensive Superiority" or O for "Offensive superiority" can be added to the diagram to indicate the situation at specific places and times. For example, an arrow has been added to Figure 13.2 to indicate that French heavy cavalry normally could defeat English light infantry in about 1250 AD. But, if the diagram was portraying the situation a century later, the arrow would have to be reversed and labeled "D" to indicate that English light infantry standing on the defensive and armed with longbows usually could prevail against French cavalry. The English advantage in the Hundred Years War disappeared not because of any improvement in French weapons, tactics or strategy, but because a 17-year old girl we know as Joan of Arc so inspired the French that they seldom lost after 1429. Morale can be a powerful factor in war!

The general notion of laying out the main weapons systems and their relative advantage in attacking or defending at particular points in time remains a useful concept. A commander may be able to force battle under circumstances that offset the advantage of the other—in one sense, that is what generalship is all about. The system is adaptable to both naval warfare and the evolution of modern weapons systems that include tactical and strategic airpower. Jones reduces strategy to three main variables. The commander can choose a defensive or offensive, a persisting or raiding, and a combat or logistic strategy. The choice among them is guided by economic, military, and political aims and capabilities. Figure 13.2 shows examples of each from World War II.

Defensive	Persisting	Combat	Russian retreat vs. German invasion
Defensive	Persisting	Logistic	Allied convoys vs. German submarines
Defensive	Raiding	Combat	Raids vs German A-bomb development
Defensive	Raiding	Logistic	Yugoslav guerrillas vs German invasion
Offensive	Persisting	Combat	Allied ground campaign vs. Germany
Offensive	Persisting	Logistic	Allied air campaign vs. Germany
Offensive	Raiding	Combat	Stirling's SAS in the western desert
Offensive	Raiding	Logistic	Allied submarine war against Japan

Figure 13.2
Strategic Combinations in World War II

Strategic Geography

Geography is at the heart of many disputes. In the post-Civil War American west, towns competed to get the railroad, knowing that only the one that succeeded would grow and prosper. In the 1950s, when the United States was designing its Interstate Highway System, towns competed to get exits, knowing that roadside services such as gas stations, motels and restaurants would bring growth and prosperity. More recently, changing values have seen towns fight against airports, halfway houses for drug addicts, prisons, waste sites and the like, the "Not In My Backyard" [NIMBY] phenomenon.

If one maps major civilizations and the resources they most need, it is easy to identify vital land and ocean trade routes. Rome depended on grain from

Egypt. The north Italian city-states became important when Central and Western Europe became wealthy enough to buy luxuries from Asia and the Near East. Portugal and Spain were perfectly sited for discovering the routes around Africa and to the New World. The Industrial Revolution favored countries with access to coal and iron. Oil gives the shipping routes from the unstable Middle East to the great industrial centers their current importance. The world's strategic centers are not fixed. Strategic geography provides a theoretical tool for understanding what is important when.

If one mapped all the world's battles on land and sea, it would quickly become apparent that battles are rare in some and common in other areas. Color-coding the battles chronologically would strengthen the impression. The chessboard provides an abstract explanation. Place three knights on a chessboard, one in a corner, one on an edge half way along the board, and one on any of the four central squares. A knight is required to move two squares parallel to one edge of the board then turn one square to the right or left. The knight in the corner can move to two, the one on the edge to four, and the one in the center to eight squares (the exercise produces similar results for the bishop, rook, queen or king). "Control of the center" is at the heart of chess strategy. Position is power.

Applied to the real world, the advantage of position can be understood in terms of "options" and "chokepoints." The more routes that go to or come from a place, and the harder it is to find routes around it, the more strategic value a place has. There are three routes large enough to move armies between Germany and France. The Belfort Gap lies between the Alps and Vosges and connects Lyon and Munich. The Lorraine Gateway lies between Vosges and Argonne (Rhine Graben to the Germans) and connects Metz and Strasbourg to the Saar. Belgium and Holland occupy the flat land between the Ardennes and the English Channel that runs all the way to Moscow. Almost all the battles between Germany and France have taken place along one of these routes. In World War II, Devers' Sixth Army used the first, Bradley's Twelfth Army Group used the second, and Montgomery's Twenty-first Army Group used the third route to invade Germany. These routes converge at Paris. This gives Paris the strategic advantage known as "interior lines" that is at the heart of de Jomini's (1971) conception of strategy. The French can keep their entire army around Paris and move it quickly to defend any one of the three invasion routes. The Germans must divide their army to defend three invasion routes.[6] Turin lies at the point where five passes through the Alps converge, giving Italy a defensive advantage over the French similar to the one France holds over the Germans.

Vienna, the second most important city in Europe, lies on the Danube just south of the Moravian Gate between the Bohemian Knot and the Carpathian Mountains. When Bismarck said "Whoever is master of Bohemia is master of

6. The French advantage is reinforced by a peculiarity of the concentric ridges facing Germany, which rise gradually from the west but fall off precipitously on the east, so are easier for the French to defend than for the Germans to attack

Europe, he meant that control of that mountain bastion made it relatively easy to invade or defend the South German basin, the North German plain, Poland, and Austria. The Moravian Gate north of Vienna gives easy access to Poland and the northern plains, the Danube gives easy access upstream to the South German Basin and downstream to the Balkans, the Black Sea and the Aegean, and the Ljublana and Peartree Passes give access to northern Italy and the Adriatic.

The world's oceans have similar chokepoints (Figure 13.3). During the Reagan presidency, a new air base in Maurice Bishop's Grenada added to two in Castro's Cuba and one in Ortega's Nicaragua made it possible for communist governments to cut off the 40% of US oil imports that arrived through the Caribbean. One might suspect that this was a larger consideration in the US decision to invade Grenada than the hypothetical danger to a few American medical students that was used to justify it. Similarly, US interest in preventing a Northern victory in Vietnam is partially explained by its position at the "Hinge of Asia," as the Japanese call it.

Europe
    Adriatic egress
    Baltic Approaches
    Bosporus & Dardanelles
    Denmark Strait
    English Channel
    Icelandic-Faroes Passage
Asia
    Formosa Strait
    Hinge of Asia[7]
    Lombok Strait
    Strait of Malacca
    Sunda Strait
    Torres Strait

Western Hemisphere
    Florida Strait
    Leeward Passage
    Mona Passage
    Panama Canal
    Strait of Magellan
    Windward Passage
Mid-East/Africa
    Bab-al-Mandab
    Cape of Good Hope
    Strait of Gibraltar
    Strait of Hormuz
    Suez Canal

Figure 13.3
Ocean Chokepoints

Siberia divides from north to south into five zones, beginning with the tundra, where winter temperatures can reach –100 degrees. Just to the south lies the taiga, the endless forests of pine and larch. Then come the grasslands that stretch from the plains of Hungary across Central Asia to the great loop of the Yangtze River. This is the previously mentioned "Nomad Route" that made possible the conquests of successive waves of horse nomads from the Huns to the Mongols. The grasslands give way to the Karakum and Gobi—cold deserts with high mountains in which one can even find glaciers. Finally, south of the deserts

---

7. The sea routes between Vietnam and Malaysia and the Philippines and Borneo

stand the mountain complex anchored by the Pamir and Armenian knots that stretch from the Alps to the Himalayas.

Americans seldom think strategically. One exception is Alfred Thayer Mahan, whose *Influence of Sea Power upon World History 1660–1783*, was published just as Americans closed their land frontier and were looking for new outlets for their energies. Mahan argued persuasively that naval supremacy explained British emergence as a world power. He explained the relationship among economics, geography, industry, national character, policy, and seaborne commerce as determinants of success. The central position of the United States with coasts on the Atlantic and Pacific gives it the advantage of interior lines on a global scale.

Under Mahan's influence, America shifted from a "green water" navy focused on coastal defense and commerce raiding to a "blue water" navy focused on command of the seas. Mahan strongly influenced Americans to acquire an overseas empire in the Caribbean and the Pacific, to establish naval bases and build the Panama Canal. The combination radically altered the world balance of power. British historian Charles Webster said that "Mahan was one of the causes of the First World War" because he supposedly sparked the British-German naval arms race. Despite that race, the German fleet remained weaker than the combined allied fleet, leading Germany to adapt the classic strategy of the weaker party, raiding enemy commerce. To this end, they used submarines, cruisers, and merchantmen converted into warships disguised to look like ships from various neutral nations.

Sir Halford Mackinder (1904) thought that the railroad made the Eurasian "heartland" the "greatest natural fortress on earth," immune from Mahan's navies so a base for control of the world. Mackinder also was influenced by the nineteenth century struggle for empire in Central Asia between Britain and Russia—the Great Game (Hopkirk, 1990). Mackinder's thinking led the negotiators at Versailles to create buffer states such as Czechoslovakia to prevent either Russia or Germany from dominating the heartland, and from it the world.

Mackinder also influenced Karl Haushofer, a multilingual German professor of geography who had been a major general in World War I and a diplomat in Japan before it. He hosted the meetings leading to the German-Japanese alliance in his home. Through Rudolph Hess,[8] one of his students, he gained access to and tried to influence the leaders of the Nazi Party. For this reason, he often is accused of being the theoretician behind the Soviet invasion. The charge is false. In fact, because he associated with the socialist wing of the Nazi Party that was destroyed in the Night of the Long Knives and advocated a German-Russian alliance to offset the American-British one, he was marginalized by the start of the war.

---

8. Haushofer convinced Hess to fly to Britain in May 1941. His brother had been part of the 20 July plot to kill Hitler. He himself was acquitted at Nuremberg but committed suicide in 1946.

During World War II, Nicholas Spykman (1944) argued that the key to controlling the world island was not Mackinder's heartland but the "rimland" between it and Mahan's oceans. Spykman's ideas influenced the "Wise Men"[9] who developed American Cold War strategy and created NATO. With the collapse of the Soviet Union, four strategic geographies have emerged to replace Spykman's vision that guided the containment strategy of the Cold War. The first, the search for a "near peer" threat to the United States, sees China replacing the Soviet Union as the bête noire of the future. The immediate challenge is xenophobic Muslim (primarily Arab and Iranian) terrorism. The larger context now is the proliferation of Weapons of Mass Destruction. Taken together, these problems suggest a replay of the Great Game in Central Asia. The region divides into two areas. Ethnic groups give the countries surrounding the Caspian Sea their names. East of them, the "stans" (from the common ending of their names) are largely Turkish or Iranian, setting up a competition within a competition between Turkey and Iran. All have substantial Russian minorities. They are strategically located to counter any alliance of China and Iran. Most important, they are oil-rich, a potential counterweight to Saudi Arabia. The second conception is an "arc of instability" formed by the Islamic states of the Near East. The third is a "clash of civilizations" (Huntington, 1996). All three seem inferior to the fourth conception, proposed by Barnett (2004).

In the first fifteen years after the Cold War, the US engaged in roughly 150 named military operations (contingency positioning, combat, evacuations, peacekeeping and relief, or show of force). About 80% involved only four countries in four continents: Haiti, Yugoslavia, Somalia, and Iraq. The common denominator is their isolation from the global economy. Similarly isolated countries divide the world into a functioning "Core" and a non-integrating "Gap" in Barnett's terminology. The Core includes Chile, Argentina and Brazil, all of North America, Russia, India, China, Japan, Australia and New Zealand, and all of Europe except the Balkans. The Gap includes western and northern South America, Central America, much of the Caribbean, all of Africa except South Africa, the Balkans, all of the Middle East, the "stans" of Central Asia, and all of South-East Asia. Barnett probably would recognize Singapore as a connected island in the midst of the Gap, and North Korea as a disconnected island in the Core.

According to Barnett, the countries in the Core live by agreed rules, are economically interdependent, and no longer resolve disputes by war. In an alternative formulation, they are "competent" (Friedman, 1999). China, the "near peer" seen by many in the Pentagon as the major threat to the United States, is more likely to continue integrating into the functioning core than to attempt anything more than regional hegemony.

Poor communications and transportation, lack of foreign investment, low life expectancy, lack of education, repression especially of women, lawlessness,

---

9. *e.g.*, Dean Acheson, George Kennan, George Marshall, Paul Nitze

and war characterize the countries in the Gap. Many depend on export of one or two raw materials for foreign exchange. Some are theocracies, others are kleptocracies, and some are both. Their rulers are for the most part above the law and likely to be removed only by coup or death. The Gap is a Hobbesian world in which life is "solitary, poor, nasty, brutish and short."

Barnett's formulation implies six main policy choices for the US. The radical fringe advocates a retreat from globalization into some sort of anarchic primitive utopia. The far left holds the Core—no more than former slavers and colonizers in their view—responsible for conditions in the Gap and advocates withdrawal of military forces, atonement through foreign aid and reparations, and treating Gap states as responsible international actors, which many are not. The reactionary fringe blames the Gap for its own problems and advocates isolationism. The mainstream left advocates dependence on joint action through the UN and defense of all possible targets at home, but no expansion of police powers to collect supporting intelligence. The mainstream right advocates short, sharp interventions to eliminate bad actors each time they crop up.

The sixth choice, advocated by Barnett (2004) is to enlarge the Core by shrinking the Gap. This strategy, which has the advantage of being an aphorism, envisions ending the conflict by creating a brighter future for the people of both the Core and the Gap. This task of decades, the equivalent of the Cold War's containment strategy, can guide foreign policy decisions such as military basing (already shifting from NATO to Central Asia), foreign aid, and encouragement of private sector investment.

In the Gap, the logical outcome of Barnett's theory is that the US must assume the role of *Leviathan*. The US must act, if necessary unilaterally and preemptively but ideally with allies—but only in the Gap. It need not do so in the Core, where there are established mechanisms to deal peacefully with almost every issue that arises. The US must lead—and hope that others will help. But, the US must do more than act. It also must explain. The US needs to clarify its goal, and then it needs to explain the goal, continually, so that the countries of the Core know that they have nothing to fear. The US has acted wisely but explained poorly.

Conclusion

Strategic geography and Jones's formulation for understanding strategy and tactics combine to provide a rational and parsimonious explanation of how wars are fought and where. Barnett's approach to strategic geography is in the tradition of optimistic conservatism, realistic but giving hope for steadily converting dispute resolution to diplomacy from war. The two concepts combine well with Expected Utility Theory (Chapter 12) as an explanation of cause to approach a complete theory of conventional interstate conflict.

Chapter 14
Asymmetric Conflict

Did my provoked jape at Vickery, that rebellion was more like peace than war, hold as much truth as haste?
—T. E. Lawrence, *Seven Pillars of Wisdom*

Asymmetric war consists of unconventional forces and methods used against conventional ones and noncombatants that are difficult to answer in kind. The qualification distinguishes asymmetric methods such as guerrilla war, "lawfare," terrorism, and the Trojan horse from symmetrical ones such as sending cavalry against infantry. In one sense, it is an application of competitive strategy (Chapter 9). Although often viewed as the strategy of the weak, in forms such as economic sanctions it is equally useful to the strong.

Economic Sanctions

Economic sanctions are one of the most common and immediate suggestions made for dealing with aggressors. Article 41 of the UN charter legitimizes economic sanctions. The targets usually are air transportation, armaments, banking, food, and oil. During World War II, the Allies tried to reduce German ability to produce explosives and hardened steel by buying mercury from Spain and cobalt from Turkey far in excess of their own needs.

Figure 14.1 contains a representative list of twenty sanctions imposed during the twentieth century.[1] Of the 20, three succeeded in achieving their aims. Sanctions against South Africa succeeded in combination with diplomacy, internal resistance, and moral suasion. Of the remaining 16, two were resolved in other ways, nine resulted in war and five continue to this day to little effect.

Muammar Qaddafi eventually turned the accused Pan Am 103 bombers over for trial in 1999, and in 2004 he agreed to halt his weapons programs and open the country to inspection. However, sanctions had nothing to do with either decision. Reagan's bombing of Muammar Qaddafi's residence (killing his daughter), the end of the Cold War, the efficiency with which the United States destroyed hostile governments in Afghanistan and Iraq, and some quiet diplomacy got Muammar Qaddafi's attention. Sanctions bothered him not a whit. Despite them, Italy bought 42% of Libyan oil, while Germany, Spain, France,

---

1. In 1998, 75 countries with two-thirds of the world population were to some degree subject to US sanctions aimed at combating drug trafficking, environmental protection, human rights violations, market access, terrorism, or weapons proliferation. Most continue ineffectively.

Greece, England, Turkey—US Allies all—and a few other countries bought the rest. Libya continued to operate more than 2300 gas stations in Italy and the refineries it controls in Germany, Italy, and Switzerland. Libya continued to reap dividends and capital gains from stocks it holds in over 120 multinational corporations.

Date	Imposed by	Result and Goal
1933	Britain	Succeeded in freeing British "spies" in USSR
1935	League of Nations	Failed to stop Italian invasion of Ethiopia
1946	Arab League	Failed to stop formation of Israel
1948	USSR	Failed to stop Yugoslav breakaway from Moscow
1954	USSR	Failed to force Australian extradition of single defector
1956	US	Succeeded in forcing French & UK withdrawal from Suez
1958	USSR	Succeeded in ending Finish repression of pro-Soviet parties
1960	US	Failed to get compensation for nationalization by Cuba
1960	USSR	Failed to stop Chinese breakaway from Moscow
1961	USSR	Failed to stop Albanian breakaway from Moscow
1965	UN	Failed to oust Portugal from African colonies
1973	OPEC	Failed to prevent western support of Israel
1974	Cyprus	Failed to force reunification of the country
1977	UN	Contributed to ending apartheid in South Africa
1980	US	Failed to force USSR out of Afghanistan
1982	EEC	Failed to force Argentine withdrawal from the Falklands
1983	Japan, others	Failed to resolve KAL Flight 007 crisis with USSR
1988	UN	Failed to resolve Pan Am 003 crisis with Libya
2000	EU	Failed to force Myanmar junta to install elected govt.
1990	UN	Failed to force Iraqi withdrawal from Kuwait

Figure 14.1

Typical Twentieth Century Economic Sanctions

Sanctions failed to induce Saddam Hussein to withdraw from Kuwait, and they failed to induce him to cooperate with UN inspectors despite treaty obligations to do so.[2] The Iraqi people have paid a very high price. During the 1990s, infant mortality rose from 3.7 to 12 percent. Inadequate food and medicine and breakdowns in sanitation and power caused a claimed 800,000 deaths mostly among children and the elderly—five times the number of people killed by the Hiroshima and Nagasaki bombs. This is not to suggest any moral equivalency. Saddam Hussein, Jacques Chirac, Vladimir Putin and the UN's mismanagement of the Oil-for-Food program imposed these evils on the Iraqi people

---

2. It became apparent within fifteen months that Saddam Hussein had bribed French President Chirac and Russian President Putin sufficiently to be assured of their veto in the UN, and several UN officials to allow him to divert over 20 billion dollars of the "oil for food" program from feeding Iraqis to his own personal purposes. Bribes often are behind the failure of sanctions, although never before on such a spectacular scale.

Theoretically, sanctions work best against governments that are susceptible to public opinion and that face a viable internal opposition. However, sanctions have not yet succeeded in Myanmar despite the National League for Democracy winning 80% of the seats in parliament in the 1990 election and the additional international support of a Nobel Peace Prize for Aung San Suu Kyi (Judge, 2004). Sanctions are most likely to work against weak allies heavily dependent on the sanctioning country for a few critical supplies for which few alternatives are available. They are more effective against allies than against enemies. They do not work well when they require the cooperation of many countries, and they do not work well if they threaten the survival of a regime, as those against Myanmar and Iraq illustrate. As these conditions for success are rare, the high failure rate for sanctions should be understandable.

Sanctions often follow legislative debate and implementation often is gradual, allowing the target country to develop defenses. The economic impact often is worse on the sanctioning countries than the target, as jobs are lost and other countries treat them as an opportunity to become suppliers. Sanctions should be the prerogative of the executive, not the legislature, so that they can be implemented hard and fast. Perhaps the worst mistake of all is to implement sanctions to satisfy public demands for "doing something," despite knowing the conditions for success do not exist.

Given the poor record of success, and the high humanitarian costs to noncombatants who do the suffering (despite recent efforts at "targeted" sanctions), we should be a lot more careful in using sanctions as an instrument of policy. When we do, we should know that conditions favor success.

Boycotts are the (primarily) domestic equivalent of economic sanctions. A boycott is simply a refusal by one group to deal with another one. Boycotts often require long-term commitment and therefore organizational ability and publicity because organizers must win and hold the loyalty of a large number of people for however long it takes to win.

Boycotts may involve no more than refusal to participate in a meeting, conference or election. Most entail refusal by employees during a labor dispute or by consumers to buy goods or services from the target company. The technique takes its name from the individual who was the target of a protest led by Charles Parnell during the Irish potato famine. Mohandas Gandhi made frequent use of boycotts in his quest for Indian independence. The Montgomery bus boycott of 1955 began when Rosa Parks refused to sit in the back of the bus as required in the segregated South.

Guerilla warfare

Guerrilla war is a raiding strategy (Chapter 13). It can be defensive or offensive, and it can target enemy troops, his logistical system, or both. Guerilla success usually requires a small ratio of force to space, better mobility than the enemy, terrain that facilitates retreat, a safe base for supply and recuperation, and the support of the local population. As guerrillas gain success, they tend to become more conventional in their strategy and tactics, and thus to lose some of their advantage. Among guerrilla campaigns illustrating all these points are the Bactrians against Alexander the Great, Welsh against the English, Seminoles against the United States, Boers against the British, Spanish against Napoleon, Yugoslavs against the Nazis, and Viet Cong against the French then the United States. The first four failed to achieve their objective. The latter four achieved theirs only when conventional forces came to their assistance. Guerilla warfare is not a guarantee of success!

T. E. Lawrence's *Seven Pillars of Wisdom* remains one of the most incredible books in the English language for the prose, for the story, and for the innovative application of general theory to specific circumstances. Chapter 33 describes his search to find an alternative end and means of war given the irrelevance of traditional military doctrine to the situation in Arabia. The alternative he chose was to ignore Turkish manpower, which Turkey viewed as expendable, so as to focus on their logistical system, which was hard to replace, vulnerable, and vital. Famously, he did so by blowing up just enough railways and bridges (ideally with trains on them) to immobilize the Turkish army but not enough to force them to retreat.

Guerilla war usually proves to be a long, exhausting, and uncertain route to victory because it depends on the aggregation of many small logistic and combat successes. Therefore, it requires astute political leadership to hold forces together. If the opponent can gradually reduce the space in which the guerrilla can operate and cut off lines of retreat, guerrillas can be defeated. As guerrillas usually depend on local support, counter-guerrilla strategy involves either "winning the hearts and minds" away from, or terrorizing the non-combatant population into abandoning, the guerrillas.

Terrorism

When people hear the word "terrorism" today, most think of Muslim groups such as al-Qaeda. In fact, Muslims perpetrated only about 25% of terrorist incidents in the late 20th and early 21st century. For example, RAND reported 1725 terrorist acts in 2002 (almost 5 a day), including 441 in Southeast Asia, 447 in the Middle East, and 214 in Europe. Groups such as the Aum Shrinri Kyo, Earth Liberation Frontt, ETA, FARC, IRA, Shining Path, and Tamil Tigers were responsible for the remaining 75%. In the radical decade of the seventies, groups such as the SLA and Baader Meinhoff Gang were responsible for their own brand of terrorism. Israeli groups such as the Irgun and the Stern Gang were among the earliest such groups. In fact, the Irgun's attack on the King David Hotel in Jerusalem that killed 91 people usually is considered the birth of modern terrorism. One of their leaders, Menachem Begin, became prime minister of Israel. However, Muslim terrorism is the major threat today, simply because the world economy cannot operate without oil.

The simultaneous hijacking of one British and two American planes in "Black September" 1970 brought Arab terrorism to the attention of the world. Attacks such as those on the *Achille Lauro* and the Munich Olympics followed. Christian, not Muslim, Arabs such as George Habash, Waddiah Haddad and Laila Khaled carried out the worst of these early attacks.

The 1990s witnessed the first attack on the World Trade Center, the attack on Khobar Towers, murders in Pakistan of five U.S. oil workers and of Daniel Pearl, attacks on U.S. embassies in Nairobi and Dar es Salaam, the attack on the U.S. Cole, the kidnapping of three missionaries in the Philippines, and the bombings of discos in Germany and Indonesia. The escalation in numbers, geographical reach and scale is apparent, and any possibility of terrorists obtaining weapons of mass destruction (WMDs) alarming.

The current wave of terrorism probably has its origin in the 1948, 1956, and 1967 defeats by Israel of the overconfident Arabs, who began to ask why and answered, as Jewish prophets and Christian preachers also have done in times of disaster, "because we have been faithless." The Serbian massacre of Muslims in Bosnia added to Muslim anger, the role of the US and NATO in ending it simply ignored. The presence of non-Muslims in Saudi Arabia (although they stay far from the holy places) was the straw that broke the camel's back for the fanatics we know as al-Qaeda, particularly after Saudi Arabia had turned Usama bin Laden down when he offered to bring his followers from Afghanistan to oppose the Iraqi invasion of Kuwait.

Terrorists and their national supporters face a significant "Catch-22." Small attacks will not change US policy significantly; while large ones risk the obliteration of whatever regime the US President sees fit to blame until he gets the right one, as the Taliban in Afghanistan and the Baathists in Iraq learned.

It is difficult to think of examples of political goals actually achieved by terrorism alone. Israeli and Mau Mau terrorism succeeded largely because Britain no longer could afford the cost of empire. The North Vietnamese assassinated over 9000 village officials in the early 1960s to little effect and succeeded in conquering South Vietnam only by a conventional military invasion. The Algerian War of independence has a similar history.

What is a terrorist? Mingst (2001) gives us the politically correct conceit that "one person's terrorist is another person's freedom fighter." Kegley and Wittkopf (2001) give us "seeking to further political objectives through the threat or use of violence usually in opposition to state governments," which does not distinguish terrorism from conventional war. Michael Walzer (1977) writes of "the systematic terrorizing of whole populations is a strategy of both conventional and guerrilla war...its purpose is to destroy the morale of a nation or a class, to undercut its solidarity; its method is the random murder of innocent people. Randomness is the crucial feature of terrorist activity." But, defining terrorism as terrorizing is not terribly helpful. Title 22 of the U.S. Code defines terrorism as "premeditated political violence perpetrated against noncombatant targets by subnational or clandestine agents." This seems satisfactory, although "noncombatants" are not defined (Chapter 15).

Liam Harte (2002) proposed a useful typology distinguishing (1) domestic and international (2) state and non-state terrorism, (3) mythic vs. non-mythic, and (4) modernist vs. anti-modern terrorism, resulting in a 2x2x2x2 taxonomy.

The non-mythic mind is rational, pragmatic and scientific. The mythic mind is traditional. Opposition to modernity is common in fundamentalist movements in all three great monotheistic religions. Mythic terrorists are satisfied only if the traditionalism permeates all aspects of life: political, economic, and cultural as well as religious. Their only demand is for everyone to become like them or die, and the demand is non-negotiable. If this is true, then the only alternative to surrendering is to destroy them. Al-Qaeda is just such a group.

The anti-modern terrorist rejects rationality, science, technology, and the like (but is willing to use its technology in attacks). The modernist terrorist wants to replace whoever governs now but if successful will use all the apparatus of modern government. These distinctions seem almost the same as that between mythic and non-mythic terrorists. Neither Harte nor I could name an anti-modernist non-mythic terrorist. The IRA is the closest we can come to identifying a modernist, non-mythic group. Further, there does not seem to be any difference in the strategic or tactical response required. With only one example in all eight non-mythic cells, and no tactical difference in responding to them, it seems reasonable to simplify Harte's taxonomy by eliminating the mythic vs. non-mythic categories, resulting in Figure 14.2

		State	Non-State
Modernist	**Domestic**	Serbs	Baader-Meinhof
		Nazis	FARC
		Soviets	IRA
	International	Nazis	Stern Gang
		Soviets	Hezbollah
Anti-Modernist	**Domestic**	Khmer Rouge	ELF
		Taliban	
	International	Iran	Al-Qaeda

Figure 14.2
Taxonomy of Terror[3]

3. Adapted from Harte, 2002

Lawfare[4]

"Lawfare," the newest form of asymmetric warfare, may be defined as an effort to defeat conventional military forces through aggressive application of law. Although some cases may be brought in national or even military courts, the venue of choice is the International Court of Justice [ICJ]. The ICJ is limited to disputes submitted by recognized states and international bodies that consent to its adjudication. This follows precedents set by The Hague Peace Conference in 1899 and the International Court established under the League of Nations. Three cases are illustrative of lawfare.

International "human rights" groups are encouraging Colombian peasants to file human rights suits on any or even no pretense against their military to raise the costs of fighting FARC and to remove commanders from duty while cases work through the multiyear court process. They are doing the same against US officers in Iraq in the hope that fear of legal action eventually will pervade the military and hamstring commanders in combat against guerrillas and terrorists.

The ICJ recently held in response to a UN General Assembly request for an "advisory opinion," that Israel's security fence violates international law, basing their opinion on conventions such as those against disrupting free movement of innocent children, plausible only if one ignores the threat from Palestinian terrorists to equally innocent Israelis. Regardless of what one thinks about the fence itself, the ICJ should not have taken the case under its own charter, and the General Assembly was circumventing the Security Council, responsible for resolving threats to peace for political purposes, the requirement that Israel consent to be judged, and the requirement that only recognized states, which Palestine is not, can bring cases to the court. Israel immediately declared that it would ignore the decision. The ruling is more likely to prove an obstacle to a negotiated peace than a contribution to it.

The International Committee of the Red Cross [ICRC] has been trying since 1993—the year of the first attack on the World Trade Center—through the ICJ and other international bodies to extend the Geneva Convention for the treatment of prisoners of war to captured terrorists despite the clear language of the convention against doing so (Chapter 15). The ICRC now argues that the rule has become "so widely accepted" that it is binding on the US even without its consent. They also argue with many others that extension of POW status is necessary so that US captives and abductees will receive humane treatment.

Nations are unlikely to compromise their survival on the basis of legal arguments. The second case increases already rampant doubts about the ability of the UN to reduce terrorism. The failure of the ICRC to protect captured Americans in the Korean, Vietnamese, and First Gulf wars and their lack of any public

---

4. This section is based on Blomley, 2003; Dunnigan 27 Feb 2005; Rabkin 17 July 2004; and Rivkin and Casey, 11 April 2005

campaign on their behalf, compared with their very public advocacy on behalf of America's enemies, exposes its politicization and destroys the claim that extending POW status to terrorists will gain more humane treatment of American prisoners. The assertion that the ICJ would only take cases on the scale of genocide is belied by the three examples given above, undermines its credibility and makes clear that it too is highly politicized. This in turn reduces the likelihood that the United States ever will join the ICJ or submit to its judgment in specific cases. Lawfare, like terrorism, is likely to backfire in the long run.

Counter-terrorism

Selecting a means to counter terrorism requires policy analysis, a method for systematic analysis of issues and options to identify the costs, benefits, risks, and consequences of each possible course of action. There are ten major options for dealing with international terrorism, considered separately below before considering how to combine them into a counter-terror strategy.

Muslims may be responsible for a minority of total terror incidents, but they are responsible for the ones that kill the most people and do the most damage to the world economy. The great fear is—or should be—the possibility of their obtaining biological or nuclear weapons. It will remain a grave threat so long as states fund, harbor, and support terrorists who have killed or injured over 10,000 people in the past ten years, destroyed millions of dollars in property, forced the diversion of billions out of more productive uses into defense and security, and taken a heavy psychological toll as well.

A major consideration in selecting a strategy to reduce terrorism is the extent of state support. One common bromide is to eliminate terrorism's "root causes." Some blame terrorism—and just about every other ill—on poverty. However, poverty is rampant in countries that have not produced international terrorists, while Usama bin Ladin was a millionaire 300 times over and the 9-11 attackers were multi-lingual upper middle class Arabs. The intractable Israeli-Palestinian conflict is a worthy candidate for a root cause. The inability of Muslims to reconcile their faith with their defeats is another. Finally, Arab scholars in the United Nation's *Arab Human Development Report* (Nader, 2002) put the blame on three Arab "deficits:" lack of political and economic freedom, illiteracy, and repression of women. Ultimately, nobody knows what the "root causes" are and the common suspects are not easily cured.

Some suggest negotiation, but the fundamental conditions for success (Chapter 8) do not exist with respect to terrorists. There are conflicting but not common interests, terrorist leaders often propose negotiation without intent to reach agreement but to allow their forces to regroup, and their leaders often make but cannot or will not keep agreements. This is primarily because a more radical, less responsible subordinate will ignore any agreement made by a leader. Moderation is not a great way for terrorist leaders to survive the fanaticism of their own followers.

Another suggestion for reducing terrorism is to rely on the police and the courts, treating terrorists as individual criminals. One difficulty is that the criminal justice system is designed primarily to arrest and prosecute rather than to prevent. Civil libertarians oppose the necessary surveillance as a violation of privacy and other rights. This conflict—between security and liberty—is an issue whenever a free country goes to war. Both concerns are legitimate and finding the balance in particular circumstances is not always easy. The first effort to do so after the attack of 11 September 2001 was the Patriot Act, hastily passed and undoubtedly in need of revision, although exactly how is less clear. An important dimension of this approach is to use the criminal justice system to destroy the financial networks of the terrorists.

Still another suggestion is a strong system of civil defense to protect targets from attack, presumably the main idea behind the new US Department of Homeland Security. However, there are too many ways to attack and too many targets in the US and abroad for this to succeed by itself. Regardless of how many terrorists are thwarted, a persisting attack by all-but-invisible agents eventually will find cracks in any defense.

Some advocate assassination[5] although of whom is not always clear. It usually is easier said than done, does not guarantee the successor will be any better, and sets a dangerous precedent and moral tone. Another bad idea is to destroy the families or neighborhoods in which every suicide bomber originates. Still worse is targeting mosques in response to terrorist attacks on "symbolic" attacks in the west. The Nazis and Israelis tried such things, and only succeeded in increasing resistance. Stealing the Black Stone from the Kaaba in Mecca[6] and threatening to fire it into space cannot be taken seriously. The worst ideas of all, advocated only by crackpots, are "turning Mecca into glass" or "annihilating all Arabs"—in other words, genocide directed at innocent millions to destroy guilty thousands. However, if the US will destroy two governments in response to a terror attack that killed 3000, the Arab world should not discount the possibility of such a reactions to any attack that kills large numbers of Americans again.

Some want to act only with United Nations approval. However, the UN is not the fair and neutral arbiter of international justice and morality these idealists imagine, and it has no way to enforce its decisions. Rather, it is a member organization consisting of governments acting in their own national interests, which is what nations do. It is becoming increasingly apparent that bribery and corruption were factors in the inability of the UN to enforce its own resolutions

---

5. The US Executive Order forbidding assassination of heads of state could be set aside or circumscribed by another Executive Order without legislative approval.
6. In 1296 King Edward I captured the Stone of Scone, a symbol of Scottish independence associated with the coronation of their kings. The English finally returned it to Edinburgh exactly 700 years later. This *may* have inspired the author of this bizarre idea.

against Iraq.[7] Many members (ironically including two on the Human Rights Commission) are guilty of horrendous human rights violations themselves. As of 2003, 44% of the membership are considered "repressive" (12 members) or "mostly unfree (72 members)."[8] It is naïve to expect these governments to support anything that would inspire their own persecuted citizens to revolt. Article 51 of the UN Charter specifically states that membership does not override a nation's right of self-defense

Some advocate containment, including inspections and sanctions, to deal with state-support for terrorism. The history of sanctions in the twentieth century (see above) suggests these methods rarely are successful and then only under conditions that do not exist in the Middle East. Terrorist groups such as al-Qaeda are even less vulnerable to containment, inspections, or sanctions. Containment probably is the most feasible and effective approach against the threat of cyberterrorism so has its place in an overall plan. Cyberterrorism seems a relatively remote threat, although, paradoxically, success against the likes of al-Qaeda may make it more likely (Weimann, 2004).

Some advocate inciting rebellion to overthrow the governments of states that support terrorism. The US tried exactly this in Iraq after the Gulf War, where the likelihood of success seemed high. There was a well-organized Kurdish resistance movement (although divided into two main and several lesser factions), strong opposition to Saddam Hussein's government among the population of the southern marshes where the tradition of guerrilla resistance goes back 4000 years, an organized government in exile, the recent decimation of the Iraqi army, and American air patrols to protect the rebellion from the air. However, the United States withdrew its promised support, the rebellion was crushed, and American credibility was eviscerated. Similar conditions do not exist in the remaining states that actively support terrorism, although discontent runs high and pro-American youth are a majority in Iran.

A successful rebellion that a deposed leader survives can result in trial or exile. The advantage of the latter is that it encourages a leader to surrender rather than fight to the end. Exile was the fate of Idi Amin, Jean-Baptiste Aristide, Jean-Claude Duvalier, Fernando Marcos, Mengistu Haile Mariam, Napo-

---

7. Security Council Resolution 1441 "deplored" Iraq's failure to comply with its commitment to stop supporting terrorism, to end repression of its population, to provide access to humanitarian organizations, to account for Kuwaiti prisoners and to return Kuwaiti property. It decided that "Iraq has been and remains in material breach of its obligations" and that Resolution 1441 was "a final opportunity to comply." The Security Council said that it was determined to "secure full compliance" and recalled repeated warnings of serious consequences of continued violations. It recalled Resolution 675 authorizing member states to "use all necessary means to uphold and implement" Resolution 687 declaring that a cease-fire would be based on acceptance by Iraq of various obligations including disarmament. (Sofaer, *WSJ* 31 January 2003).
8. Freedom House publishes an annual assessment based on a clear methodology of what is meant by each of its four categories

leon, Reza Pahlavi, Charles Taylor, and Wilhelm II. But, many died as they resisted that fate till the end. Why not, then, make it attractive, by providing a
"Last Resort" on some beautiful island such as Socotra exclusively for dictators,
who could arrive anytime with all their cash, no questions asked, but never
leave. They would find luxurious accommodations and all modern conveniences
and amenities, at exorbitant rates. Rulers who ran out of money would become
members of the resort staff, cleaning rooms and cooking meals for recent arri-
vals.[9] Unfortunately, it does little to prevent the ex-dictator's cronies becoming
equally bad successors. Even worse, the idea is only satire.

Finally, some advocate traditional interstate war to destroy states that support terrorists. President Bush chose this option in Afghanistan and Iraq[10] in
what he warned would take a long time to resolve. The Bush administration,
after attempting the UN option, put together a strategy combining the criminal
justice system, civil defense, diplomacy and war options. It obtained significant
support from several, and minor support from many nations, despite the accusa-
tion that it was going it alone. The outcome is uncertain and the stakes are
enormous.

Much like the Normandy "D-Day" invasion during World War II in which
so much energy went into planning how to get ashore that there was none left to
plan what to do next, the Bush administration failed to plan adequately for winning the peace. There seems to have been little attention to possible reactions of
former adherents of the regime, Iran, or of al-Qaeda. The insurrections in Falu-
jah and Najaf were allowed to fester. Little provision seems to have made fo.
dealing with the many divisions within Iraqi society. Opposition by some US
officials to the exiles of the Iraqi National Congress delayed creation of an Iraqi
government and lent credibility to charges of US imperialism. However, these
mistakes were tactical rather than strategic, and were belatedly recognized and
corrected.

As of February 2005, the number of terror incidents in Iraq is declining, and
the number of people willing to provide intelligence is increasing. Many of the
senior leaders of al-Qaeda, if not the most dangerous three or four, have been
captured or killed, including several key imams in Saudi Arabia. Their finances
and communications have been badly disrupted. Over 10,000 fundamentalist
schools have been closed, recruitment is down and al-Qaeda web sites are complaining of "hypocrites," suggesting infiltration by spies and recruits willing to
sell out for rewards. Yemen has taken an innovative approach worth emulating
in holding Quranic debates between pro- and anti-terrorist clerics, to the discom-
fort of the latter.

---

9. The Last Resort, *Atlantic Monthly*, April 1992.
10. Given the focus among critics on the failure to find WMDs, it is worth noting that the
Congressional resolution giving President Bush authority to attack included 23 clauses,
only one of which mentioned them.

Afghanistan, Iraq, and Palestine all have elected governments now. In Iraq, many Sunni who boycotted the elections are realizing they may be left behind if they do not change tactics, and are planning to vote in the next round. In Palestine, Arafat is dead, Hamas is showing signs of shifting to politics, although it is too early to be completely optimistic, and negotiations have resumed with Israel, which is showing some flexibility.[11] Syria seems to be in retreat from Lebanon although it undoubtedly will leave agents behind and Hezbollah remains a threat. Saudi Arabia has been forced into local elections and Egypt is talking about real ones (we must expect and live with elections that select some governments and officials that are not as friendly toward us as we might wish).

Iran remains a major threat, particularly as efforts to prevent it building nuclear weapons remain ineffective, but it now is surrounded, with the American fleet controlling the Indian Ocean and Persian Gulf, and American troops stationed in friendly countries to the west in Iraq, the north in the "stans," and the east in Afghanistan. Iranian youth—over half the population—are not enthusiastic about rule by the ayatollahs, and are likely to become less so if they like what they see of secular rule in Afghanistan and Iraq.

Borrowing a term from the Soviet Union, in what the Middle East might call the "near abroad," revolution against centuries of authoritarian rule seems to be continuing its spasmodic course despite occasional backtracking in states such as Georgia, Kazakhstan, Kyrgystan, Romania, and Ukraine, with rumblings even in Belarus and Turkmenistan. The struggle against terrorism is merely the latest chapter in Man's long search for peace, to which we now turn.

Conclusion

Asymmetric war is a tool both of state and non-state actors. The former use it as an ancillary tactic, the latter as a basic strategy. Economic sanctions, a favorite tool of liberal governments, have not proved effective because the conditions for success are rare. Guerilla warfare has many forms, including resistance to invaders, revolt against colonial masters, and ancillary support for traditional campaigns. It often is romanticized and perceived as more effective than it has been in practice until it grows into a conventional campaign using regular forces. Terrorism is associated with non-state actors and took its modern form under the Irgun and Stern Gang. As with economic sanctions, political goals seldom have been achieved by terror alone unless very unusual conditions exist.

---

11. The essential tradeoff is almost certain to involve Palestine giving up its "right" of return in exchange for Israeli withdrawal from its "settlements." However, both concessions will face huge internal opposition.

Chapter 15
The Search for Peace

You cannot simultaneously prevent and prepare for war.
—Albert Einstein
Let him who desires peace prepare for war.
—Flavius Vegetius Renatus

This chapter takes up man's efforts to end or limit war. The Just War tradition and Truce of God provide the intellectual foundation for modern state-based efforts such as arms control, world government, peacekeeping, and the balance of power. Their failures have inspired nontraditional alternatives. The oldest and most idealistic ones are pacifism and non-violence. Reconciliation and its associated activities of restorative justice and truth commissions can moderate behavior and reduce tensions that can lead to the resumption of civil wars. The amorphous methods collectively know as Track II diplomacy can hurt and might help. This chapter describes and analyzes each of these approaches.

Just War Theory

St. Augustine and subsequent Catholic thinkers developed Cicero's notion of "Just War" into a highly influential theory dividing the question of morality with respect to war into two independent issues. The first is when war is just; the second is how to fight justly.

Jus ad bellum, the question of when war is just, was answered by St. Augustine with six propositions that have undergone relatively little change in fifteen centuries, so that we hear echoes of them whenever modern democracies debate the war option:

War must be the last resort
War must redress violated rights or defend against unjust threats
War must be openly declared by properly constituted governments
There must be a reasonable prospect of victory.
The means must be proportionate to the ends
The victorious can punish but must not humiliate the vanquished.

The following corollaries follow from these propositions:

Independent states form an international society
States have the right to territorial integrity and political sovereignty
Force or threats by one state against another constitutes aggression

Aggression justifies self-defense aided by any other states
Violation of a truce or treaty reopens the original conflict
Nothing but aggression can justify war

Just War theory encourages alternatives to war and tries to limit the violence if it occurs. Attacking a neighbor never can be just; defending oneself even
preemptively can be; friendly nations can but are not obligated to assist. Thus,
Article 51 of the United Nations Charter provides that "nothing" in the Charter
"shall impair the inherent" right of self-defense. The attack need not be on sovereign territory, but can be on an ally or on "national interests," a slippery concept generally including economic interests, embassies and consulates, ships at
sea, airplanes in flight, satellites in space, citizens and their property overseas,
and even abstract values such as credibility and values.

The "last" resort is difficult, probably impossible, to identify objectively
and unambiguously: ultimately, it is a matter of judgment. Aggressors trying to
appear just in their actions claim to be acting defensively, provoke others into
attacking them, or even fake an enemy attack on their own territory to justify
their aggression. The principles date most clearly from the 1648 Treaty of
Westphalia that ended the Thirty Years War and originated the modern state
system. This system was based on the principles of balance of power and non-
intervention in the internal affairs of nations. The latter assumed that states were
the surest protectors of the rights of their own citizens.

The Helsinki Accords can be interpreted as international recognition that
twentieth century events have refuted this assumption.[1] Thus, for example, US
Catholic bishops in 1993 declared a duty of intervention in cases of human
rights violations regardless of sovereignty. The American Declaration of Independence, the French Declaration of the Rights of Man and the Helsinki Human
Rights Accord exhibit the same reasoning. Some religious leaders make the peculiar argument that the United States should intervene only if its own national
interests are *not* also served, but exempt other nations from the same requirement. Their effort to add pure selflessness to Just War Theory but only for the
United States is pure bias.

Just War theory evolved as centralized government collapsed in Western
Europe and barbarian migrations, Norse raiders, and private armies made for a
Hobbesian world. As order began to reemerge, Just War theory was called upon
in an effort to eliminate private wars and to reduce overall violence by limiting it
to recognized states. However, doing so also eliminates the right to rebel against
an occupying power or an oppressive government. The UN wrestled with the
problem following WWII and declared:

---

1. Hitler's Germany, Stalin's Russia, Mao's China, Ho Chi Minh's Vietnam, Pol Pot's
Cambodia, Castro's Cuba, Mugabe's Zimbabwe, Amin's Uganda and many others.

Nothing in this definition can prejudice the right to self-determination, freedom and independence, as derived from the charter, of peoples forcibly deprived of that right, particularly of peoples under colonial and racist regimes or other forms of alien domination; nor the right of these peoples to struggle to that end and to seek and receive support…

This declaration allowed great powers and local hegemonic ones to intervene wherever their strategic interests dictated while ignoring cases such as Tibet where the right of rebellion was exercised against a power too dangerous to confront.

Aggressors can be punished but not humiliated. Of course, they must first be defeated before they can be punished. Deterrence, reform, restraint, and retribution are possible purposes. Equally unclear is whether to punish particular individuals or the aggressor state itself, and if the latter, how to do so.

Jus in Bello, how to fight justly, has evolved with time and with changes in technology and is likely to continue to do so. In medieval Europe, war supposedly was an honorable undertaking that was to be fought chivalrously—although the code could be set aside when fighting heretics or non-Christians. Capture while fighting in enemy uniform or fighting or spying while dressed as a civilian traditionally legitimates the death penalty.

Some weapons are judged unjust. Today, biological, chemical and nuclear weapons are so considered, although the first two have been used even after being declared illegal. Just War Theory treats those who make war materiel, as opposed to those who make the normal necessities of life, as legitimate targets. The distinction began to erode during Spanish Civil War and all but disappeared in World War II, partly to rationalize area bombing, but more fundamentally because nations mobilized every resource for war. Thus, terrorists should expect shorter shrift even than guerillas, as should those who hide, train, supply, finance, lead, or otherwise directly support them.

Just War theory emerged from western Christian thought. Some argue that it therefore is not universal, so irrelevant in a global context. But, there is no universal moral code, leaving each society a choice between following its own moral code, surrendering its sovereignty to an international body, or putting all morality aside to pursue its own self-interest without restraint. In democracies, elections provide a mechanism for voters to affirm or deny the policy and morals of their leaders.

Truce of God

The Peace of God tried to protect consecrated persons, places and times (essentially, priests, churches and sacred days) and led to the Truce of God. It was an effort in an anarchical age to limit war by forbidding it on Sunday beginning in 1027 AD. It was extended to Saturday in memory of the Resurrection, then to Friday in memory of the Passion, and then to Thursday in memory of the Ascension. It was extended to other consecrated days and periods, such as Advent through Epiphany and Mardi Gras through Easter. Ultimately, it limited war to only 80 days each year, twice the usual period of feudal service. In theory, the Truce of God was enforced by penance, exile (for up to thirty years) and excommunication. It applied to most of France, Germany, Italy and the Low Countries for about two centuries, by which time kings and dukes were again becoming capable of enforcing peace within their own domains. Magna Carta (1215) is part of this process, the barons giving up the right to make private war in exchange for the protection of the rights enumerated in the document (Knight, 2003).

Arms Control vs. Peace through Strength

The belief that arms races cause wars (Chapter 14) logically suggests arms control as the way to peace. Arms control bets national security on the assumption that potential enemies will reduce armaments mutually below safe levels. The opposite view, peace through strength, assumes that victory can be made so expensive that a potential aggressor will not attack (Chapter 12).

The term "arms race" describes a rapid, iterative increase in the quantity or quality of weapons in peacetime that increases the chances of war. The most common example given is the arms race leading up to World War I and the idea that the assassination in Sarajevo led to an accidental war. In the twenty years or so before the war, French and British spending doubled, and German spending increased ten-fold from a much smaller base. Inconveniently for the theory, non-defense spending increased even faster in all three countries. Also inconvenient, nations that never got into World War I such as Sweden and Switzerland also vastly increased their arms spending. Even today, these perpetual neutrals are among the best-armed states in the world.

Most inconvenient of all, we now know from sources such as diplomatic correspondence and minutes of their cabinet meetings that Germany aimed to displace Britain as Europe's power broker, eliminate France as a world power, dominate Russia and end its hope of controlling Constantinople, and unite middle Europe under its own sway. We now know from an exhaustive study of these primary sources that the German arms build up of the previous two or three decades did not drive but implemented policy (Fischer, 1967). A vast increase in arms expenditures did precede World War I, but as statisticians continually warn us, correlation is necessary but not sufficient to prove causation.

Arms race theorists have argued that failing to respond to an arms buildup will prove lack of hostile intent and prevent war. Thus, the one-sided arms buildup that preceded World War II is equally inconvenient for arms race theory. France hunkered down behind its Maginot Line. Russia trusted German promises. Britain ignored the warnings of Winston Churchill. Although Germany was not threatened, it attacked. The German arms build up did not drive but implemented policy.

Cold War policy makers using game theory (Chapter 2) coordinated arms control and arms buildup on the assumption that the superpowers shared a common interest in avoiding nuclear war. Arms control theory evolved from "first strike" capability into Mutually Assured Destruction—in effect, a game of Prisoners' Dilemma (Chapter 2). Betting on the rationality of the nuclear powers, the idea was to make sure that any country launching an attack would suffer total destruction, making the acronym for the doctrine, MAD, a description of the mind set required to start nuclear war. It worked: The Cold War arms race did not result in a nuclear war between the communist and free world.[2]

Arms control faces new problems with the end of the Cold War. Barnett (2004) probably is right in judging it irrelevant in the Core and futile in the Gap countries (Chapter 13). The increasing number of nuclear powers, the pursuit of chemical and biological weapons, the failure of the most dangerous states to keep agreements, and the growth of global terrorism—and particularly the possibility that terrorists might obtain weapons of mass destruction [WMDs] invalidate the assumptions on which arms control is based.

The United States has become so powerful militarily that no likely alliance has the means to force it to change any policy it deems vital to its national interests. If anything, the US preponderance is becoming even larger, as it continues to develop weapons that are even more exotic and powerful. Yet there is no peace. In a perfect example of Merton's Law of Unintended Consequences (Chapter 9), America's enemies have turned to asymmetric strategies (Chapter14) despite a significant "Catch-22."[3] Small attacks will not change US policy while large ones risk the almost random obliteration of whatever regime the US President sees fit to blame until he gets the right one, as the Taliban in Afghanistan and the Baathists in Iraq learned.

The domestic equivalent of arms control is gun control. The United States is a notoriously violent country, with around 30,000 gun deaths each year (about 80 a day).[4] As so often is the case, the devil is in the details. About a third of the total are murders and two-thirds of murder victims have criminal records.[5] Suicide accounts for most of the remainder, with the rest being accidents. Two-thirds of all gun deaths occur among 18-22 year olds.

---

2. Of course, the conclusion is uncertain. There is a joke about a charm that keeps wild polar bears away from Florida, the proof that it works being the lack of polar bears there.
3. Note 1, Chapter 4
4. Measured by murders per capita, seven countries are worse: South Africa (approximately 35 times worse than the US), Colombia, Thailand, Zimbabwe, Mexico, Costa Rica and Belarus. The United States, Uruguay, and Lithuania are tied at approximately 2 murders per 100000 people per year.
5. Chicago Police Department, (n.d.) *Murder Analysis*, and FBI Uniform Crime Reports.

Making guns difficult to obtain does not reduce suicides, with most shooters becoming leapers.[6] Gun control advocates always select Britain and Japan for their examples: they never select Switzerland and Finland, both of which have higher gun ownership and lower murder rates.

Gun advocates often speak of an individual's right to self-defense as a matter of faith. Armed robberies went up 44 percent, assaults 8.6%, and homicides 3.2% a year after Australians surrendered 640,381 personal guns.[7] US data from the National Crime Victimization Study [NCVS] suggest about 80,000 Defensive Gun Incidents [DGIs] per year in the United States. However, the NCVS survey is not anonymous and is carried out by Department of Justice employees, effectively warning respondents that they risk prosecution if they admit defending themselves.

Twelve surveys without this weakness conducted during the 1990s yield estimates varying from 700,000 to 2.2 million DGIs annually! Defenders feared for their lives in 400,000 cases, about forty times higher than the number of murders (Kleck and Gertz, 1995).[8] Two or more attackers were involved in 53% of DGIs; 46% of the defenders were women. Seventy-four percent of attackers were strangers, 63% took place outside the home, and only 10% involved family members or acquaintances. These data are consistent with a separate study that concluded that assault, murder, rape, and robbery are significantly lower in areas of the United States where permits for concealed firearms are obtained easily (Lott, 1997). The media routinely reports gun crimes, but rarely if ever reports DGIs. The result is a badly distorted picture of firearm use in the United States.

In the largest study of crime in America ever conducted, John Lott (1998) examined data on gun ownership, crime, arrests, and convictions separately for each of the United States' 3045 counties annually for 18 years. He found that state-imposed waiting periods and criminal background checks required by the Brady Act had no impact on violent crime rates. Non-discretionary carry permits (available in 32 of the 50 states when he did the study) reduce the number of gun crimes attempted, and for the ones that are attempted, 98% of the time merely brandishing a gun stops an attack without it being fired. High-crime urban areas experience the greatest improvements. Women benefit more than men and the improvement is not limited to those with weapons. This is a case where the free rider effect (Chapter 10) is positive!

A close examination of specific cases is not kind to the arms race theory. Germany's behavior was typical of rising hegemonic powers facing the great

---

6. Rich, Young, Fowler, Wagner and Black, March 1990. Guns and Suicide: Possible Effects of Some Specific Legislation. *The American Journal of Psychiatry*
7. Ed Chenel, Internet communication.
8. Cook and Ludwig (n.d.) concluded that DGIs would number 4.7 million if the original study had not been limited to one incident per individual.

power of the day.[9] It is common for an arms race to be initiated by a state interested in changing the status quo. The Cold War example suggests that sometimes it is difficult even to distinguish an "arms race" from a policy of "peace through strength." Similar conclusions follow at the domestic level from efforts to reduce violence through gun control.

Balance of Power

Some view balance of power as the most reliable basis for peace in an anarchic international system, that is one in which there is no greater power than the state. Balance of power theory asserts that a rising hegemon will provoke other states to form alliances to protect themselves against it, making successful conquest unlikely. This balance can operate regionally, globally or both. Thus, Hans Morgenthau (1948/1973) wrote:

> This being inherently a world of opposing interests and of conflict among them, moral principles can never be fully realized, but must at best be approximated through the ever- temporary balancing of interests and the ever-precarious settlement of conflicts. This school, then, sees in a system of checks and balances a universal principle for all pluralist societies. It appeals to historic precedent rather than to abstract principles, and aims at the realization of the lesser evil rather than the absolute good.

Analysts of this approach such as Henry Kissinger (1994) recognize about a dozen periods in history of actual balance of power systems (Figure 12.4). Crises and wars were common to these periods. That is, balance of power does not guarantee peace but prevents dominance by a single state and keeps wars short and limits the victor's gains. Professionals rather than citizen levies tend to fight balance of power wars. They are fought, not for great causes or national survival, but for strategic and policy reasons at the margins of empire. Citizens tend not to understand so often oppose them. Korea was the first such battle of the Cold War. Subsequently, the US and the USSR intervened selectively and strategically around the world, often using proxies to avoid direct confrontation.

With the end of the Cold War, some conclude from the increasing number of democracies, global interdependence, the dominance of the United States, and the disruptions of sub-state actors that balance of power no longer is relevant. This view makes four assumptions. First, democracies do not attack one another (Chapter 12). Second, the United States is so powerful economically, militarily, and technologically that no challenge to it is likely to succeed. Third, globalization of trade and investment is so pervasive that attacking another country amounts to attacking oneself. Fourth, the threat of Islamic terrorism will drive

---

9. Rome's buildup against Carthage and China's against the United States are two examples widely separated in time.

most other major powers into alliance to defeat it. So far, that has not happened, although that could change if terrorism expands and the corruption of the French, Russian, and UN leaders becomes more widely known.

World Government and Peacekeeping

Immanuel Kant (1795) generally is credited with being the first to propose world government as the route to world peace. Specifically, he proposed six "preliminary articles" and three "definitive articles" for perpetual peace:

Preliminary articles:

No treaty of peace shall be held valid in which there is tacitly reserved matter for a future war.

No independent states, large of small, shall come under the dominion of another state by inheritance, exchange, purchase, or donation

Standing armies shall in time be totally abolished.

National debts shall not be contracted with a view to the external friction of states.

No state shall by force interfere with the constitution or government of another state.

No state shall, during war, permit such acts of hostility which would make mutual confidence in the subsequent peace impossible: such are the employment of assassins, poisoners, breach of capitulation, and incitement to treason in the opposing state.

Definitive articles:

The civil constitution of every state should be republican.

The law of nations shall be founded on a federation of free states.

The law of world citizenship shall be limited to conditions of universal hospitality [sic].

The first significant effort to implement Kant's vision emerged from the horrors of World War I. The resulting League of Nations failed partly because the United States was not a member and partly because the League would not apply its own principles to condemn Italy's invasion of Ethiopia. Some draw a parallel with the UN failure to enforce numerous resolutions during the 1990s with respect to Iraq.

The United Nations replaced the League of Nations after World War II. It has provided a useful forum that has defused many disputes that could have ended in war.[10] It has reduced the violence of many disputes. Its peacekeeping

---

. 10. Like good news, the many successes tend to be forgotten in the face of the few failures.

forces have reduced the violence in others. Theory in the form of an analytical process has guided UN officials in deciding whether, when and how to intervene in a conflict. The first of three phases involves early warning analysis aimed at understanding the background, situation, causes, extent, and dynamics of the conflict. The completed phase includes actions that the UN could take to prevent escalation.

The second phase focuses on UN capabilities to carry out proposed actions, probable positive and negative consequences of each, and development of assessment criteria. Tasks such as caring for and repatriating·refugees, clearing mines, conducting elections, disarming and demobilizing combatants, humanitarian relief, maintaining public order, patrolling cease-fire lines, and rebuilding economies and civil society may be required. Finally, the UN identifies the political, human, and financial resources needed to carry out the preferred strategy and spells out coordination, timing, and sequencing requirements.

The third phase is implementation planning. The key UN departments and agencies are brought together, lead departments selected, mandates for action drawn up, agreements finalized, clearances and other operational requirements are obtained. Partnerships are formed with local actors, regional organizations, contact groups and NGOs. Evaluation and exit criteria are established and data collection mechanisms are arranged to determine progress. Plans for transition to local authorities are developed.

Despite what is supposed to happen, each time a new peacekeeping mission is authorized, UN officials must scramble to find governments willing to commit equipment, money and personnel. Apart from the time-consuming three-phase process outlined above, this alone has proven to be an agonizingly slow process at a time when speed can make all the difference between success and failure. The contingents sent often are poorly trained and equipped, particularly as to transport, logistics, and communications. Once on scene, national contingents of peacekeeping missions all too often refuse or second-guess orders from the mission commander. UN commanders are so pressured to avoid casualties among their troops that they appease the strongest local force, tolerating its abuses. As the strongest local force varies throughout each country, a coherent policy is almost impossible. The relief agencies often perpetuate the refugee camps that preserve the resentments across generations (Renner, September 2000).

UN peacekeeping divides naturally into two phases. During the Cold War, between 1948 and 1989, the largest concern was prevention of escalation and confrontation that might lead to global nuclear war between the United States and Soviet Union. Eighteen UN operations were begun during this period, of which nine ended before and five ended after 1989. The remaining four continue to this day. They focused on preventing violence, monitoring ceasefires, demilitarization, and policing and tried to provide conditions for a negotiated settlement based on the Westphalian state system.

With the likelihood of escalation into nuclear war reduced by the end of the Cold War, major powers were less concerned with restraining their allies. Long-simmering disputes boiled over. Forty-eight UN operations were begun in the fourteen-year period following 1989, of which eight[11] continue as of this writing. The goal gradually shifted from peacekeeping to peace building under the changed circumstances of the post-Cold War world. Peacekeeping gradually became less strategic and more humanitarian. The Helsinki Accords provided some justification for selective intervention in the internal affairs of states that violate the rights of their own citizens.[12] Finally, the shift reflected the study of past successes and failures by governments, NGOs, think tanks and universities that led to new ideas as to what was possible and desirable.

There have been a significant number of peacekeeping successes. To cite a few, El Salvador ended with free and fair elections after UN implementation of a peace accord following 12 years of civil war. Cambodia saw the establishment of a new constitution and government after destruction of weapons and mines, provision of human rights training, and repatriation of 370,000 refugees. In Mozambique, the UN demobilized local troops, monitored withdrawal of foreign ones, destroyed weapons, facilitated the return of 1.5 million refugees, and organized and monitored free elections. A ceasefire and withdrawal of foreign troops followed by repeal of repressive legislation and creation of a new government was achieved in Namibia. In West New Guinea the UN oversaw the successful transfer of powers from the Netherlands to Indonesia, maintained order, and improved economic, health and education services.

There have been failures too, most prominently in Lebanon, Rwanda and Somalia. Finally, there are cases that have gone unresolved for decades, most prominently the Middle East (since 1948), Kashmir (since 1949) and Cyprus (since 1964). The failures along with cases where no intervention has been possible have led to the suggestion that peacekeeping is fundamentally flawed. Luttwak (1999) suggests that UN intervention prevents rather than encourages resolution of the underlying conflicts. A forced ceasefire protects the weaker side from the consequences of defeat that leads to peace. It diverts resources from rebuilding ravaged societies to preparing for another round of war. Knowing there would be no such intervention could dissuade the weaker side from risking war. Where they do break out, letting them run their course usually leads to relatively rapid and realistic resolution through surrender and negotiation.

The theoreticians argued that peace was a complicated, multi-dimensional process involving a multitude of actors working on a vast swathe of activities designed to construct a liberal state. Threats to the peace such as poverty, ethnic and religious wars, terrorism, human rights abuses and the breakdown of civil society are beyond the capability of the traditional Westphalian system (Lederach, 1997).

---

11. East Timor, Kosovo, Ivory Coast, Liberia, Congo, Ethiopia and Eritrea, Sierra Leone, and Western Sahara.
12. Interventions still must be logistically, militarily and politically feasible.

Theoreticians distinguish between negative and positive peace. The former is reactive and imposed by outside peacekeepers. The latter assumes that democracy, development, and reconciliation can remove the causes of war. These assumptions are implicit in UN documents such as *An Agenda for Peace, An Agenda for Democratization,* and *An Agenda for Peace* (Ghali, 1992, 1994, 1996). These documents are based on the supposedly universal ideals of the UN Charter. They advocate targeting "the deepest causes of social injustice and political oppression." Major goals were disarmament, repatriation of refugees, restoration of order, economic development, formal and informal processes of political participation, election monitoring, protection of human rights and governmental reform.

Peacekeeping assumes governance will devolve upon local inhabitants once the situation is stable. But this might never happen, leading to essentially permanent peace missions (*e.g.*, Cyprus, Israel). Theoreticians differ as to how to interpret this result, the two main camps being those who see peacekeeping as a duty and those who see it as "neo-imperialism."

There are two important problems with the critique. First, the critics have provided no evidence that the underlying UN assumptions actually are wrong. They speak in generalities and possibilities rather than specifics and probabilities. *Which* people do not want some form of democracy, exactly what do they desire instead, and is the desire acceptable?[13] Second, the alternative to peacekeeping is war. Luttwak may be right that letting people fight it out is the quickest and cheapest route to peace. It might also lead to expanded or perpetual war. Predictors to distinguish the two might be useful, so that the better decisions can be made on whether or not to intervene.

The UN was unable to summon the will to enforce its own resolutions in Iraq. Instead, the US formed a coalition in what critics termed a "unilateral" intervention to overthrow Saddam Hussein although it had twice as many countries as are represented in the Security Council. It hardly was auspicious to learn that the two main opponents of intervention, France and Russia, and several high UN officials, were taking bribes from Saddam Hussein or that the UN long resisted efforts to investigate the charges. Nor is it encouraging that the UN withdrew from Iraq over the protests of its own dying representative when it suffered a few casualties. The UN seldom has been effective without the active involvement of a major power, usually the United States, occasionally Britain or France. Where this has not been the case, such as in Rwanda, events have been left to run their disastrous course.

Because every country eventually gets its turn on every commission, we have absurdities such as Libya, Sudan and Cuba on its Human Rights Commission and Iran and Iraq on its Disarmament Commission. It is as if civil rights

---

13. There are groups that desire non-democratic alternatives such as the Iranian ayatollahs and the Syrian Baathists. However, these do not hold much hope for a just and peaceful world.

organizations were required to extend membership to the KKK and the Nazis and to give them a chance in the rotation as chairman. UN members bring their own agendas to every vote—which should be no surprise, as that is what nations do. Thus, for example, China's vote on vote on, say, Cyprus or Sudan, has less to do with justice or facts, and everything to do with avoiding precedents that might affect its control of Tibet or its claims to Taiwan.

Focusing on the UN's failures has led to proposals for reform as well as proposals for an alternative international organization limited to democratic states that adhere to the rule of law. The rewards of membership, both financial and defensive, could motivate non-members to become more democratic, assumed, probably correctly, to be a good thing. Setting up criteria for membership poses some practical difficulties given the practice of modern dictators running rigged elections. Setting up a mechanism to eject or suspend governments that regress poses an even greater difficulty. NATO, trying like so many institutions to preserve its existence after the problem it was designed to solve not longer exists, could be converted into the military arm of this new organization. Serious negotiations directed at creating such an institution might even motivate reform of the UN, making the new one unnecessary.

Pacifism and Nonviolence

In 1660, the Quakers declared to Charles II:

> We utterly deny all outward wars and strife, and fightings with outward weapons, for any end, or under any pretense whatever; this is our testimony to the whole world. The Spirit of Christ by which we are guided is not changeable, so as once to command us from a thing as evil, and again to move unto it; and we certainly know, and testify to the world, that the Spirit of Christ, which leads us into all truth, will never move us to fight and war against any man with outward weapons, neither for the kingdom of Christ, nor for the kingdoms of this world.

Western pacifism is largely rooted in obedience to Jesus's example of self-sacrifice.[14] The Amish, Mennonites, Seventh Day Adventists and Society of Friends (Quakers) are best known. They are willing to die but not to kill for their beliefs. The best did not flee their obligations as citizens, but sought alternative ways to serve, often as medics or in ambulance units. Many served heroically and two received the Medal of Honor.

---

14. This does not imply that pacifism is exclusively rooted in Christianity. The classical Greek playwright Euripedes (*Trojan Women, Hecuba*) was a pacifist. Mohism, founded by Mo Zi, a contemporary of Confucius, opposes any form of aggression. One of Islam's most famous and influential philosophers was Al-Ghazali, a pacifist. There are similar examples from virtually every civilization.

A. A. Milne (1934, Hitler's second year as chancellor) proposed a thought experiment in "The Pacifist Spirit." The leaders of England, France, Germany, and Italy were to be killed if they led their country into war, even in self-defense even against a fifth leader not subject to the same constraint.[15] He concludes that, "there would be no more war if the makers of it were always the first victims," proving to his satisfaction that war is not a "biological necessity."

Milne never tells us who was to do the killings. Biological necessity is not the only explanation for war, one alternative being his fellow pacifist William James's (1906) assumption that war is motivated by glory, plunder, and the pleasures of pillage. This book treats many other possibilities without claiming to be complete. However, the fundamental problem with stand alone "thought experiments" is that, just like the plot of a novel, they always can be made to come out the way the author wants. The serious theoretician should not take them too seriously. Even in real experiments, preconceptions can affect interpretation of results. Bertrand Russell joked that American rats in maze experiments would run about until they accidentally found the food while German rats would sit quietly while they evolved the solution in their inner consciousness. The so-called Pygmalion effect warns us of the tendency of experimenters to find whatever they are looking for. It is the reason for doing experiments "double blind"—that is, so neither the observer or care giver knows whether the subject received the treatment or a placebo. It is one more reason experiments, especially those involving human behavior, require replication and great care in interpreting results.

Pacifism is not passive. Nonviolence requires courage and action. Jeanette Rankin's votes in the US Congress against both WWI and WWII are examples of belief put into practice. Aung San Suu Kyi, Gandhi, King, Mandela, and Thoreau are famous practitioners imprisoned for their beliefs. All are admired. Excepting the first, who remains under house arrest, each achieved his goal but suffered setbacks when followers could not be controlled and turned to violence in contradiction of their principles. Pacifism and non-violence are individual moral choices based on the conviction that war is wrong.

Martin Luther King (1963) specifies six requirements for nonviolent resistance. First, following Thoreau, it requires willingness to suffer consequences. Second, following Gandhi, nonviolent resistance requires courage and discipline. Third, its goal is friendship and reconciliation rather than victory. Fourth, it targets evil, not people. Fifth, one must not do violence to others or to one's own spirit. Sixth, it requires faith that justice will triumph.

Holmes (1990) names six examples of successful nonviolent resistance. The first is a report by an anthropologist of an isolated tribe that frowns on disagreements of even the mildest sort. The second is that of Gandhi's and his disciple Badshah Khan's movements for Indian and Pushtun independence from Britain. The third is Norwegian and Dutch resistance against the Nazis. The

---

15. Such as Stalin, who ruled Russia at the time Milne made this suggestion.

fourth is Cesar Chavez's farm labor movement in California, the fifth that of the Druze in the Golan Heights directed against the Israelis, and the sixth led to the overthrow of Ferdinand Marcos in the Philippines.

Of these cases, the isolated tribe is irrelevant to modern conditions in which most people live in interdependent states participating in a world economy. Gandhi and Badshah Khan succeeded only because Britain already had decided to abandon India because it no longer could afford the costs of empire. Integration had begun in the US Army, professional sports, the schools, and many workplaces over a decade before King began his work. Israel, the Philippines, and South Africa were nominally democratic and under intense international pressure. The Norwegian and Dutch resistance succeeded only because of Allied armies fighting a conventional war. India, Pakistan, and South Africa often turned violent.

In "Nonviolent acts that break oppression's chains," Peter Ackerman[16] (*Christian Science Journal*, February 2003) does not give a single example of nonviolence succeeding against oppression. Instead, typically, he tells us of his hopes and why these methods *should* work in much the same way medieval scholastics argued that a spider as a manifestation of evil should not be able to pass a barrier of ground unicorn horn that was a manifestation of virginal purity. Nobody ever tried nonviolent resistance against Hitler, Kim Il Sung, Mao Tse Tung, Pol Pot, Saddam Hussein, or Stalin for reasons that expose its limitations.

However, nine recent and ongoing nonviolent movements require that we reserve judgment. Lech Walesa's Solidarity Movement in Poland and Vaclev Havel's Velvet Revolution in Czechoslovakia, both with considerable covert help from the United States, successfully opposed satellites of the dying Soviet Union. The most impressive exception is the Orange Revolution in Ukraine, which came under the dictatorship of Leonid Kuchma with the fall of the Soviet Union. He rid the country of his opponents by methods that were revealed when tape recordings became public of him ordering his Interior Minister to dispose of several individuals. This led to public and peaceful protests that created a viable opposition and prevented Kuchma's nomination for a third presidential term. He rigged the election of his chosen successor so blatantly that tens of thousands of Ukrainians turned out in a sustained and peaceful protest that gained the backing of much of the world. The Ukrainian Supreme Court ordered new elections in December 2004, which were widely accepted as fair. As noted above, peaceful revolutions are beginning to take hold against other successor dictatorships in other former Soviet Satellites.

Nobel laureate Aung San Suu Kyi leads another nonviolent movement in Myanmar. The Dalai Lama, also a Nobel laureate, leads one on behalf of but from outside Tibet. More amorphous ones are directed at the governments of Iran and China. Early in 2005, the Kyrgyz dictator fell to a peaceful protest, although it was motivated primarily by clan competition. Another nonviolent ef-

---

16. *Christian Science Journal*, February 2003

fort whose outcome remains unknown is the Varela Project, essentially a peti-
tion for democracy in Cuba that Fidel Castro has repressed but not destroyed,
and the related Ladies in White, some 30 wives of prisoners of conscience in the
Cuban gulags. Each Sunday since early 2004, these women have marched after
mass in St. Rita's church some ten blocks in silent protest at Fidel Castro's oppressive regime.

Track II Diplomacy

Track II diplomacy[17] evolved from Eisenhower's "People-to-People" program. A myriad of educational, private and government cultural exchange and
service programs followed, among them Experiment in International Living,
Fulbright Fellowships, Junior Year Abroad, Peace Corps, and Sister Cities.
Track II Diplomacy now includes "non-state actors" such as churches, think
tanks, humanitarian organizations, student exchanges, and former government
officials.

Conflict theorists and practitioners see Track I and Track II diplomacy as
complementary. Track I diplomacy can resolve issues such as boundaries, distribution of political power, and economic structure, all of which are beyond the
capability of Track II diplomacy. Conversely, Track II is better suited than
Track I to resolving issues of identity, relationships, and understanding. Positive
peace is not possible without resolving both types of issues. The idea is to provide a safe non-judgmental process in which individuals caught up in intractable
conflicts can explore their fears, hopes, ideas, needs and perceptions so as to
develop mutual understanding and learn problem-solving methods. In some
cases, the process seeks to influence public opinion or Track I negotiators.

Chiagas (2003) identifies three Type II activities. The first involves unoffi-
cial actors serving as intermediaries between people and government. The intermediaries often are former government officials, the most prominent example
being Jimmy Carter.[18] A second occurs when neutrals bring key individuals together in their personal rather than their official capacities, for off-the-record
talks focused on trust building. A third occurs when citizens take the initiative
and the lead in trying to stimulate progress in official negotiations.

Another set of activities focus on problem solving, usually following models developed by scholars such as Burton (1969), Fisher (1989), or Saunders
(1996). These "engage representative citizens from the conflicting parties in
designing steps to be taken in the political arena to change perceptions and
stereotypes, to create a sense that peace might be possible, and to involve more
and more of their compatriots [in achieving it]" (Saunders, 1969). Knowledge-

---

17. Joseph Montville of the US Department of State coined the term, to contrast it with
official or "Track I" diplomacy.
18. However, Carter seems too friendly to dictators and too certain of his own rectitude,
and therefore something of a loose canon.

able, skilled, and neutral scholars or practitioners usually act as trainers and fa-
cilitators. Participants are drawn from involved and politically influential member of the community, such as journalists, scholars, and government personnel.

Track II seeks to affect intangibles, so is difficult to assess. Evaluation usually comes in the form of questionnaires completed by participants at the end of
Track II activities. Those who participate tend to be enthusiasts for peace who
may not—in fact usually clearly are not—representative of their community.
They take place at the end of the activity when friendships and feelings are
warmest. However, there is nothing to suggest that Track II activities are harmful and much to suggest that they may be helpful. At their best, Track II efforts
can open channels of communication, reduce stereotyping, strengthen the moderate members of the community, and weaken the fanatics. Track II diplomacy
can create a climate in which Track I diplomats can make concessions and create the rudiments of an infrastructure for reconciliation and peace (below).

To accomplish all this, Track II activists usually must overcome considerable obstacles. They must face the opprobrium of their society, the hostility of
often state-controlled media, the propaganda of their educational system, and the
obstacles to meeting counterparts created by their governments. As some wit
said, Track II diplomacy is least likely where it is most needed.

Reconciliation

When a civil war winds down, reconciliation, sometimes called restorative
justice, is an essential element of efforts to create or restore civil society.[19] Maynard (2000) proposes a five-step model for community reconciliation following
civil war based on her experience in Bosnia. The first two steps are preparatory.
Establishing safety for people and property is the first step because nothing is
possible without it. Training an honest police force representative of the warring
population has a very high priority. It leads to "communalization," during which
traumatic experiences are shared in a safe environment in conjunction with a
period of mourning over losses.

The next two steps initiate the healing process itself. The third step is reconstructing relationships with former adversaries. It starts small—buying bread
from and selling milk to the baker who was on the other side, for example. Joint
committees often work to eliminate disparagement and stereotyping in educational materials. Re-establishing personal and moral codes set aside in war is the
fourth and perhaps the most difficult step. "Quick Impact Projects [QIPs]" rebuilding infrastructure are undertaken that require former adversaries work toward a common end.[20] QIPs serve the same role as and may be indistinguishable

---

19. The domestic equivalent is restitution or victim offender mediation. Its opposite is
vigilantism, which is most common when law enforcement is weak or corrupt.

.   20. One famous QIP is the rebuilding from one end by the Muslims and from the other
by the Croats of the bridge at Mostar in Bosnia-Herzegovina. Built in 1566, destroyed in

from Confidence Building Measures [CBMs], the tool of traditional diplomacy. Osgood (1962) proposed a similar approach in gradual reciprocated tension reduction that is based on the tit-for-tat strategy devised from the study of Prisoners's Dilemma (Chapter 2).

The final step is full restoration of civil society, including shared governance. Truth commissions have proved important to the entire reconciliation process. National governments or international organizations establish them to ferret out and report on human rights violations that occurred during a specific conflict or period. Truth commissions take testimony from perpetrators, victims, relatives, and anyone else with knowledge of past abuses. Their purpose is to promote national reconciliation. They often help distinguish a new government from the one guilty of abuses, legitimating its authority. Approximately two-dozen have been established, and at least a dozen others additional ones called for (Hayner, 1994; Kritz, 1995).

Among the more successful instances is the South African Commission of Truth and Reconciliation, set up in 1995 to investigate apartheid-era human rights investigations over the previous 35 years. Chaired by Archbishop Desmond Tutu, the commission held public hearings in 12 languages throughout the country at which former victims of human rights abuses told their stories and 7112 individuals applied for amnesty (Hayner, 1994). As of November 2000, the commission had granted 849 amnesties, and refused 5392. The remaining 871 included duplicate applications, withdrawn applications, or other dispositions (www.doj.gov.za/trc).

The UN Transitional Administration in East Timor provides an example established by an international body. It gave the Commission for Reception, Truth, and Reconciliation three tasks. The first was to investigate human rights violations committed in East Timor between April 1974 and October 1999. The second was to facilitate reconciliation and reintegration of individuals who confessed to minor crimes. The third was to recommend measures to prevent future abuses and address the needs of victims. Between 25 and 30 regional commissioners had two years to complete their work (Hayner, 2001).

Conclusion

When one takes account of the many causes and types of war, and the many different means of fighting, it becomes less surprising that peace has proved so elusive. A common theme one hears among peace activists is the need for better relationships among people, by which method alone they expect to eliminate all war. However, not all people are like the other like-minded enthusiasts they

---

1993, reopened in July 2004, it had long been a tourist attraction. It is featured on a Bosnian stamp along with Emir Balic, 13 times the winner of the sometimes fatal head-first diving contest from the bridge to the water 20 meters (65 feet) below.

meet, and such a *reductio ad absurdum* is unlikely to prove efficacious. International organizations fall short for reasons discussed above, with the best hopes probably to be found in a combination of economic growth, democratization, and sophisticated strategic thinking.

Chapter 16
Prolegomena to a Theory of Conflict

To go boldly where no man has gone before
—*Startrek* motto

This chapter summarizes and synthesizes conflict theory and methods. It begins with a brief assessment of the theoretical ideas discussed in the text. A similar assessment of the methods for managing conflict follows. The chapter closes by suggesting a coherent but very preliminary synthesis written with the criteria for good theory in mind.

<u>Status of Theories</u>

Figure 16.1a-f rates theoretical ideas discussed in the book. It dichotomizes each as applicable or not at each level of conflict, and if applicable as either strong (capital letters) or weak (lower case letters) as to empirical support (E), falsifiability F), logic (L), parsimony (P), and usability (U). the more columns in which a concept is rated the more generalizable, the final criterion for good theory, it is. The ratings are subjective, audacious and debatable.

Twenty-nine ideas pertain to individual conflict, fifteen of them exclusively so. These are evolutionary and biological, for which the scientific evidence seems relatively strong, or psychological and psychiatric, for which the evidence is ambiguous. The ideas related to personality are potentially useful for conflict management tasks such as team formation. The usefulness of the other ideas seems low, as it is difficult in normal circumstances to control any of them in any meaningful way. Of the remaining fourteen, five appear applicable across all levels of conflict. One of these pertains to risk, one to stress, and three to aspects of Merton's Law of Unintended Consequences. All enjoy reasonably strong scientific support, so probably are essential components of any general theory of conflict.

Fifty-nine ideas are applicable to interpersonal conflict, thirteen of them exclusively so. Those pertaining to culture interact with personality and education, so are difficult to apply but have potential for conflict management in intercultural situations. The Dual Concern model probably provides a more useful approach to understanding interpersonal situations. Five of the ideas apply to six, and two of them to all seven levels of conflict. Two originate with game theory and two with cultural studies. The most important to conflict theory are "fairness" and the underlying philosophical assumptions of conflict participants.

Theory	Chapter	Individual aggression	Interpersonal conflict	Community conflict	Intellectual conflict	Organization conflict	Intra-state conflict	International conflict
Evolution: aggressive or pacific nature	3	EflPu						
Sociobiology: Predation	3	EFLpu						
Sociobiology: Anti-predation	3	EFLpu						
Biology: Brain physiology	3	EFLPu						
Biology: Hormones	3	EFLPu						
Aggression as Instinct	4	EfLpu						
Hydraulic theory of aggression	4	efLpU						
The Unconscious & Repressed Memory	4	eflpu						
Ego, Id, and Superego	4	eflpu						
Eight stages of human development	4	efLpu						
Personality: authoritarian	5	efLPU						
Personality: Sensing-Intuition	5	efLPU						
Personality: Extroversion-Introversion	5	efLPU						
Personality: Thinking-Feeling	5	efLPU						
Personality: Judging-Perceiving	5	efLPU						
Sociobiology: Sexual aggression	3	EfLpu	EfLpu					
Social learning	4	EfLpU	EfLpU					
Frustration-Aggression	4	eflpU	eflpU					

Theory	Chapter	Individual aggression	Interpersonal conflict	Community conflict	Intellectual conflict	Organization conflict	Intra-state conflict	International conflict
Evolution: Benign aggression	4	EfLPu	EfLPu					
Alcohol	3	EfLpU	EfLpU					
Drugs of abuse	3	EfLpU	EfLpU	EfLpU				
Psychiatry: Malignant aggression	4	eflpu	eflpu	eflpu			eflpu	eflpu
Unintended consequences self-defeating action	9	efLPU	efLPU	efLPU		efLPU	efLPU	efLPU
Human Needs Theory	4	EfLpU	EfLpU		EfLpu			
Attitudes toward risk	2	EFLPU	eFLPU	EFLPU	EFLPU	EFLPU	EFLPU	EFLPU
Psychology: Stress	7	EFLPU	EFLPU	EFLPU	EFLPU	EFLPU	EFLPU	EFLPU
Unintended consequences: Values distort judgment	9	eflPU	eflPU	eflPU	eflPU	eflPU	eflPU	eflPU
Unintended consequences: Erroneous appraisal	9	eflPU	eflPU	eflPU	eflPU	eflPU	eflPU	eflPU
Unintended consequences: partial information	9	eflPU	eflPU	eflPU	eflPU	eflPU	eflPU	eflPU
Gender: Relational aggression	6		EfLPu					
Culture: Assertiveness	5		EFLpU					
Culture: Space	5		EFLpU					
Culture: Time	5		EFLpU					
Culture: Relational vs. Substantive	5		EFLpU					
Culture: Formal vs. informal	5		EFLpU					
Culture: Optimistic vs. pessimistic	5		EFLpU					

Theory	Chapter	Individual aggression	Interpersonal conflict	Community conflict	Intellectual conflict	Organization conflict	Intra-state conflict	International conflict
Sociobiology: Dominance	3		EfLpu					
Sociobiology: Moralistic Aggression	3		efLpu					
Sociobiology: Parental discipline	3		eflpu					
Sociobiology: Weaning	3		eflpu					
Dual Concern Models	5		EfLPU					
Communication: gender	6		eFlpu					
Generation Gap	5		efLPu	efLPu				
Communication: Linguistic models	5		EF	EF		EF		
Communication: Social models	5		EFLPU	EFLPU		EFLPU		
Communication: System models	5		efLu	efLu		efLu		
Prisoner's Dilemma	2		EFLPU	EFLPU		EFLPU	EFLPU	EFLPU
Definitions of fairness	2		EFLPU	EFLPU		EFLPU	EFLPU	EFLPU
Culture: Individual vs. collective culture	5		EFLpU	EFLpU		EFLpU		EFLpU
Nash stabilities	2		EFLPU	EFLPU		EFLPU	EFLPU	EFLPU
Sociobiology: territory	3		EfLpu	Eflpu			Eflpu	EfLpu
Culture: Power distance	5		EFLpU	EFLpU	EFLpU	EFLpU		EFLpU
Power	5		EFLPU	EFLPU	EFLpU	EFLPU	EFLPU	EFLPU
Underlying philosophical assumptions	11		EfLpU	EfLpu	EfLpU	EfLpu	EfLpu	EfLpu

Theory	Chapter	Individual aggression	Interpersonal conflict	Community conflict	Intellectual conflict	Organization conflict	Intra-state conflict	International conflict
Gangs as nation states	7			efLPU				
Hostage or crisis negotiation	7			EFlpU				
Social order (Parsons)	7			EFlpu				
Functions of conflict: Safety valve	7			eflpU		eflpU	eflpU	eflpU
Functions of conflict: Warning	7			eflpU		eflpU	eflpU	eflpU
Deliberative assemblies	10			EFLPU			EFLPU	EFLPU
Ethnic Conflict	7			Efl_pU			EfLpU	EfLpU
Functions of conflict: Adjust power	7			Efl_pU			EfLpU	EfLpU
Functions of conflict: boundaries	7			EfL_pU			EfLpU	EfLpU
The Matriarchal Past	6			eFlpu				eFlpu
Class Conflict	7			eFLPu		eFLPu	eFLPu	eFLPu
Voting	10			EfLPU		EfLPU		eflpu
Search for Peace: pacifism & nonviolence	15			eFlPU			eFIPU	eFIPU
Search for Peace: Reconciliation	15			Efl_pU			EfLpU	EfLpU
Search for Peace:Track II Diplomacy	15			efl_pU			efLpU	efLpU
Free Rider Problem	10			EflPU			EflPU	
Tragedy of the Commons	10			EflPU			EflPU	
Search for Peace: Arms Control	15			efLPU				efLPU

Theory	Chapter	Individual aggression	Interpersonal conflict	Community conflict	Intellectual conflict	Organizaton conflict	Intra-state conflict	International conflict
Search for Peace: Peace through Strength	15			EFLPU				eflPU
Functions of conflict: Develop consensus	7		EflpU	eflpU	eflpU	eflpU	eflpU	eflpU
Authority: charismatic	7		eflpu	EFLpu	EFLpu	EFLpu	EFLpu	EFLpu
Behavioral model of labor-management	9					EFLPU		
Sexual Harassment	6					EFLpU		
Authority: bureaucratic	7					EFLPU	EFLPU	EFLPU
Causes of war: Relative Deprivation	12						Eflpu	
Causes of War: Correlates of War	12						EFLpu	EFLpu
Causes of war: territorial imperative	12						EFLpU	EFLpU
Methods of war: Guerrilla	13						EFLpU	EFLpU
Methods of war: Strategic Geography	13						EFLPU	EFLPU
Methods of war: Strategy	13						EFLPU	EFLPU
Methods of war: Tactics	13						EFLPU	EFLPU
Methods of war: Terrorism	13						eflPU	eflPU
Aggression as therapy	4						exxxu	exxxu
Search for Peace: Democracy	15						EfLPU	EfLPU
Search for Peace: Just War	15						XXLPu	XXLPu
Types of War	13						EFLpu	EFLpu

Theory	Chapter	Individual aggression	Interpersonal conflict	Community conflict	Intellectual conflict	Organization conflict	Intra-state conflict	International conflict
Women and Peace	6						eFIPU	eFIPU
Causes of War: Arms Races	12							EFLPU
Causes of War: Borders	12							eFLPu
Causes of war: Ecological Equilibrium	12							eFIPu
Causes of war: Expected Utility	12							EFLPU
Causes of war: Nation-State System	12							eFIpu
Causes of war: Polarity	12							EFLPu
Causes of war: Reproductive Success	12							EfLPu
Origins of war: Archaeology	13							Eflpu
Search for Peace: Balance of Power	15							efLPU
Search for Peace: World Government	15							efLPU
Capitalism	11		EFLPU	EFLPU	EFLPU	EFLPU	EFLPU	eFIPU
Marxism	11		Eflp	Eflp	Eflp	Eflp	Eflp	eFIPU
Theological disputes	11		FLp	FLp	FLp	FLp'		
Evolution vs. creationism	11		EFLPU	EFLPU	EFLPU			
Intractable conflict	14						efl	eflpu
Checks and balances	11			EFLPU		EFLPU		

Thirty-three ideas seem applicable to community conflict, only three exclusively so. Of these, treating gangs as a facsimile of the nation-state system—or as a parody of its worst elements—has led to some useful methods for dealing with them. Hostage negotiation theory and method are developing in concert. The remaining ideas carry over to the next three, four, or even five levels of conflict, charismatic authority being the most general concept in this group, although it seems of limited usefulness to a conflict manager.

Only eleven ideas seem applicable to intellectual conflict, none exclusively so. The paucity of methods to resolve intellectual conflict may partially explain why they go on for so long. Academic debates are famously bitter because they involve articulate, egotistical, and intelligent people with lots of discretionary time. Theological ones often end in schism.

Twenty-five ideas are applicable to organizational conflict. All but three apply at lower levels already discussed. Sexual harassment is a narrow issue. The behavioral theory of labor negotiations is broader but primarily pertains to unionized corporations. Despite its breadth and sophistication, which makes it useful at this level, it is unlikely to be part of a general theory of conflict, except perhaps for some of its insights into negotiation. Bureaucracy is a pervasive form of organization, but a general theory of conflict probably will have to be broader, and aim at relating form of organization to types and methods of conflict resolution.

Forty ideas are applicable at the intra-state level. Two-thirds of them apply at lower levels. Of the remaining thirteen, most pertain to violent conflict, which is to say the causes, methods, and resolution of civil war and revolution. Aggression as therapy, relative deprivation, strategy, tactics, territorial imperative, and women and peace, are unlikely to be components of a general theory of conflict. Guerrilla war and terrorism must be integrated into a taxonomy of types of war that also must incorporate the findings of the Correlates of War project. Strategic geography seems to have great applicability, although it requires continual updating to reflect the precise global situation. Just war theory and democracy are likely to remain major components of a general theory, despite the philosophical rather than scientific dimensions of both.

Fifty-three ideas are applicable to interstate conflict, forty-three of which apply at lower levels as well. The remaining ideas pertain to the causes and resolution of interstate war. Two of these, ecological equilibrium and reproductive success, apply at best to intertribal war, so are not of much relevance to the world with which most of are concerned. The archaeology of war may tell us something of the origins of interstate war and can provide an evolutionary perspective in developing a conflict taxonomy. Of the remaining ideas, a general theory of conflict requires resolution of the arguments between arms through strength and peace through strength and between the nation state system and world government. Polarity theory can incorporate balance of power theory. Expected utility, which incorporates risk and cost-benefit analysis, almost certainly must be part of a general theory.

Applicability of Methods for Managing Conflict

Figure 16.2a-c summarizes the methods for managing conflict discussed in the book. Unlike theory, there are no generally accepted criteria for judging methods. The best we probably can do is to say that what works without unintended consequences is good. Every method works some of the time; no method works all of the time. In effect, the subjective judgments in Figure 16.2 are normative rather than prescriptive. In the end, managers must choose a method or combination of methods based on situation-specific factors such as the number of stakeholders and the issues.

It is immediately apparent that no one method works at all seven levels of conflict: there is no general solution to the problem of managing conflict. Only two methods, mediation and stability analysis, appear useful across six levels. They are complementary rather than contradictory. Mediators can facilitate or bring disputants to agreement. Stability analysis can help the mediator to identify possible solutions and make the process more efficient. Adjusted winner, proportional allocation, arbitration, and negotiation, are the next most general methods, applicable across five levels of conflict. The first two of these are largely limited to division of tangible assets of all kinds, while the second two are general, differing primarily in whether or not a third-party is assisting in reaching agreement. The remaining methods are increasingly limited both between and within levels.

The methods available tend to increase in number and variety with the level of the conflict, but so do the types of conflict experienced within each. Therapeutic techniques are the only methods available for reducing individual aggression. Stress management appears to be adequate for normal people, and drug therapies are available for those who are overly aggressive. Catharsis finds little support in the scientific literature and psychoanalysis is best for those with minor neuroses and plenty of time and money. The academic literature, in a characteristic bias, gives relatively little attention to the problems of the overly pacific. Perhaps the omission can be corrected by adding training in becoming more, not less aggressive to the methods in Figure 16.2.

Fourteen methods appear applicable to resolving interpersonal disputes, but ten are limited to special circumstances. Hostage and crisis negotiation is a tool of law enforcement. Voluntary cooperation is useful only if the benefits are high, the costs are low, and the people involved know each other well enough for social pressure to ensure long-term compliance. Restitution, in the form of victim-offender mediation, is an alternative to torts. The four mathematical techniques (adjusted winner, proportional allocation, imaginary auction, and Steinhaus procedure) are useful in dividing property among claimants. Stability analysis requires special skills in mathematics and computer programming. Gun control may be efficacious if it prevents someone getting to a gun when angry— but that almost certainly also prevents getting to one needed for self-defense.

Method	Chapter Reference	Individual aggression	Interpersonal conflict	Intellectual conflict	Community conflict	Organizational conflict	Intra-state conflict	International conflict
Adjusted winner	2		xx		xx	xx	xx	xx
Advisory Boards and Committees	9				xx	xx	xx	xx
Aggression as therapy	4						xx	xx
Appeal to higher authority	5	xx	xx	xx	xx	xx	xx	
Arbitration	8		xx		xx	xx	xx	xx
Argument & Debate	11		xx	xx				
Arms Control	15							xx
Assassination	14		xx				xx	xx
Assimilation	7						xx	
Avoidance	5	xx	xx	xx	xx	xx	xx	xx
Balance of Power	15							xx
Boulwarism	9				xx			
Boycott	14				xx	xx		
Boycott	14		xx			xx	xx	xx
Capitulation	5	xx	xx	xx	xx	xx	xx	xx
Catharsis	3	xx						
Civil disobedience	14				xx	xx	xx	
Competitive Strategy	9					xx		xx
Coup	12					xx	xx	xx
Crisis planning	9				xx	xx	xx	xx
Deliberative assemblies	10				xx		xx	xx
Denial	5	xx	xx					
Drug therapies	3	xx						
Economic Sanctions	14						xx	xx
Economic Sanctions	14						xx	xx
Expulsion	7						xx	
Fire or exile	14					xx	xx	xx
Forced migration	7						xx	
Genocide	7						xx	

Figure 16.2a
Conflict Management Methods

Method	Chapter Reference	Individual aggression	Interpersonal conflict	Intellectual conflict	Community conflict	Organizational conflict	Intra-state conflict	International conflict
Guerrilla War	14						xx	xx
Gun Control	15		xx		xx			
Hostage and crisis negotiation	7		xx					
Impeach	10				xx	xx	xx	
Just War Theory	15						xx	xx
Law enforcement	14	xx	xx		xx	xx	xx	
Lawfare	14				xx	xx	xx	xx
Legislation	10				xx	xx	xx	xx
Listening skills	5		xx	xx	xx	xx	xx	xx
Markets	11		xx			xx	xx	xx
Mediation	8		xx	xx	xx	xx	xx	xx
Negotiation	8		xx		xx	xx	xx	xx
Nuclear response	14							xx
Pacifism and Non-violence	15				xx		xx	xx
Peace through Strength	15				xx		xx	xx
Peacekeeping	15						xx	xx
Pluralism	7						xx	
Policy analysis	14				xx	xx	xx	xx
Price fixing	11		xx			xx	xx	xx
Privatization	10				xx		xx	
Proportional allocation	2		xx		xx	xx	xx	xx
Psychoanalysis	3	xx						
Rebellion	14					xx	xx	
Recall election	10				xx		xx	
Reconciliation	15				xx		xx	xx
Redistricting	10				xx		xx	
Regulation	10				xx		xx	
Reparations	15							xx
Restitution	15		xx		xx		xx	xx

Figure 16.2b
Conflict Management Methods

Method	Chapter Reference	Individual aggression	Interpersonal conflict	Intellectual conflict	Community conflict	Organizational conflict	Intra-state conflict	International conflict
Segregation	7						xx	
Silent auction	2		xx		xx	xx		
Stability analysis	2		xx	xx	xx	xx	xx	xx
Steinhaus procedure	2		xx		xx	xx		
Strategy	13						xx	xx
Stress management	7	xx						
Strikes	9					xx		
Tactics	13						xx	xx
Tariffs	11							xx
Terrorism	14						xx	xx
Torts	8		xx		xx	xx	xx	
Track II Diplomacy	15						xx	xx
Tradition	11	xx	xx	xx	xx	xx	xx	xx
Truce of God	15						xx	xx
Vigilantism	15				xx		xx	
Voluntary cooperation	10		xx					
Voting	10				xx	xx	xx	xx
World Government	15						xx	xx

Figure 16.2c
Conflict Management Methods

Torts provide a remedy only for substantial damages caused by a party unwilling to compensate victims for injuries. Argument, debate, discussion, mediation, and negotiation remain the most likely methods of resolving interpersonal disputes.

At best, only five methods are available for resolving intellectual conflicts. Authority is common but seldom successful, while argument and conferences based on fact-finding and further research undoubtedly is the most powerful. Mediation is rare, and probably only occurs in such contexts as church councils in which the price of failure is schism. Oftentimes, these debates take place in settings such as conferences and academic journals.

Twenty-three methods are applicable to managing community disputes. Again, the four mathematical techniques (adjusted winner, proportional allocation, imaginary auction, and Steinhaus procedure) are most useful in dividing real property among claimants. Gerrymandering now uses exceptionally sophisticated computer models and census data in combination with political maneuvering to resolve election district boundaries. Stability analysis can operate in concert with several other methods. Some methods—gun control vs. widespread concealed carry permits and privatization vs. regulation—appear to be mutually contradictory although mixed solutions are possible. Even the most liberal concealed carry states do not extend the privilege to felons or individuals with a history of mental illness.

Community conflicts sometimes pit neighbor against neighbor but more significantly pit opposing groups of citizens such as pro-development and pro-environment groups against one another. Citizen-corporate conflicts also are common. Some citizens will oppose almost every idea a governing body considers. Finally, disputes can develop within and between the various departments of government itself.

In citizen-citizen disputes other than civil war[1], likely methods include adjusted winner, arbitration, deliberative assemblies, imaginary auctions, mediation, negotiation, privatization, proportional allocation, reconciliation, regulation, restitution, stability analysis, Steinhaus procedure, and voting. The issues, the number of stakeholders, and the degree to which the opposed groups are organized will help determine the best of these methods in any particular circumstance.

In citizen-corporate disputes, likely conflict management methods include citizen advisory boards, arbitration, boycott, crisis planning, mediation, negotiation, privatization, regulation, restitution, stability analysis, and torts. In citizen-government disputes, likely methods include citizen advisory boards, deliberative assemblies, gun control, mediation, negotiation, pacifism and non-violence, peace through strength, privatization, regulation, restitution, stability analysis, torts, and voting.

In some intra-government disputes, the superior can try to impose a decision, but subordinates have many ways to sabotage those with which they disagree. More success is likely through methods such as adjusted winner, advisory boards, arbitration, deliberative assemblies, mediation, negotiation, privatization, proportional allocation, regulation, and stability analysis.

Fifteen methods are available to manage organizational conflicts. The major ones occur within and between organizations, between citizens and businesses, and between organizations and government. Again, the four mathematical techniques (adjusted winner, proportional allocation, imaginary auction, and Steinhaus procedure) are useful in settling disputes involving property. Stability analysis can help identify potential solutions. Protest groups often attempt boycotts, which in the hands of some organizations can be hard to distinguish from blackmail. Consumers rely on arbitration, mediation, and torts. Advisory boards and crisis planning are preventative measures, and competitive strategy helps to

---

1. Treated below as intra-state conflict

gain an edge on other businesses. Labor disputes are settled by Boulwarism (unless illegal), negotiation, strikes, and sometimes by intervention often in the United States with assistance from the Federal Mediation and Conciliation Service.

Thirty-four methods appear applicable to intra-state conflicts. Five (aggression as therapy, expulsion, genocide, segregation, and terrorism) are reprehensible under any circumstance. The best way to make sense of the remaining methods is to classify them by the political situation. Arbitration, mediation, negotiation, and stability analysis may work to prevent conflict, control crises, and restore stability. Nine methods appear applicable in politically stable situations. As in the community case, gerrymandering now uses exceptionally sophisticated computer models and census data in combination with political maneuvering to resolve election district boundaries. Assimilation, pluralism, and *voluntary* internal migration are approaches to ethnic conflict. Advisory boards, deliberative assemblies, and torts are general methods useful in politically stable situations.

Privatization, regulation, or combinations of both are specialized techniques to solve conflicts originating from the tragedy of the commons or free rider problem. Crisis planning, peace through the strength of domestic police forces, voting, and UN intervention can prevent conflicts, although we seldom hear of successes by the latter. Stability analysis, adjusted winner, proportional allocation, just war theory, pacifism, non-violence, Track II diplomacy, and UN intervention all are useful in preventing crises degenerating into open war, particularly in combination with the basic techniques of arbitration, mediation, or negotiation. When everything fails and civil war does break out, traditional and asymmetric military strategy and tactics come into play depending on whether the rebellion takes the form of guerrilla, terror, or traditional warfare. Sometimes such wars are fought to a conclusion, sometimes they result in mediated or negotiated peace, and sometimes in international intervention and peacekeeping followed by efforts at reconciliation and restitution that may or may not succeed.

Twenty-eight methods appear applicable to interstate conflicts. The primary diplomatic methods are, of course, arbitration, negotiation, and mediation, all of which could but rarely actually use techniques such as adjusted winner, proportional allocation, and stability analysis to identify potential solutions. The League of Nations then the United Nations brought deliberative bodies and voting to the diplomatic scene, albeit with mixed success. Competitive strategy has proved a formidable alternative to war in a world where power increasingly is determined by economic power.

Preventive measures include advisory groups, crisis planning, arms control, peace through strength, balance of power, Just War Theory, and World Government. Crisis—the condition where war is likely but not yet certain—is addressed with much the same tools, although citizens may become involved. Among the methods employing violence, neither aggression as therapy or terrorism ever is warranted. Where the Middle Ages saw such efforts as the Truce of

God, today we have pacifism and nonviolence. When everything fails and inter-state war does break out, traditional and asymmetric military strategy and tactics again come into play depending on whether the rebellion takes the form of guer-rilla, terror, or traditional warfare. Just War theory remains applicable to mini-mizing and limiting the violence. Wars seldom end in unconditional surrender, but usually are ended by negotiation and sometimes by mediation.[2] Conflict management texts focus on peacekeeping, reconciliation, and restitution as means of stabilizing the peace, but historically war losers usually have faced reparations and loss of territory.

Toward a general theory of conflict

This section is a thought experiment (*Gedankenexperiment*)[3] leading to a theory of conflict based on the strengths and weaknesses of the theories dis-cussed in the preceding chapters. Three initial tasks face theoreticians attempt-ing to develop a single theory of conflict. The first is developing a taxonomy such as the Linnaean system[4] on which biology rests or the periodic table on which chemistry rests. A system can provide a uniform and internationally agreed nomenclature, put the myriad of conflicts into an agreed context, aid re-trieval of information, and guide design and interpretation of research. The or-ganization of this book into seven levels of conflict is a starting point. The ideal system would assign every type of conflict to one and only one category (a goal not achieved in this book), would accommodate new forms of conflict, and would tell researchers where to look for them.

The second major task is to put bad theories out to pasture. Social scientists seem more reluctant to do so than natural scientists.[5] Working toward some agreed upon set of criteria for eliminating bad ideas seems essential to develop-ing a successful general theory of conflict. This book suggests six. The best cur-rent theory is consistent with the facts, falsifiable, generalizable, logical, parsi-monious, and usable (Chapter 1).

---

2. Theodore Roosevelt won the Nobel Peace Prize for mediating the Russo-Japanese War, but many intractable conflicts, such as those between Israelis and Palestinians, Indi-ans and Pakistanis, and Turkish and Greek Cypriots, have resisted resolution.
3. Examples include Zeno's paradox, Galileo's ship, Maxwell's demon, Schrodinger's cat, Wagner's friend, Putnam's twin earth (*Wikipedia Online Encyclopedia*), Brams's fair division (Chapter 2) and Milne's on preventing war (Chapter 15).
4. Any good encyclopedia outlines the issues and methods.
5. Natural scientists once advocated but now have abandoned ideas such as alchemy, Aristotelian physics, astrology, caloric theory, ether as the carrier of light waves, bodily humors, the geocentric and heliocentric universe, Lamarckism, miasma theory of disease, phlogiston, phrenology, plum pudding theory of the universe, and spontaneous genera-tion.

The third task is to identify a small number of powerful variables that provide a general explanation of the causes, processes, and outcomes of conflict, the three main components of a complete theory of conflict.

Maslow's hierarchy of needs provides a reasonably complete and parsimonious starting point for the causes of individual conflict, although its extension to complex organizations and states is problematic.

Processes are best explained by a modified dual concern model with attitude toward risk on one axis, and desired relationship with opponent on the other (Figure 16.3) as independent variables serving as predictors of process. As attitude toward risk shifts from avoidance to seeking, willingness to take chances and use force increases. Force always is risky both in terms of impact on relationships and on likelihood of achieving goals. Therefore, it seems logical that willingness to use more forceful methods would be greater toward the right and toward the bottom of the diagram, but also with the importance of the specific issue in dispute.

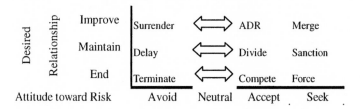

Figure 16.3
Conflict Preferences, Considerations, and Processes

If attitude toward risk determines management strategy, then presumably there are four main strategies to coincide with the four main attitudes toward risk. Specific methods will depend both on the level of conflict and the attitude toward the relationship. An individual who wishes to avoid risk presumably also wishes to avoid conflict, so can deny its existence, delay dealing with it, remove the source of the conflict, or surrender. The level of the conflict will further determine the specific methods possible. A classic device in organizations for delaying a confrontation is to appoint a committee, selecting people who are bound to have difficulty reaching agreement and giving it lots of resources and time to do so. Anger management can avoid conflict. Termination—divorce, firing, a new supplier—usually involve short-term conflict but long-term avoidance. Easing curfew rules on a teenager or paying what the IRS demands are forms of surrender. Appeal to authority (a boss, a parent, a lawsuit, an arbitrator) is a means of passing the conflict to someone else.

The individual who is risk neutral in a particular conflict is the least predictable, as by definition he does not care whether he avoids further conflict or accepts it. The risk neutral individual may also simply tolerate the conflict or let others resolve it. Consulting policies and regulations, reassigning personnel, and voting may appeal to the risk neutral conflict manager.

The risk-accepting individual will take calculated risks and turn to rational approaches, so is likely to propose methods such as competitive strategy, fair division, negotiation or mediation. Risk accepting individuals may not like the process but are willing to undertake it so as to achieve a satisfactory outcome and resolution.

The risk-seeking individual is willing to take high risk approaches that promise very high payoffs but also risk very high losses. A risk-seeking individual is likely to turn to more aggressive methods, again varying with the level of the conflict but The final major approach is confrontation, ranging from imposition through reliance on the courts to escalation. As with the other three approaches, additional methods such as sanctions, and forceful methods such as strikes or war are available at specific levels of conflict.

Outcome is the third major element in a complete theory of conflict. Preference vectors based on strategic choice (Chapter 2) are the most powerful and useful method for identifying stable outcomes. Treating unintended consequences as the equivalent of an error term incorporates them into outcomes. The distinction between equality, equity, and need may help to identify why people disagree as to problems and solutions to them.

Hierarchy of needs, attitude toward risk and relationships, and preference vectors combine into a complete theory of the causes, processes, and outcomes of human conflict. Whether the three can combined into a coherent and parsimonious theory that can be supported empirically, stand up to efforts at falsification and to scrutiny of the logic, and will prove generalizable and usable remains to be seen: the combination stems only from a thought experiment. Focusing research on testing theory—this or some other—is a major improvement on the current tendency of researchers to focus on perfecting instruments and statistical methods to measure ever more variables with ever more precision, perhaps in conjunction with some narrow, often trivial, "theoretical" concept.

Whether the approach suggested holds any promise of understanding conflict raises even grander epistemological questions that have challenged people since the birth of civilization and perhaps even before. Perhaps the most important among them is whether the logical-positivist assumptions of this book are warranted. Three special difficulties are worth mentioning. First, researchers often have a desire to reform the world to their own vision, whether it be conservative, continental liberal, Anglican liberal, or radical. Second, as the problem of Type I and Type II errors (chapter 1) reminds, it is possible to find the truth but not recognize it, or to mistake error for truth. Third, humans can read and adapt theory to their advantage, invalidating it in the process. Just as a football coach may call a draw in an obvious passing situation in an effort to catch the defense off guard, people in conflict situations can gain the advantage of surprise by doing something theory does not predict.

Conclusion

William Perry (1963) remarked that we often dismiss ideas as "bull" but seldom as "cow." He went on to define "cow" as facts without relevance. "Bull," on the other hand, is relevance without fact, opinion without evidence. Student papers consisting of cow invariably earn "C" grades, while bull earns either an "A" or an "F" depending on whether or not it is detected.

Much the same can be said for many of our theoretical ruminations about human conflict. Academics have both a tendency to lose the forest for the trees and to be impressed by obscure ideas elaborately expressed. Advances in knowledge require solving the problem, as Galileo did for physics, of what facts to study that make the results relevant but also the need for objective criteria to assist everyone in judging the resulting theories (Chapter 1). So, let us continue our research, but let us also search out an appropriate context in which to interpret the results and to put them into context. Then, and only then, might "theory" cease to be an object of derision and fulfill its promise as a powerful tool for understanding and managing conflict.

Appendix
Major Fallacies in Logic[1]

'Contrariwise,' continued Tweedle, 'if it was so, it might be; and if it were so, it would be: but as it isn't, it ain't. That's logic.

—Lewis Carroll, *Through the Looking Glass*

Question Framing

Baconian: Conducting research without specific questions or hypotheses
Declarative: Making an assertion instead of answering a question
False Dichotomy: Implying incorrectly that only two possibilities exist
Fictional question: Answering by speculation
Many questions: Demanding one answer to complex or multiple questions
Metaphysical question: Answering a non-empirical question empirically
Semantic: Supporting a position with opinion not evidence
Shallow question: Asking a question nobody needs answered
Tautology: Asking a question so that it is true by definition

Proof

Circular: Assuming what is to be proved
Hypostatized: Refusing to consider contrary evidence
Insufficient: Asserting a proof rather than providing one
Irrelevant: Answering a question that was not asked
Misplaced Precision: Using greater precision than warranted
Negative: Claiming something is true by proving its opposite false
Possible: Confusing possibility for probability
Presumptive: Demanding disproof rather than providing proof
Pseudofacts: Using false or slippery facts

Semantic Distortion

Accent: Distorting by emphasis or innuendo
Amphiboly: Obscuring meaning by syntax or euphemism
Equivocation: Using a term in two ways
Quibbling: The only difference is the way the term is defined

---

1. Adapted from D. Fisher (1970)

Significance

Aesthetic: Placing elegance or beauty above truth
Antinomian: Treating quantification or measurement as dehumanizing.
Essences: Using an unobservable characteristic as proof
Furtive: Explaining the unexplainable by asserting a conspiracy
Holist: Selecting trivial facts to fit a theory, ignoring major exceptions
Moralistic: Judging friends and foes by different standards
Pragmatic: Selecting trivial facts to support a cause
Prodigious: Exaggerating the significance of a common event
Quantitative: Treating only quantified facts as important

Generalization

Extrapolation: Assuming a trend will continue unchanged
Gamblers: Assuming probabilities operate in the short run
Impressionism: Treating impressions as precise data
Interpolation: Assuming all data lies on a straight line.
Lonely Fact: Generalizing from a single instance
Special Pleading: Obscuring inconvenient data with rhetoric
Sampling: Treating sample size as more important that sampling method

Narration

Anachronism: Ascribing something to the wrong time
Didactic: Bending facts to extract a predetermined lesson or meaning
Genetic: Mistaking process for outcome
Periodization: Setting inappropriate temporal boundaries
Presentism: Interpreting the past in terms of current values
Static: Treating events as having a foreordained conclusion
Tunnel Vision: Separating related events

Causation

Cum hoc, Propter hoc: Mistaking correlation for causation
Identity: Assuming the cause must resemble the effect
Indiscriminate pluralism: Making the simple seem complicated
Mechanistic: Assuming parts of a whole work independently
Post hoc, Propter hoc: Assuming the first event caused the second
Pro hoc, Propter hoc: Putting the effect before the cause
Reductive: Oversimplifying

Analogy

Absurd: Claiming similarities that are ridiculous
False: Drawing analogy from a mistaken similarity
Literalist: Taking metaphors, myths, or figures of speech literally
Perfect: Mistaking partial for total resemblance
Prediction by Analogy: Assuming that the future will be like the past

Motivation

Apathetic: Treating animate creatures as objects
Historians: Assuming participants knew outcomes of events beforehand
Man-Mass: Using one individual to represent everyone in a group
Mass Man: Treating all people in a group as being the same
One-dimensional Man: Explaining everything by one characteristic
Pathetic: Attributing animate behavior or feelings to inanimate objects
Universal man: Ignoring cultural, historical, and individual differences

Substantive Distraction

Ad Antiquitam: Assuming something is true because it is old
Ad Baculum: Assuming that might makes right
Ad Crumenem: Measuring truth by money
Ad Hominem: Attacking the person not the argument
Ad Nauseum: Sustaining a thesis by repetition
Ad Novitam: Assuming something is true because it is new
At Temperatum: Assuming the truth lies midway between the extremes
Ad Verecudiam: Appealing to (often irrelevant) authority or expertise

Bibliography

Some books are to be tasted, others to be swallowed, and some
few to be chewed and digested.

—Francis Bacon

Chapter 1.   Criteria for Good Theory

Atkins, P. (2003). *Galileo's Finger; The Ten Great Ideas of Science*. New York: Oxford.

Boorstin, D. (1985). *The Discoverers*. New York: Vintage.

Bronowski, J. and B. Mazlish (1960). *The Western Intellectual Tradition*. New York: Harper & Bros.

Fisher, D. H. (1970). *Historians' Fallacies*. New York: Harper & Row.

Herman, A (2001). *How the Scots Invented the Modern World*. New York: Three Rivers.

Popper, K. (1959). *The Logic of Scientific Discovery*. London: Hutchinson

Roberts, D. (April 2002). The Word Sleuth, *Readers Digest*.

Tarnas, R. (1991). *The Passion of the Western Mind*. New York: Harmony Books.

Van Doren, C. (1991). *A History of Knowledge*. New York: Ballantine Books.

Wynn, C. and A. Wiggins (1997). *The Five Biggest Ideas in Science*. New York: John Wiley & Sons.

Chapter 2.   Conflict Analysis

Axelrod, R. (1985). *The Evolution of Cooperation* New York: Basic Books.

Brams, S. and A. Taylor (1996). *Fair Division: From Cake Cutting to Dispute Resolution*. Cambridge: Cambridge University.

Brown, A. (1975). *Bodyguard of Lies*. New York: Harper and Row.

Fraser, N. and K. Hipel (1984). *Conflict Analysis: Models and Resolutions*. Amsterdam: Elsevier Science.

Howard, N. (1971). *Paradoxes of Rationality: Games, Metagames, and Political Behavior*. Cambridge: MIT.

Keegan, J. (2003). *Intelligence in War*. New York: Alfred A. Knopf.

Lee, L. (2004). *100 Most Dangerous Things in Everyday Life And What You Can Do About Them*. New York: Broadway.

Luce, R. (1989). *Games and Decisions*. Mineola, NY: Dover.

Nash, J. (1950). The Bargaining Problem. *Econometrica 18*.

Oye, K. (1986). *Cooperation Under Anarchy*. Princeton, NJ: Princeton University.

Raiffa, H. (1982). *The Art & Science of Negotiation*. Cambridge, MA: Harvard University.

Rapoport, A. (1960). *Fights, Games and Debates*. Ann Arbor: The University of Michigan.

Rapoport, A. (1970). *N-Person Game Theory: Concepts and Applications*. Ann Arbor: University of Michigan.

Ridley, M. (1988). *The Origins of Virtue*. New York: Penguin.

Ropeik, David (2000). *Risk: A Practical Guide for Deciding What's Really Safe and What's Really Dangerous in the World Around You*. Houghton Mifflin.

Tucker, A. (1950). *Prisoners' Dilemma*. Unpublished lecture delivered at Stanford University.

Tversky, A. and D. Kahneman (1974). Judgment under Uncertainty: Heuristics and Biases. *Science 185*.

Tversky, A. and D. Kahneman (1981) The Framing of Decisions and the Psychology of Choice. *Science 211*.

Von Neumann, J. and O. Morgenstern (1944). *Theory of Games and Economic Behavior*. New York: John Wiley.

Wahlke, J. (1979). Prebehavioralism in Political Science. *American Political Science Review*.

Chapter 3.   Nature of Man

Ardrey, R. (1965). *African Genesis* New York: Collins.

Ardrey, R. (1966). *Territorial Imperative*. New York: Atheneum.

Barlow, G. (1980). *Sociobiology: Beyond Nature/Nurture*. Boulder, CO: Westview.

Brunet, M. *et al.* (2002): A New Hominid from the Upper Miocene of Chad, Central Africa, *Nature*.

Caspi, A. *et. al.* (18 July 2003). Influence of Life Stress or Depression: Moderation by a Polymorphism in the 5-HTT Gene. *Science*.

Chagnon, N. (1990). *Yanomamo: The Fierce People*. New York: Harcourt, Brace, Jovanovich.

Dabbs, J. (2000). *Heroes, Rogues and Lovers: Testosterone and Behavior*. New York: McGraw-Hill.

Dart, R. (1959) *Adventures with the Missing Link*, New York: Harper Brothers.

Davie, M. (2003). *Evolution of War: A Study of Its Role in Early Societies*. Mineola, NY: Dover.

Dawkins, R. (1989). *The Selfish Gene*. New York: Oxford University.

Dugatkin, L. (September 2003). Homebody Bees and Bullying Chimps. *Cerebrum.*

Eibl-Eibesfeldt, I. (1979). *The Biology of Peace and War*. New York: Penguin.

Feh C. (1999) Alliances and Reproductive Success in Camargue Stallions. *Animal Behavior*.

Ferguson, R. (1984). *Warfare, Culture and Environment*. Amsterdam: Elsevier Science.

Goodall, J. (May 1979). Life and Death at Gombe. *National Geographic*.

Haldane, J. B. S. (1955). Population Genetics. *New Biology, 18*.

Hamer, D. and P. Copeland (1998). *Living with Our Genes*. New York: Anchor Books.

Hamilton, W. (1964). The Genetical Evolution of Social Behavior I and II. *Journal of Theoretical Biology*.

Heinsohn, R. & C. Packer, C. (1995). Complex Cooperative Strategies in Group-Territorial African lions. *Science*.

Leakey, L. (1965). *Olduvai Gorge 1951–61*. Cambridge: Cambridge University.

Lewin, R. (1998). *The Origin of Modern Humans*. New York: Scientific American Library.

Manson, J. and R.Wrangham (1991).Intergroup Aggression in Chimpanzees and Humans. *Current Anthropolog*.

Montagu, A. (1962) *Culture and the Evolution of Man*, New York: Oxford University.

Montagu, A. (1978). *The Nature of Human Aggression*. New York: Oxford University.

Montagu, A. (1980). *Sociobiology Examined*. New York: Oxford University.

National Institute on Alcohol Abuse and Alcoholism (October 1997, October 2000). *Alcohol Alert*. Washington, DC: U.S. Department of Health and Human Services).

Nelson, R. (2000). *An Introduction to Behavioral Endocrinology*. Sunderland, MA: Sinauer.

Miller, M. (1996). *Drugs and Violent Crime*. New York: Rosen.

Moffit, T. (1993). The Neuropsychology of Conduct Disorder. *Development and Psychology*.

Otterbein, K. (1989). *The Evolution of War*. New Haven, CT: Human Relations Area Files.

Potter-Effron, R and P. Potter-Effron (1997). *Anger, Alcohol and Addiction*. New York: W. W. Norton and Company.

Ruse, M. (1984). *Sociobiology: Sense or Nonsense*. Dordrecht, Netherlands: Kluwer Academic.

Schiavi, R. (January 1984). Sex Chromosome Anomalies, Hormones and Aggressivity, *Archives of General Psychiatry 41*.

Turney. H. (1991) *Primitive War: Its Practice and Concepts*. Columbia, SC: University of South Carolina.

Vayda, A. (1976). *War in Ecological Perspective*. Dordrecht, Netherlands: Kluwer Academic.

Wilson, E. (2000). *Sociobiology: The New Synthesis*. Cambridge: Harvard University.

Wood B. (2002): Hominid revelations from Chad, *Nature*.

Zuckerman, M (2002). Genetics of Sensation-Seeking in J. Benjamin *et. al.*, *Molecular Genetics and the Human Personality.* Washington, DC: American Psychiatric Association.

Zuckerman, M. (2003). Biological Bases of Personality in T. Millon and M. Lerner, *Handbook of Psychology* 5. Hoboken, NJ: Wiley.

Zukerman, M. (November/December 2000). Are You a Risk-Taker? *Psychology Today.*

Chapter 4   Aggression and the Mind

Adorno, T. *et. al.* (1950) *The Authoritarian Personality.* New York: Harper and Row.

Bandura A. (1986). *Social Foundations of Thought and Action.* Englewood Cliffs, NJ: Prentice-Hall.

Bandura, A. (1973). *Aggression: A Social Learning Analysis.* Englewood Cliffs, NJ: Prentice-Hall.

Baumeister, R., *et. al.* (1994). *Losing Control: How and Why People Fail and Self- Regulation.* San Diego: Academic.

Begley, S. (13 July 1998). You're OK, I'm Terrific: 'Self-Esteem" Backfires. *Newsweek.*

Berkowitz, L. 1978. *Group Processes.* New York: Academic.

Bushman, B., R. Baumeister, and C. Phillips (2001). Do People Aggress to Improve their Mood? *Journal of Personality and Social Psychology,* 81.

Dollard, J. *et. al.* (1980) *Frustration and Aggression.* Westport, CT: Greenwood.

Erikson, E. (1963). *Childhood and Society.* New York: W.W. Norton and Company

Fanon, F. (1976). *Wretched of the Earth.* London: Grove/Atlantic

Freud, S. (1984). *Civilization and Its Discontents.* New York: H. W. Norton and Company.

Fromm, E. (1973) *Anatomy of Human Destruction.* New York: Henry Holt and Company.

Goode, E. (9 March 1999). Letting Out Aggression Is Called Bad Advice. *New York Times.*

Gruen, L. and P. Singer (1987). *Animal Liberation: A Graphic Guide.* London: Unsourced Publlisher.

Harlow, H. (1973). *Learning to Love.* New York: Random House.

Hobson, J. (1988). *The Dreaming Brain.* New York: Basic Books.

Hobson, J. (2003). *Dreaming: An Introduction to the Science of Sleep.* New York: Oxford University.

Loftus, E. (1996). *The Myth of Repressed Memory.* New York: St. Martin's.

Lorenz, K. (1974). *On Aggression.* New York: Harvest.

Maslow A., *et. al.* 1987. *Motivation and Personality.* New York: Addison Wesley.

Mauldin, B (1945). *Up Front*. Cleveland, OH: The World Publishing Company.

McCain, J. and M. Salter (2004). *Why Courage Matters*. New York: Random House.

Miller, N. (1941). The Frustration-Aggression Hypothesis. *Psychological Review 48.*

Rokeach, M. (1960). *The Open and Closed Mind: Investigations into the Nature of Belief Systems and Personality Systems.* New York: Basic Books.

Rollin, B. (1981). *Animal Rights and Human Morality.* Buffalo, NY: Prometheus.

Stannard, D. (1980). *Shrinking History.* New York: Oxford University.

Storr, A. (1996). *Feet of Clay. Saints, Sinners, and Madmen: A Study of Gurus.* New York: The Free Press.

Sulloway, F. (1992). *Freud, Biologist of the Mind.* Cambridge, MA: Harvard University.

Whiting, J. (1941). *Becoming a Kwoma.* New Haven, CT: AMS.

Yates, A.(1962). *Frustration and Conflict.* New York: John Wiley & Sons.

Chapter 5   Interpersonal Conflict

Axtell, R. (1985). *Do's and Taboos Around the World.* New York: John Wiley.

Bolton, R. (1992). *People skills.* New York: Prentice Hall.

Bostrom, R. (1990). *Listening Behavior: Measurement & Application.* New York: Guilford.

Burton, J. (1969). *Conflict and Communication*, London: Macmillan.

Chernev, I. and F. Reinfeld (1948) *Winning Chess.* New York: Simon and Schuster.

Cialdini, R.(1984) *Influence: The New Psychology of Modern Persuasion.* New York: Quill.

Comaroff, J. and S. Roberts 1986). *Rules and Processes: Cultural Logic of Disputes in an African Context.* Chicago: University of Chicago.

Erickson, M. and E. Rossi (1979). *Hypnotherapy.* New York: Irvington.

Festinger, L. (1962). *A Theory of Cognitive Dissonance.* Stanford, CA: Stanford University.

Gilin, D. and S. Mestdagh (2004). The Paradox of Perspective Taking Ability in Conflict and Negotiation. Paper presented at the annual meeting of the International Association for Conflict Management Pittsburgh, PA.

Goffman, E. (1974). *Frame Analysis: An Essay on the Organization of Experience.* New York: Harper & Row.

Grimshaw, A. (1990). *Conflict Talk.* Cambridge: Cambridge University.

Hall, E. (1959). *The Silent Language.* New York: Doubleday.

Hall, L. (1993). *Negotiation Strategies for Mutual Gain: The Basic Seminar of the Harvard Negotiation Project on Negotiation.* Newbury Park, CA: Sage

Haritos-Fatouros, M. (1988). The Official Torturer: A Learning Model for Obedience to Authority. *Journal of Applied Social Psychology 18*).

Hase, S., A. Davies and B. Dick (1999). The Johari Window and the Dark Side of Organizations. http://multibase.rmit.edu.au.

Hofstede, G. (2004). *Cultures and Organizations: Software for the Mind*. New York: McGraw-Hill.

Kochman, T.(1983). *Black and White Styles in Conflict*. Chicago: University of Chicago.

Larson, C. (1989). *Persuasion: Reception and Responsibility*. Bellmont, CA: Wadsworth.

Littlejohn, W. (1989). *Theories of Human Communication*. Belmont, CA: Wadsworth.

Luft, J. (1969) *Of Human Interaction*, Palo Alto, National Press Books

Milgram, S. (1963). Behavioral Study of Obedience. *Journal of Abnormal and Social Psychology 67.*

Milgram, S. (1983). *Obedience to Authority: An Experimental View*. New York: Harper Collins.

Nemko, M. (26 February 2004) Becoming a Human Lie Detector. www.content.monster.com/martynemko/articles/archive/lying.

Pruitt, D. (1988). *Negotiation Behavior*. New York: Academic Press.

Pruitt, D. and J. Rubin (1986). *Social Conflict: Escalation, Stalemate, and Settlement*. New York: Random House.

Pruitt, D. & P. Carnevale,. (1993). *Negotiation and Social Conflict*. Pacific Grove, CA: Brooks/Cole.

Putnam, L. and M. Roloff (1992). *Communication and Negotiation*. Newbury Park, CA: Sage.

Rahim, M. (1990). *Theory and Research in Conflict Management*. Westport, CT: Greenwood Publishing Group.

Reiser, M. and M. Sloane (1983). "The Use of Suggestibility Techniques in Hostage Negotiations." In L. Freedman and Y. Alexander. *Perspectives on Terrorism*. Wilmington, DE: Scholarly Resources.

Sapir, E. (1979). *Language*. Woodstock, NY: Beckman.

Singer, L. (1994). *Settling Disputes: Conflict Resolution in Business, Families, and the Legal System*. Boulder, CO: Westview.

Sommers, C. and S. Satel (2005). One Nation Under Therapy: How the Helping Culture is Eroding Self-Reliance. New York: St. Martin's.

Weaver, R. (1990). *Understanding Interpersonal Communication*. Glenview, IL: Scott, Foresman Company.

Weiss, S. (1994). Negotiating with "Romans": A Range of Culturally Responsive Strategies. *Sloan Management Review 35.*

Whorf, B. (1926). *Language, Thought, and Reality*. Cambridge, MA: MIT.

Wilmot, W. and L. Hocker (1997). *Interpersonal Conflict*. Dubuque, IA: Wm. C. Brown

Wolff, F. and N. Marsnik (1992). *Perceptive Listening*. Fort Worth, TX: Harcourt, Brace, Jovanovich.

Wolvin, A. and C. Oakley (1992). *Listening*. Dubuque, IA: William C. Brown.

Chapter 6.   Gender Conflict

Barth, J. and P. Raymond. (1995). The Naïve Misuse of Power: Nonconscious Sources of Sexual Harassment. *Journal of Social Issues, 51.*

Borisoff, D. and D. Victor, 1989. *Conflict Management: A Communication Skills Approach*, Englewood Cliffs NJ: Prentice Hall

Dahlerup, D, (n.d.) Gender quotas. www.idea.int/gender/index.htm

Davis, P. (1998). *The Goddess Unmasked: The Rise of Neopaganism Feminist Spirituality.* Dallas, TX: Spence Publishing.

Crick, N., et. al. (in press). Childhood Aggression and Gender in D. Bernsetin, *Nebraska Symposium on Motivation.* Lincoln: The University of Nebraska Press.

Crick, N. and M. Bigbee (1998). Relational and Overt Forms of Peer Victimization: A Multi-informant approach. *Journal of Consulting and Clinical Psychology, 66.*

Eisler, R. (1998). *The Chalice and the Blade.* New York: HarperCollins

Eller, C. (1995). *Living in the Lap of the Goddess.* Boston: Beacon.

Eller, C. (2001). *The Myth of Matriarchal Prehistory: Why an Invented Past Will Not Give Women a Future.* Boston: Beacon.

Equal Employment Opportunity Commission (27 June 2002). *Facts About Sexual Harassment.* DC: Author.

Fraser, A. (1980). *Warrior Queens.* New York: Random House.

Garbarino, J. (1999). *Lost Boys: Why Our Sons Turn Violent and How We Can Save Them.* New York: Free Press.

Gimbutas, M. (1989) *The Language of the Goddess.* New York: HarperCollins.

Gimbutas, M. (1997) *The Civilization of the Goddess: The World of Old Europe.* New York: HarperCollins.

Hofmann, C. 1994. *Issue Brief on Quota Systems for Women's Political Participation.* Quezon City, Philippines: Women in Politics Program, Congressional Research and Training Service.

Inter-Parliamentary Union. (2000) *Participation of Women in Political Life.* Geneva: Inter-Parliamentary Union.

Katz, M (2003). Reconsidering Attraction in Sexual Harassment. *Indiana Law Journal, 79.* http://ssrn.com/abstract=495563

Kelleher, M. and C. Kelleher (1998). *Murder Most Rare: The Female Serial Killer.* Westport: CT: Praeger.

Kirsta, A. (1994). *Deadlier than the Male.* London: Harper Collins.

Lips, H, (1981). *Women, Men, and the Psychology of Power.* Englewood Cliffs, NJ: Prentice Hall.

Norris, P. (2000). Women's Representation and Electoral Systems in Rose, R. (ed.) *The International Encyclopedia of Elections.* Washington DC: CQ Press.

Pizan, C. (1982). *The Book of the City of Ladies*. New York: Persea.

Pollock, W. (1998). *Real Boys: Rescuing Our Sons from the Myths of Boyhood*. New York: Random House.

Prothrow-Stit, D. and H. Spivak (2005). Sugar & Spice and No Longer Nice. San Francisco: Jossey –Bass.

Seagrave, K. (1992). *Women Serial Killers and Mass Murderers 1580–1990*. Jefferson, NC: McFarland & Co.

Sommers, C. (2001). *The War Against Boys*. New York: Simon & Schuster.

Tannen, D. (1990). *You Just Don't Understand: Women and Men in Conversation*. New York: William Morrow.

Tannen, D. (1995). *Gender and Discourse*. New York: Oxford.

Taylor, A. and J. Bernstein-Miller (1994). *Gender and Conflict*. Creskill, NJ: Hampton.

Taylor, J. (1999). *What to Do When You Don't Want to Call the Cops*. New York: New York University.

Tiger, L. (2000). *The Decline of Males*. New York: St. Martins.

Veraldi, L (1995). Academic Freedom and Sexual Harassment. *Education Digest, 6.*

Wood, J. (1994). Saying It Makes It So: The Discursive Construction of Sexual Harassment, in S. Bingham (Ed.). *Conceptualizing Sexual Harassment as Discursive Practice*. Westport, CT: Praeger

Wyatt, N. (2000) http://www.de.psu.edu/harassment/generalinfo/theory.html

Chapter 7   Community Conflict

Allport, G. (1958). The Nature of Prejudice. New York: Anchor Books.

Avruch, K, P. Black, and J. Scimecca (1991). *Conflict Resolution: Cross-Cultural Perspectives*, London: Greenwood.

Azar, E. (1990). *The Management of Protracted Social Conflict,* Hampshire, UK: Dartmouth Publishing.

Berenbaum, M. (Ed.) (1997). *Witness to the Holocaust: An Illustrated Documentary History of the Holocaust in the Words of its Victims, Perpetrators, and Bystanders*. New York: Harper Collins.

Blalock, H. (1989). *Power and Conflict*. Newberry Park, CA: Sage.

Button. J. 1978. *Black Violence: Political Impact of the 1960s Riots*. Princeton, NJ: Princeton University.

Cohen, R. and F. Deng (1998). *The Forsaken People; Case Studies of the Internally Displaced.* Washington, DC: Brookings Institute.

Collins, R. (1975). *Conflict Sociology: Toward an Explanatory Science.* New York: Academic Press.

Coser, L. (1956). *The Functions of Social Conflict*. New York: Free Press

Dahrendorf, R. (1959). *Class and Class Conflict in Industrial Society*. Stanford, CA: Stanford University.

Davis, K. and W. Moore (1945) Some Principles of Stratification. *American Sociological Review 10.*

FBI (1985, 1992). Hostage Negotiations Seminar. Quantico, VA

Fitzduff, M. (1994). *Approaches to Community Relations Work.* Belfast: Community Relations Council.

Gurr, T. and B. Harff (1994). *Ethnic Conflict in World Politics,* Oxford: Westview.

Hart, A. (1991). *Adrenaline and Stress.* Dallas, TX: Dallas World.

Jackson, W. and A. Jackson (1995). *Toward a Common Destiny: Improving Race and Ethnic Relations in America.* San Francisco: Jossey-Bass.

Jenkins, B. *et.al* (1977). Numbered Lives: Some Statistical Observations from Seventy-Seven International Hostage Episodes. Santa Monica CA: RAND Corporation.

Kiernan, B. (1996). *The Pol Pot Regine: Race, Power, and Genocide in Cambodia under the Khmer Rouge.* New Haven: Yale University.

Klein, M. (1995). *The American Street Gang.* New York: Oxford University.

Kreisberg, L. (1973). *The Sociology of Social Conflicts.* Englewood Cliffs, NJ: Prentice Hall.

Kuper, L. (1982). *Genocide: Its political use in the Twentieth Century.* New Haven: Yale University.

Leng, R. and E. Henderson. (1996). Managing Intergang Conflict: Norms from the Interstate System. Presented at the annual meeting of the International Association for Conflict Management, Ithaca, NY.

Levitt, S. and S. Dubner (2005). Freakonomics: A Rogue Economists Explores the Hidden Side of Everything. New York: William Morrow.

McMains, M.. and W. Mullins (1996). *Crisis Negotiations: Managing Critical Incidents and Hostage Situations in Law Enforcement and Corrections.* Cincinnati, OH: Anderson Publishing Co.

Merton, R. (1968). *Social Theory and Social Structure.* New York: Free Press

Merton, R (1936). *The Unanticipated Consequences of Purposive Social Action, American Sociological Review 1.*

Miller, A. (1980). *Terrorism and Hostage Negotiations.* Boulder, CO: Westview.

Mindell, A. (1995). *Sitting in the Fire: Large Group Transformation Using Conflict and Diversity.* Portland, OR: Lao Tse.

Myrdal, G. (1944). *An American Dilemma.* New York: Harper.

Nyankanzi, E. (1997). *Genocide: Rwanda and Burundi.* Rochester, Vermont: Schenkman.

Padilla, F. (1992). *The Gang as an American Enterprise.* New Brunswick, NJ: Rutgers University.

Park, R. and E. Burgess. (1921). *An Introduction to the Science of Sociology.* Chicago: University of Chicago.

Parsons, T. (1977). *The Evolution of Societies.* Englewood Cliffs, NJ: Prentice-Hall

Pincus, F and H. Ehrlich. (1999). *Race and Ethnic Conflict: Contending Views on Prejudice, Discrimination and Ethnoviolence.* Boulder, CO: Westview.

Porter, M. (1980). *Competitive Strategy.* New York: Free Press.

Quick, J. and J. Quick (1984). *Organizational Stress and Preventive Management.* New York: McGraw-Hill.

Richmond, O. (1998). *Mediating in Cyprus: The Cypriot Communities and the UN,* London: Frank Cass.

Ritzer, G. (1983). *Sociological Theory.* New York. Alfred A. Knopf

Rothchild, D. (1997). *Managing ethnic conflict in Africa: Pressures and incentives for cooperation.* Washington, DC: Brookings Institution.

Schlossberg, H. (1979). Hostage Negotiation School. Austin, TX: Texas Department of Public Safety.

Schneirov, R. (1998) *Labor and Urban Politics: Class Conflict and the Origins of Modern Liberalism.* Champagne-Urbanna: University of Illinois.

Secher, R (2003). *A French Genocide: The Vendee.* Chicago: University of Notre Dame.

Simmel, G. (1955). *Conflict and the Web of Group Affiliations.* New York: Free Press.

Sorokin, P. (1967). *The Sociology of Revolution.* New York:: Fertig Howard.

Soskis, D. and C.Van Zandt (1986). "Hostage Negotiation: Law Enforcement's Most Effective Non-Lethal Weapon." *FBI Law Management Quarterly 6.*

Steinbeck, J. (1966). *America and Americans.* New York: Viking.

Strentz, T. (1982). A Hostage Psychological Survival Guide." *FBI Law Enforcement Bulletin 48.*

Strentz, T. (1994). Thirteen Indicators of Volatile Negotiations. *The U.S. Negotiator,* Winter.

Strozier, C. & Flynn, M., (1998). *Genocide, War, and Human Survival.* Lanham, Maryland: Rowman & Littlefield.

Tanaka, Y. (1998). Hidden Horrors: Japanese War Crimes in World War II. Boulder, Colorado: Westview.

Thrasher, F. (1963). The Gang: A Study of 1313 Gangs in Chicago. Chicago: University of Chicago.

Volkan, V. (1997). *Bloodlines: From Ethnic Pride to Ethnic Terrorism.* New York: Farrar, Strauss, & Giroux.

Weber, M. (1968). *Economy and Society.* Totowa, NJ: Bedminster.

Weine, S. (1999). *When History is a Nightmare: Lives and Memories of Ethnic Cleansing in Bosnia-Herzegovina.* New Brunswick, NJ: Rutgers University.

Williams, W. (1982). *The State Against Blacks.* New York: New Press/McGraw-Hill.

Chapter 8   Dispute Resolution

American Arbitration Association (1992). *Arbitration and the Law.* Washington, DC: Author.

Beer, J.and E. Steif (1997). *Mediator's Handbook.* Gabriola Is, BC, Canada: New Society.

Bennett, S. (2002). *Arbitration: Essential Concepts* New York: American Lawyer Media.

Burgess, H. and G. Burgess (n.d). *Encyclopedia of Conflict Resolution.*

Burton, J. (1990). *Conflict: Resolution and Prevention.* New York: St. Martin's.

Bush, R and J. Folger. (2004). *The Promise of Mediation.* New York: John Wiley.

Campbell, T. (1995). The Causes and Effects of Liability Reform: Some Empirical Evidence. Working Paper # 4989. National Bureau of Economic Research, Inc.

Churchman, D. 1995, *Negotiation: Process, Tactics and Theory.* Lanham, MD: University Press of America.

Deutsch, M. & Coleman, P.T. (2000). *The Handbook of Conflict Resolution.* San Francisco: Jossey-Bass.

Doob, L. W. (1993). *Intervention: Guides and Perils.* New Haven: Yale University.

Fisher, R., W. Ury and B. Patton (1991). *Getting to Yes: Negotiating Agreement Without Giving In.* New York: Penguin.

Fleming, J. (1988). *The American Tort Process.* Oxford: Oxford University.

Folberg, J. & Taylor, A. (1984). *Mediation.* San Francisco: Jossey-Bass.

Garry, Patrick (1997). *A Nation of Adversaries.* New York: Insight Books.

Ikle, F. (1964). *How Nations Negotiate.* New York: Frederick A Praeger.

Kellor, F. (1999). *American Arbitration: Its History, Functions and Achievements.* Washington, DC: Beard Books.

Kolb, D. & Associates (1994). *When Talk Works: Profiles of Mediators.* San Francisco: Jossey-Bass.

Lax, D. and J. Sebenius, (1986). *The Manager as Negotiator: Bargaining for Cooperation and Competitive Gain.* New York: The Free Press.

Lewicki, R. *et. al.* (1997). *Essentials of Negotiation.* Chicago: Irwin.

Mitchell, C. & Banks, M. (1996). *Handbook of Conflict Resolution: The Analytical Problem Solving Approach.* London: Pinter.

Moore, C. (1996). *The Mediation Process: Practical Strategies for Resolving Conflict.* San Francisco: Jossey-Bass.

Northrup, H. (1964). *Boulwarism.* Ann Arbor, MI: The University of Michigan.

Science Magazine (10 April 1992). Is Liability Slowing AIDS Vaccines? *Science Magazine.*

Committee on Commerce, Science, and Transportation (19 June 1997). Product Liability Reform Act of 1997. *Report 105-32*. Washington, DC: Author.

Ury, W. (1991). *Getting Past No: Negotiating with Difficult People*. New York: Bantam.

Ward, K. Associates (15 March 1993). *A Study to Address Relationships between Economic Development and the Need for Tort Reform*. Washington, DC: Author.

Zartman, W. and M. Berman (1982). *The Practical Negotiator*. New Haven: Yale University.

Chapter 9   Organizational Conflict

Bennis, W., *et. al.* (1985). *The Planning of Change*. New York: Holt, Rinehart & Winston.

Blake R. and J. Mouton (1994). *The Managerial Grid*. Amsterdam: Elsevier Science.

Bucholz, T. (n.d.). *Economic and Social Upheavals That Will Shake Your Financial Future--and What to Do About Them*. New York: Harper Business

Burnett, John (2002) *Managing Business Crises: From Anticipation to Implementation*. Westport, CT: Quorum Books.

Burton, J. and F. Dukes (1990). *Conflict Practices in Management, Settlement, and Resolution*. New York: St. Martin's.

Killman and Thomas, (January 1978). Four Perspectives on Conflict Management: An Attributional Framework for Organizing Descriptive and Normative Behavior. *Academy of Management Review, 3*, 1.

Boulware, L. (1969). *The Truth About Boulwarism*. Washington DC: Bureau of National Affairs.

Matlock, Jr., J. (2004). *Reagan and Gorbachev: How the Cold War Ended*. New York: Random House.

Meyers, G. and J. Holusha 1986. *When it Hits the Fan: The Nine Crises of Business*, New York: Houghton Mifflin.

Oregon School Boards Association (2004). *Crisis Management*. Salem, OR: Author

Peterson, W. (April 1991). Boulwarism: Ideas Have Consequences. *The Freeman*.

Rees, A. (October 1952), Industrial Conflict and Business Fluctuations, *Journal of Political Economy 60*.

Schweizer, Peter (1994). *Victory: The Reagan Administration's Secret Strategy that Hastened the Collapse of the Soviet Union*. New York: The Atlantic Monthly.

Walton, R. and R. McKersie (1965, 1991). *A Behavioral Theory of Labor Negotiations*. New York: McGraw-Hill Book Company.

Wildlife on Wheels (2000). *Crisis Management Plan*. Unpublished.

Chapter 10   Political Conflict

Borda, J. (1781). Memoire sur les elections au scrutin, in *Histoire de l'Academie Royale des Sciences*. Paris.

Brams, S. and P. Fishburn (1991). Alternative Voting Systems In L. Maisel, *Political Parties and Elections in the United States: An Encyclopedia,* vol 1. New York: Garland.

Clark, G. (2004). *Stealing Our Votes: How Politicians Conspire to Control Elections.* Pittsburgh: PA: Dorrance.

Condorcet, Marquis de (1785). *Essai sur l'application de l'analyse a la probabilite des decisions rendues la pluralite des voix.* Paris.

De Young, R. (1999). Tragedy of the Commons. In D. Alexander and R. Fairbridge *Encyclopedia of Environmental Science.* Hingham, MA: Kluwer Academic.

Eckstein, H. (1980). Theoretical Approaches to Explaining Collective Political Violence. In T. Gurr, *Handbook of Political Conflict.* New York: The Free Press

Einstein, A. and Freud, S. (1932). *Why War?* Paris: International Institute of Intellectual Cooperation.

Erikson, E.(1969). *Young Man Luther: A Study in Psychoanalysis and History.* New York: W. W. Norton and Company.

Gurr, T. (1980) On the Outcomes of Violent Conflict. In T. Gurr, *Handbook of Political Conflict.* New York: The Free Press.

Hardin, G. (1968). The Tragedy of the Commons, *Science.*

Kelly, J. (1987). *Social Choice Theory: An Introduction.* New York: Springer-Verlag.

Lasswell, H. (1960). *Psychopathology and Politics.* New York. Viking.

Mazlish, B. (1976). *The Revolutionary Ascetic: Evolution of a Political Type.* New York: Basic Books.

Napolitano, A. (2005). *Constitutional Chaos.* Nashville: Thomas Nelson

Nardin, T. (1980). Theory and Practice in Conflict Research. In T. Gurr, *Handbook of Political Conflict.* New York: The Free Press.

Nurmi, H. (1987). *Comparing Voting Systems.* Dordrecht, Holland: D. Reidel.

Pirages, D. (1980). Political Stability and Conflict Management. In T. Gurr, *Handbook of Political Conflict.* New York: The Free Press.

Rejai, M. (1980) Theory and Research in the Study of Revolutionary Personnel. In T. Gurr, *Handbook of Political Conflict.* New York: The Free Press.

Robert, H. (1876, 1951). *Robert's Rules of Order* Chicago: Scott, Foresman and Company.

Weber, M. (1964). *The Theory of Social and Economic Organization.* New York: Free Press.

Wolfenstein, E. (1967). Revolutionary Personality: Lenin, Trotsky, Gandhi. Princeton, NJ: Princeton University.

Zimmerman, E. (1980). Macro-Comparative Research on Political Protest. In T. Gurr, *Handbook of Political Conflict.* New York: The Free Press.

Zinnes, D. (1980). Why War? Evidence on the Outbreak of International Conflict. In T. Gurr, (1980). *Handbook of Political Conflict.* New York: The Free Press.

Chapter 11   Intellectual Conflict

Abraham, R. (1994). *Chaos, Gaia, Eros.* Harper Collins.

Asch, S. (1995). Opinions and Social Pressure. In E. Aronson *Readings about the Social Animal.* New York: W. H. Freeman.

Baden, J. (1994). *Environmental Gore.* San Francisco: Pacific Research Institute for Public Policy.

Baumer, F. (1977) *Modern European Thought.* New York: Macmillan.

Bikhchandani, S. *et al.* (1998). Learning from the Behavior of Others: Conformity, Fads, and Informational Cascades. *Journal of Economic Perspectives*

Bronowski, J. and B. Mazlish (1962). *The Western Intellectual Tradition.* New York: Harper & Row.

Bunyard, P. (1996). *Gaia in Action: Science of the Living Earth.* Edinburgh: Floris Books.

Burnham, J. (1987). Medical Practice à la Mode: How Medical Fashions Determine Medical Care. *New England Journal of Medicine.*

Carson, R. (2002). *Silent Spring.* Boston: Houghton-Mifflin

Commager, H. (1925). *Living Ideas in America.* New York: Macmillan.

Dawkins, R. (1987). *The Blind Watchmaker.* New York: W. W. Norton and Company.

Downs, R. (1963). *Books that Changed the World.* New York: Mentor.

Ehrman, B. (2003). *Lost Christianities.* Oxford: Oxford University.

Eisner, R. (1994). *The Misunderstood Economy: What Counts and How to Count it.* Boston: Harvard Business School.

Ellsaesser, H. (1994). With Respect to the Ozone Hole—Gore is Part of the Problem. In J. Baden, *Environmental Gore.* San Francisco: Pacific Research Institute for Public Policy.

Esser, J. (1998). Alive and Well after Twenty-Five Years: A Review of Groupthink Research. *J. Organizational Behavior and Human Decision Processes.*

Fromkin, D. (1999). *The Way of the World.* New York: Alfred A. Knopf.

Gore, A. (1992). *Earth in the Balance.* Boston: Houghton Mifflin.

Hahn, R. (1994). Toward a New Environmental Paradigm. In J. Baden, *Environmental Gore.* San Francisco: Pacific Research Institute for Public Policy.

Heilbroner, R. (1962), *The Making of Economic Society*, Englewood Cliffs NJ: Prentice Hall.

Heyne, P. (1973), *The Economic Way of Thinking*, Chicago: Science Research Associate.

Janis, I. (1982), *Groupthink*. Boston: Houghton Mifflin.

Jones, R. (1978). *The Wizard War: British Scientific Intelligence 1939–1945*. New York: Coward, McCann & Geoghegan, Inc.

Kassim, S and K. Kiechel (1996). The Social Psychology of False Confessions: Compliance, Internalization, and Confabulation. *Psychological Science*.

Kline, M. (1953). *Mathematics in Western Culture*. New York: Oxford University.

Lennox, J. (1994). The Environmental Creed According to Gore: A Philosophical Analysis. In J. Baden, *Environmental Gore*. San Francisco: Pacific Research Institute for Public Policy.

Lindzen, R. (1994). The Origin and Nature of the Alleged Scientific Consensus. In J. Baden, *Environmental Gore*. San Francisco: Pacific Research Institute for Public Policy.

Lott, J. (1994). Gore's Environmental Views and the Economy. In J. Baden, *Environmental Gore*. San Francisco: Pacific Research Institute for Public Policy.

Lovelock, J. 1979. *Gaia: A New Look at Life on Earth*. Oxford University.

Lovelock, J. 1991. *Healing Gaia*. Harmony.

Margulis, L. and Sagan, D. 1997. *Slanted Truths: Essays on Gaia, Evolution and Symbiosis*. New York.

Mill, J. (1972) On Liberty in J. Mill, *Utilitarianism*. London: Everyman's Library.

Peterson, R. et. al. (1998). Group Dynamics in Team Management Teams: Groupthink, Vigilance and Alternative Models of Organizational Failure and Success. *J. Organizational Behavior and Human Decision Processes*.

Rothkrug, L. (1965) *Opposition to Louis XIV: The Political and Social Origins of the French Enlightenment*. Princeton, NJ: Princeton University.

Sowell, T. (1987). *A Conflict of Visions*. New York: William Morrow

Sowell, T. (1985), *Marxism: Philosophy and Economics*. London: Unwin.

Stewart, R. (1997) *Ideas that Shaped Our World*. San Deigo: Thunderbay.

Sunstein, C. (2003). *Why Societies Need Dissent*. Cambridge, MA: Harvard University.

Thompson, J. and E. Johnson (1937). *An Introduction to Medieval Europe 300–1500*. New York: W. W. Norton and Company.

Turner, M. and A Pratkanis (1998). Twenty Years of Groupthink Theory and Research: Lessons from the Evaluation of a Theory. *J. Organizational Behavior and Human Decision Processes*.

Vernadsky, V. (1929). *La Biosphere*. Paris: Felix Alcan

## Chapter 12	Causes of War

Aristotle (1997) *The Politic* In J. Barnes, *The Complete Works of Aristotle.* *Princeton, NJ: Princeton University.*

Blainey, G. (1991). *The Causes of Wars.* New York: Simon and Schuster.

Berndt R. and C. Berndt (1951) *Sexual Behavior in Arnhem Land.* New York: Viking, New York

Boulding, K. (1962). *Conflict and Defense: A General Theory* New York: Harper and Row.

Brown, S. 1994 *The Causes and Prevention of War* New York: St. Martin's

Bueno de Mesquita, B. and D. Lalman. (1992). *War and Reason.* New Haven: Yale University.

Bueno de Mesquita, B. (1981). *The War Trap.* New Haven: Yale University.

Bueno de Mesquita, B. (1985). "The War Trap Revisited." *American Political Science Review* 79.

Dominguez, J. *et. al.* (2003). *Boundary Disputes in Latin America.* Washington, DC: United States Institute of Peace.

Garnham, D. (1976). Dyadic International War, 1816–1965: The Role of Power Parity and Geographical Proximity. *Western Political Quarterly.*

Geller, D. and D. Singer, 1998. *Nations at War: A Scientific Study of International Conflict.* Cambridge: Cambridge University.

Goldstein, J. (n.d.). *Long Cycles: Prosperity and War in the Modern Age.*

Gurr, T. (1970). *Why Men Rebel.* Princeton, NJ: Princeton University.

Harris, M. (1974). *Cows, Pigs, Wars and Witches.* New York: Random House

Harris M. (1978) *Cannibals and Kings: the Origins of Cultures.* New York: Vintage Books, New York, 1978.

Harris M. (1980), *Culture, People, Nature: An Introduction to General Anthropology.* New York: Harper & Row.

Herek, G., I. Janis and P. Huth (1987) Decision Making during International Crises: Is Quality of Process Related to Outcome. *Journal of Conflict Resolution.*

Holsti, K. (1991). *Peace and War: Armed Conflicts and International Order 1648–1989.* Cambridge: Cambridge University.

Howard, M. (1983). *The Causes of War and Other Essays.* London: Unwin.

Huntingdon, S. (1996). *The Clash of Civilisations and the Remaking of World Order,* New York: Simon and Schuster.

Intriligator, M. and D. Brito, (February 2000). Arms Races. *Defence and Peace Economics*

Intriligator, M. (1964). *Some Simple Models of Arms Races.* Rand RM-3903-PR. Santa Monica, CA: Rand Corporation.

Kagan, D.1(995). *On the Origins of War and the Preservation of Peace.* New York: Doubleday.

Keegan, J. (1993) *A History of Warfare.* New York: Alfred A. Knopf

Kegley, C. and G Raymond (1994). *A Multipolar Peace.* New York: Worth/St. Martin's.

Lenin, V. (1990). *Imperialism: The Highest Stage of Capitalism.* New York: International Publishers.

Majeski, S. and D. Sylvan (1984). Simple Choices and Complex Calculations: A Critique of the War Trap. *Journal of Conflict Resolution.*

McNeill, W. (1982) *The Pursuit of Power.* Chicago: University of Chicago.

Midlarsky M. (1975) *On War: Political Violence in the International System.* New York: Free Press.

Modelski, G. (1983). Long Cycles of World Leadership. In William R. Thompson, *Contending Approaches to World System Analysis.* Beverly Hills: Sage.

Naroll R. (1969). Imperial Cycles and World Order. *Peace Research Society International Papers.*

Ray, J. (1995). *Democracy and International Conflict: An Evaluation of the Democratic Peace Proposition.* Columbia: University of South Carolina.

Richardson, L. (1960), *Statistics of Deadly Quarrels.* Pittsburgh: Boxwood.

Richardson, L. (1960). *Arms and Insecurity.* Pittsburgh: Boxwood.

Sabrosky, A. (1985). *Polarity and War: The Changing Structure of International Conflict.* Boulder: Westview.

Schelling, T. (1960). *The Strategy of Conflict.* Oxford: Oxford University.

Singer, D. (1979). *The Correlates of War I: Research Origins and Rationale.* New York: Free Press.

Singer, D. and M. Small 1993 *Correlates of War Project: International and Civil War Data, 1816–1992* [Computer file]. Ann Arbor, MI.

Singer, D. and M. Small. (1972). *The Wages of War, 1816–1965: A Statistical Handbook.* New York: John Wiley and Sons.

Singer, D. and P. Diehl (1990). *Measuring the Correlates of War.* Ann Arbor: University of Michigan.

Thucydides, (1954). *The Peloponnesian War.* New York: Penguin.

Tuchman, B (1962). *The Guns of August.* New York: Dell.

van der Dennen, J. (n.d.). Why is the Human Primitive Warrior Virtually Always the Male of the Species? http://rint.rechten.rug.nl/rth/dennen/warrior.

Chapter 13   Interstate Conflict

Barnett, T. (2004). *The Pentagon's New Map.* New York: G. P. Putnam's Sons.

Chaliand, G. (1994). *The Art of War in World History.* Berkeley: University of California.

Chandler, D. (1976) Art of War in the Age of Marlborough. New York: Hippocrene Books.

Clausewitz C. (1976). On War. Princeton: NJ: Princeton University.

Farrington, H (1989). *Strategic Geography.* London: Routledge.

Fehrenbach, T (1963). *This Kind of War*. New York: Macmillan.

Ferrell, A. (1985). The Origins of War from the Stone Age to Alexander the Great. London: Thames and Hudson.

Foch F. (1938). *Des principes de la guerre*. Paris: Berger Levrault.

Friedman, T. (1999). *The Lexus and the Olive Tree: Understanding Globalization*. New York: Farrar, Straus and Giroux.

Hart, B. (1954). *Strategy*. New York: Praeger.

Hopf, T. (1994). *Deterrence Theory and American Foreign Policy 1965–1990*. Ann Arbor: The University of Michigan.

Hopkirk, P. (1990). *The Great Game*. New York: Kodansha International

Hufbaauer, G. (2000). *Economic Sanctions Reconsidered*. Washington, DC. Institute for International Economics.

Huntington, S. (1996). *The Clash of Civilizations and the Remaking of the World Order*. New York: Simon and Schuster.

Ibn Khaldun (1969). *The Muqaddimah*. Princeton, NJ: Princeton University.

Jomini H. (1971). *The Art of War*. Westport, CT: Greenwood.

Jones, A. (1987). *The Art of War in the Western World*. New York: Oxford University.

Keegan (1993). *A History of Warfare*. New York: Alfred A. Knopf.

Keeley, L. (1996) *War Before Civilization*. New York: Oxford University.

Kleveman, L. (2003). *The New Great Game*. New York: Grove Press.

Luttwak, E. (1987). *Strategy: The Logic of War and Peace*. Cambridge, MA: Harvard University.

Lynn, J. (2003). *Battle: A History of Combat and Culture*. Boulder, CO: Westview.

MacDonald, D. (1991). The Truman Administration and Global Responsibilities: Birth of the Falling Domino Principle in R. Jervis and J. Snyder, eds. *Dominos and Bandwagons*. New York: Oxford University.

Mackinder, H. (April 1904). The Geographical Pivot of History" *Geographical Journal*.

Mahan, A. (1957). *The Influence of Seapower Upon History*. New York: Hill & Wang.

May, E. (2000). *Strange Victory: Hitler's Conquest of France*. New York: Hill and Wang.

Miyagawa, M.(1992) *Do Economic Sanctions Work*? New York: St. Martin's.

Modelski, G and W.Thompson (1987). *Seapower in Global Politics*. Seattle: University of Washington.

Phillips, T. (1985). *Roots of Strategy*. Mechanicsburg, PA: Stackpole.

Ritter, E. (1978). *Shaka Zulu*. New York: Penguin.

Spykman. N. (1944). *The Geography of Peace*. New York: Harcourt, Brace and Company.

Sun Tzu (1963). *The Art of War* London: Oxford University.

Wright Q (1942). *A Study of War*. Chicago: University of Chicago.

von Moltke, H. (1909). Sur la stratégie: Mémoire de l'annee 1871. In Chaliand, G. (1994). *The Art of War in World History.* Berkeley: University of California.

X [George Kennan] (July 1947). The Sources of Soviet Conduct. *Foreign Affairs.*

Chapter 14.   Asymmetric War

Blomley, N. (March 2003). Law, Property and the Geography of Violence. *Annals of the Association of American Geographers.*

Dunnigan, J. (27 Feb 2005). Lawfare Gives Terrorist an Edge. www.strategypage.com

Fergany, N. et. al. (2002). *Arab Human Development Report.* New York: United Nations Development Program.

Harte, L (2002). The Taxonomy of Terror: Mythic and Modernist Terrorism in Theory and Practice Paper presented at the California State University Conference on Terrorism.

Judge, M. (19 July 2004). Are Sanctions Evil? *Wall Street Journal.*

Kegley, C. and E. Wittkopf, (2001). *World Politics: Trends and Transformation.* Bedford: St. Martins.

Lawrence, T. (1935). *Seven Pillars of Wisdom* Garden City, NY: Doubleday, Doran & Company, Inc..

Lewis, B. (2002). *The Assassins: A Radical Sect in Islam.* New York: Basic Books.

Lewis, B. (2002). *What Went Wrong.* Oxford: Oxford University.

Michalak, S. (November 2002). *What College Students Learn About Terrorism: A Case Study of IR Textbooks.* Foreign Policy Research Institute

Mingst, Karen 2001. *Essentials of International Relations* New York: W. W. Norton and Company,

Papp, D. (2002). *Contemporary International Relations.* New York: Longman

Pearson, F. and J. Rochester (1997). *International Relations: The Global Condition in the Twenty-First Century.* New York: McGraw-Hill

Peters, R. (1990). *Fighting for the Future.* Mechanicsburg, PA: Stackpole

Rabkin, J. (17 July 2004). Lawfare. *Opinion Journal* www.WSJ.com

Rivkin, D. and L. Casey (11 April 2005). Rule of Law: Friend or Foe. *Wall Street Journal.*

Walzer, M. (1977). *Just and Unjust Wars.* New York: Basic Books.

Weimann, G. (2004). *Cyberterrorism: How Real is the Threat.* Washington, DC: United States Institute of Peace. Special Report 119.

Zeigler, D. (2000). *War, Peace, and International Politics.* New York: Addison, Wesley.

Chapter 15   The Search for Peace

Bailey, S. (1982). *How Wars End: The United Nations and the Termination of Armed Conflict 19461964.* Oxford: Clarendon.

Bercovitch, J. (1996). *Resolving International Conflicts: The Theory and Practice of Mediation,* London: Lynne Rienner.

Berridge, G. (1991). *Return to the United Nations: UN Diplomacy in Regional Conflicts,* Basingstoke: Macmillan.

Bull, H. (1984). *Intervention in World Politics,* Oxford: Clarendon.

Chiagas, D. (2003). *Track II Diplomacy* Boulder: Intractable Conflict Knowledge Base Project at the University of Colorado.

Churchman, D. (2002). The Cyprus Problem. Paper presented at the annual conference of the International Association of Conflict Management.

Cohen, R. (1991). *Negotiating Across Cultures.* Washington, DC: United States Institute for Peace.

Cook, P. and J. Ludwig. *Guns in America: National Survey on Private Ownership and Use of Firearms.* Washington, D.C.: National Institute of Justice.

Crocker, C. & Hampson, F. (1996). *Managing Chaos.* Washington, DC: United States Institute of Peace.

Debrix, F. (1991). *Re-Envisioning UN Peacekeeping,* Minneapolis: University of Minnesota.

Deutsch, M. (2000). Competition and Cooperation in P. Coleman and M. Deutsch, eds. *Handbook of Conflict Resolution: Theory and Practice.* San Francisco: Jossey-Bass.

Diamond, L. & MacDonald, J. (1996). *Multi-track Diplomacy: A Systems Approach to Peace.* West Hartford, CT: Kumarian.

Diehl, P. (1993). *International Peacekeeping,* Baltimore and London: Johns Hopkins University.

Durch, W. (1994). *The Evolution of UN Peacekeeping,* Houndmills, Basingstoke: Macmillan.

Fischer, F. (1967). *Germany's Aims in the First World War.* New York: W.W. Norton and Compan.

Fisher, R (1989). Prenegotiation Problem Solving Discussions. In J. Stein. *Getting to the Table.* Baltimore: Johns Hopkins University.

Fisher, R. (1997). *Interactive Conflict Resolution.* Syracuse, NY: Syracuse University.

Gandhi, M. (1986). On Satyagraha in R. Iyer *The Moral and Political Writings of Mahatma Gandhi,* New York: Oxford University.

Ghali, B. (1992). *An Agenda For Peace: Preventative Diplomacy, Peacemaking and Peacekeeping,* New York: United Nations.

Gobbi, H. (1994). *Building Peace and Development,* New York: United Nations.

Gordenker, L. and T. Weiss. (1991). *Soldiers, Peacekeepers and Disasters,* Basingstoke: Macmillan.

Gow, J. (1997). *Triumph of Lack of Will: International Diplomacy and the Yugoslav War,* London: Hurst and Company.

Haas, R. (1990). *Conflicts Unending: The United States and Regional Disputes.* New Haven: Yale University.

Hammarskjold, D. (July 1960).Summary Study of the Experience Derived From the Establishment and Operation of the Force: Report of the Secretary-General, in *Official Records of the General Assembly, Thirteenth Session: Annexes. A/3943, 9 October 1958.* New York: United Nations.

Hampson, F (1996). *Nurturing Peace: Why Peace Settlements Succeed or Fail,* Washington, DC: United States Institute of Peace.

Hayner P. (14 November 1994). Fifteen Truth Commissions–1974 to 1994: A Comparative Study. *Human Rights Quarterly.*

Hayner, P. (2001), *Unspeakable Truths: Confronting State Terror and Atrocity,* New York, Routledge.

Henderson, M. (1996). *The Forgiveness Factor.* London: Grosvenor Books.

Holbroke, R. (1998). *To End A War.* New York: , Random House

Holmes, R. (1990). *Nonviolence in Theory and Practice.* Belmont, CA: Wadsworth Publishing Company

James, W. (1906) *The Moral Equivalent of War* City. Speech given at Stanford University reprinted in W. James (1911). *Memories and Studies.* New York: Longman Green and Co.

Kant, I. (1795). *Perpetual Peace and Other Essays on Politics, History and Morals.* Indianapolis, IN: Hackett.

Kegley, C. and G. Raymond (1999). *How Nations Make Peace.* New York: St. Martin's/Worth.

Kennedy, R. (1969) *Thirteen Days: A Memoir of the Cuban Missile Crisis.* New York: W. W. Norton and Company.

King, M. (1976). Letter from a Birmingham Jail. In M. King, *Why We Can't Wait.* New York: Signet

Kissinger, H. (1994). *Diplomacy.* New York: Simon & Schuster

Kleck, G. and M. Gertz, (Fall 1995.) Armed Resistance to Crime: The Prevalence and Nature of Self-Defense with a Gun, *The Journal of Criminal Law & Criminology.*

Knight, K. (2003). Truce of God. *The Catholic Encyclopedia, Volume.* (1912) Volume 15. Online edition: Robert Appleton Company.

Kriesberg, L. and A. Thorson (1991). *Timing the De-escalation of International Conflicts.* Syracuse: NY University.

Kritz, N. (1995). *Transitional Justice: How Emerging Democracies Reckon with Former Regimes,* Washington, DC: U.S. Institute of Peace.

Lederach, J. (1995). *Preparing for Peace: Conflict Transformation Across Cultures,* Syracuse: Syracuse University.

Lederach, J. (1997). *Building Peace: Sustainable Reconciliation in Divided Societies,* Washington, DC: United States Institute of Peace.

Liddell Hart, (1954). *Strategy.* New York: Praeger.

Lott, J. (1998) *More Guns, Less Crime: Understanding Crime and Gun Control*. Chicago: University of Chicago.

Lott, J. and D. Mustard (January 1997). Crime, Deterrence, and Right-to-Carry Concealed Handguns. *Journal of Legal Studies*.

Love, M. (1995). *Peace Building through Reconciliation in Northern Ireland*. Idershot: Aveburg

Luttwak, E. (July/August 1999). Letting Wars Burn. *Foreign Affairs*

Mayall, J. (1996). *The New Interventionism, 1991–1994 : United Nations Experience in Cambodia, Former Yugoslavia, and Somalia,* Cambridge: Cambridge University.

Maynard, K. (2000). *Healing Communities in Conflict*. New York: Columbia University.

Michele G. (1999). "Retrenchment, Reform, and Regionalisation: Trends in UN Peace Support Operations", *International Peacekeeping*.

Milne, A. (1934).*Peace with Honour*. New York: E. P. Dutton.

Montville, J. (1991). *Conflict and Peacemaking in Multiethnic Societies*. Lexington, MA: Lexington Books.

Morgenthau, H. (1948/1973) *Politics Among Nations*. New York: Knopf

Osgood, C. (1962). *Alternative to War and Surrender*. Urbana: University of Illinois.

Paris, R. (2002). "International Peacebuilding and the 'Mission Civilisatrice'", *Review of International Studies*.

Parsons, T. (1995). *From Cold War to Hot Peace: United Nations Interventions 1947–1994,* London: Penguin.

Ratner, S. (1997). *The New UN Peacekeeping*. London: Macmillan.

Renner, M. (September 2000). UN Peacekeeping an Uncertain Future. *Foreign Policy in Focus*.

Roberts, A. and B. Kingsbury (1994), *United Nations, Divided World*. London: Oxford University.

Rothman, J. (1997). *Resolving Identity Based Conflict in Nations, Organizations and Communities*. San Francisco: Jossey-Bass.

Saunders, H (1996). Prenegotiation and Circumnegotiation: Arenas of the Peace Process. In C. Crocker and F. Hampson, *Managing Global Chaos: Sources of and Responses to International Conflict*. Washington DC: United States Institute of Peace

Sisk, T. (1996). *Power Sharing and International Mediation in Ethnic Conflicts*. Washington, DC: United States Institute for Peace

Tavuchis, N. (1991). *Mea Culpa: A Sociology of Apology and Reconciliation*. Stanford, CA: Stanford University.

Tolstoy, L. 1987. *Writings on Civil Disobedience and Nonviolence*. Philadelphia: New Society.

Tolstoy, L. (1987) Letter to Ernest Howard Crosby in L. Tolstoy, *Writings on Civil Disobedience and Nonviolence*. Philadelphia: New Society.

Truth and Reconciliation Commission Amnesty Committee (14 April 1999). http://www/truth.org.za/amnesty.htm (April 14, 1999).

United Nations (1996). *The Blue Helmets- A Review of UN Peacekeeping* (3rd ed.), New York: Author.

Ury, W. (2000). *The Third Side: Why We Fight and How We Can Stop.* NY: Penguin Books.

Woodhouse, T and O. Ramsbotham (2000). *Peacekeeping and Conflict Resolution*, London: Frank Cass, 2000.

Woodward, S. (1996). *Balkan Tragedy: Chaos and Dissolution after the Cold War,* Washington, DC: Brookings Institution.

Zartman, W. (2000). Ripeness: The Hurting Stalemate and Beyond in P. Arwen and D. Druckman, *International Conflict Resolution after the Cold War.* Annapolis:: Naval Academy.

Zartman, W. (1995). *Elusive Peace: Negotiating an End to Civil Wars,* Washington, DC: The Brookings Institution.

Chapter 16   Prolegomena to a Theory of Conflict

Bartos, O. (2002). *Using Conflict Theory.* Cambridge: Cambridge University.

Bronowski, J. (1965) *Science and Human Values.* New York: Harper & Row.

Greene, B. (2003). *The Elegant Universe: Superstrings, Hidden Dimensions, and the Quest for the Ultimate Theory.* New York: W. W. Norton and Company

Jeong, H. (1999). *Conflict Resolution: Dynamics, Processes and Structure,* Aldershot: Ashgate.

Johnson, D. and R. Johnson (1989). *Cooperation and Competition: Theory and Research.* Edina, MN: Interaction Book Co.

Kriesberg, L. (1998). *Constructive Conflicts: From Escalation to Resolution.* Lanham, MD: Rowman & Littlefield.

Kuhn, T. (1970). *The Structure of Scientific Revolutions.* Chciago: University of Chicago.

Miall, H., O. Ramsbotham, and T. Woodhouse (1999). *Contemporary Conflict Resolution,* Boston: Polity.

Perry, W. (1963). Examsmanship and the Liberal Arts: Examining in Harvard College. Cambridge, MA: Harvard University

Sandole, D. & Van der Merwe, H. (1993). *Conflict Resolution Theory and Practice.* Manchester, UK: Manchester University.

Sowell, T. (1980). *Knowledge & Decisions.* New York: Basic Books.

Ury, W., J.Brett, and S. Goldberg, (1989). *Getting Disputes Resolved: Designing Systems to Cut the Costs of Conflict.* San Francisco: Jossey-Bass

Index

Half-way through the labour of an index to this book, I recalled the practice of my ten years' study of history; and realized I had never used the index of a book fit to read.

—T. E. Lawrence, *Seven Pillars of Wisdom*

Author Biography

In a moderately long life, I have learned three important things: that it is better to be know than to be ignorant, better to tell the truth than to lie, and better to be free than be a slave.

—*The Gallant Hours*

David Churchman is professor *emeritus* of Behavioral Science and of Humanities, California State University. As chairman of the Behavioral Science Graduate Program he founded a degree in conflict management that soon was awarding some 100 masters degrees each year. He taught courses in conflict theory and negotiation tactics both in the traditional classroom and on worldwide on interactive Internet television. As professor of humanities, he taught courses in ancient, Arab, and Byzantine history.

David is co-founder and director *emeritus* of Wildlife on Wheels, which provides live wild animal education programs to approximately 100,000 Los Angeles basin children annually and works with International Bird Rescue and Research Corporation to rescue wildlife from oil spills.

David has been a Fulbright Scholar in Cyprus and Ukraine and a Malone Scholar in Saudi Arabia. He has been a National Science Foundation program officer, high school teacher, social worker, and infantry officer. He earned his bachelors and masters degrees in Near Eastern History at The University of Michigan and, with the support of a fellowship from the U.S. Department of State and American Association of School Administrators, his doctorate in program evaluation at UCLA. His avocations include chess, cooking, photography, rifle marksmanship, and travel.